Adventures in Physics and Pueblo Pottery

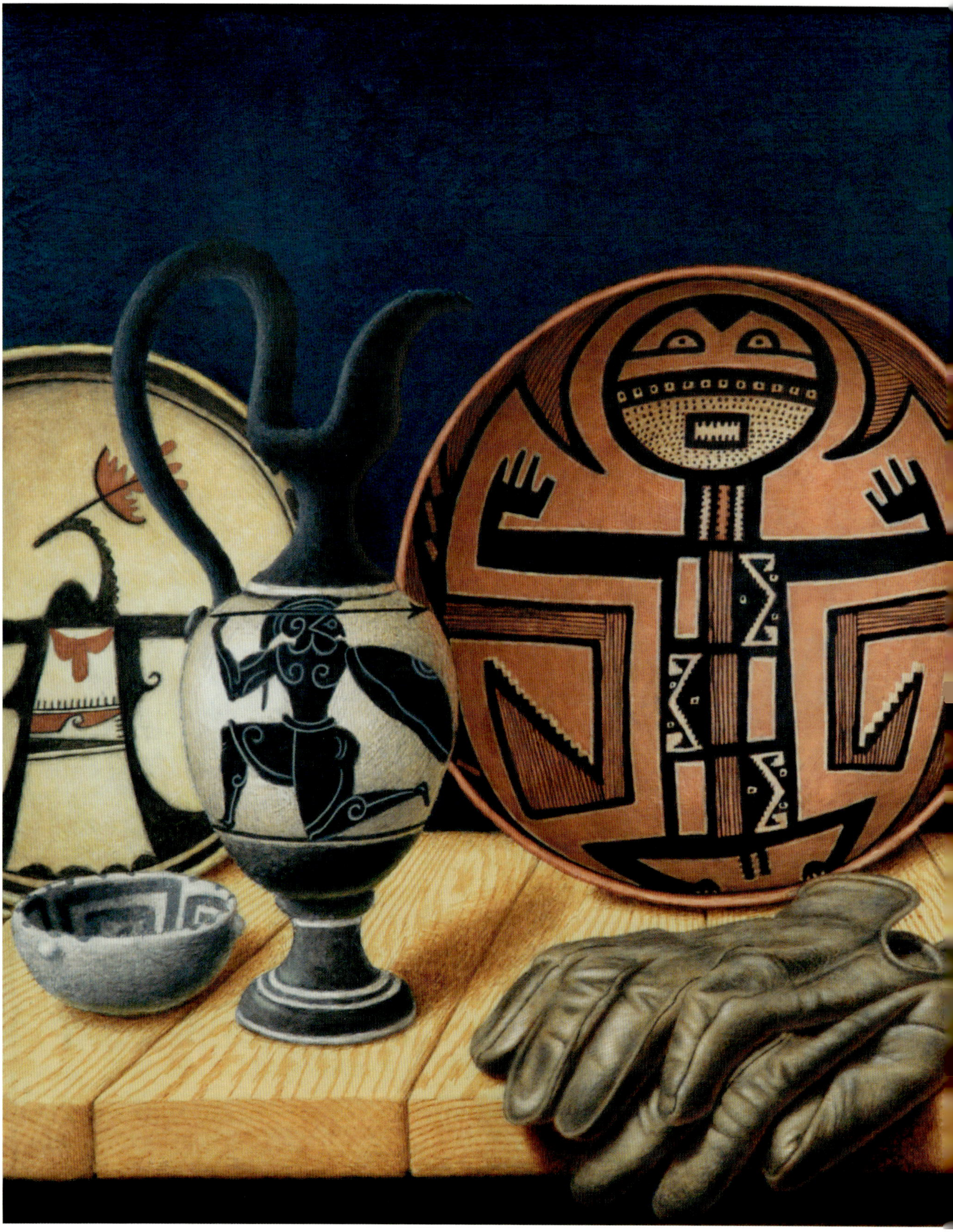

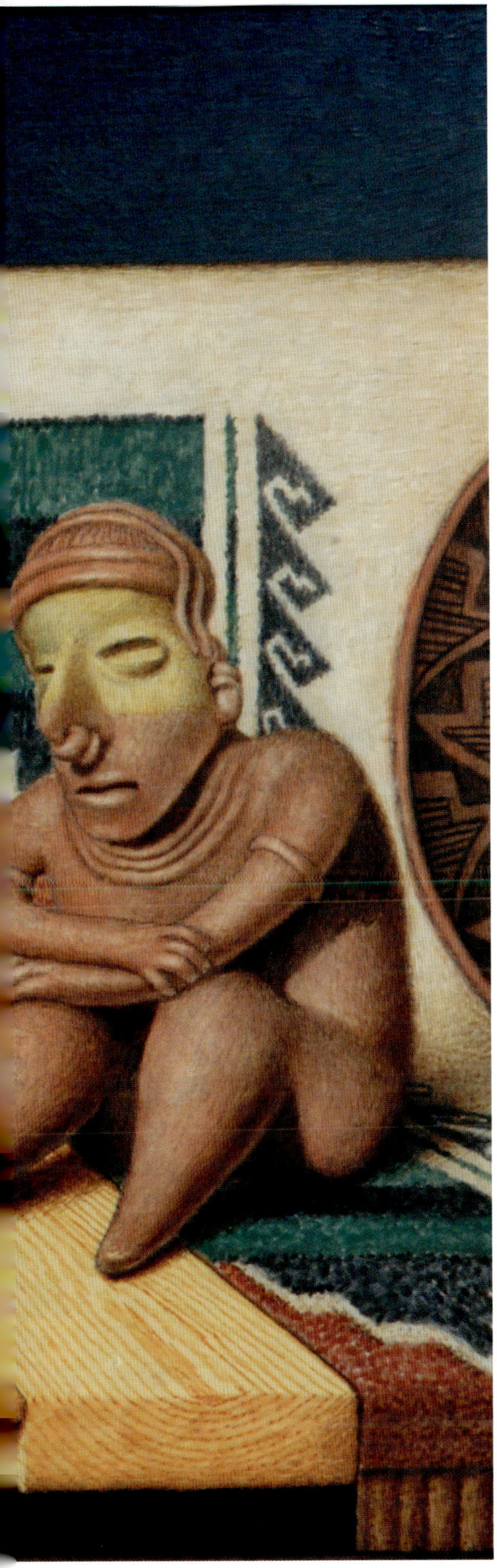

Adventures in Physics and Pueblo Pottery

Memoirs of a Los Alamos Scientist

by Francis H. Harlow
with Dwight P. Lanmon

Museum of New Mexico Press
Santa Fe

The Museum of New Mexico Press is a division of the New Mexico Department of Cultural Affairs.

Project editor: Lisa Pacheco
Design and production: David Skolkin
Composition: Set in ITC New Baskerville and Din
Manufactured in China
10 9 8 7 6 5 4 3 2 1

Library of Congress Cataloging-in-Publication Data
Names: Harlow, Francis H. (Francis Harvey), 1928- | Lanmon, Dwight P.
Title: Adventures in physics and Pueblo pottery : memoirs of a Los Alamos scientist / by Francis H. Harlow ; with Dwight P. Lanmon.
Description: Santa Fe : Museum of New Mexico Press, [2016] | Includes bibliographical references.
Identifiers: LCCN 2015041012 (print) | LCCN 2016001083 (e-book) | ISBN 9780890136157 (cloth) | ISBN 9780890136164 (e-book)
Subjects: LCSH: Harlow, Francis H. (Francis Harvey), 1928- | Physicists—United States—Biography. | Los Alamos National Laboratory—Officials and employees. | Pottery—Collectors and collecting—New Mexico. | Indian pottery—New Mexico. | Pueblo pottery—New Mexico.
Classification: LCC QC16.H285 L36 2016 (print) | LCC QC16.H285 (e-book) | DDC 530.092—dc23
LC record available at http://lccn.loc.gov/2015041012

ISBN 978-0-89013-615-7 cloth
ISBN 978-0-89013-616-4 e-book

Museum of New Mexico Press
PO Box 2087
Santa Fe, New Mexico 87504
www.mnmpress.org

The most wonderful parts of my life are the devotion, care, and encouragement I have received from Patricia over our more than sixty-two years of marriage. Without her presence, many of the things described in this book would never have happened. To her this book is most lovingly dedicated.

CONTENTS

ACKNOWLEDGMENTS 9

PREFACE 11

- 1 The Seattle and Bremerton Years 13
- 2 My Time in the Army 21
- 3 The University Years 31
- 4 Family and Homes 37
- 5 Los Alamos National Laboratory 53
- 6 Fossils 75
- 7 Motorcycles 89
- 8 The Pueblo Indians of New Mexico 103
- 9 Pueblo Indian Pottery Studies and Collecting 129
- 10 Our Pueblo Indian Pottery Collection 151
- 11 Paintings and Art 173
- 12 Album of Some of My Favorite Paintings 183

BIBLIOGRAPHY OF HARLOW PUBLICATIONS ON PUEBLO POTTERY AND PALEONTOLOGY 198

ACKNOWLEDGMENTS

DWIGHT LANMON MADE IMPORTANT CONTRIBUTIONS TO THIS BOOK. They include excellent editorial suggestions, detailed processing of illustrations and text, frequent interactions with the publisher, and much more. Without his activities, this book would never have been completed. And, most especially, Dwight is a wonderful friend.

In addition, I gratefully acknowledge the many people with whom I have interacted during the activities described in this book. I also thank Valerie Verzuh of the Museum of Indian Arts and Culture (MIAC) in Santa Fe and Blair Clark of the Museum of New Mexico, who photographed all the pottery from our gift to the MIAC illustrated in this book (see especially chapter 10). Heather McLanahan and Rebecca Collinsworth of the Los Alamos History Archives were also very helpful in reproducing images from their collection.

PREFACE

THIS BOOK RECOGNIZES THE WONDERFUL OPPORTUNITIES that have filled my many years of life. The text describes the three fields of published research that have been of importance to me: the physical dynamics of disturbed materials; the history of the oceans that covered this area with ancient life; and the history of the Pueblo Indians, especially the pottery they produced. I also discuss the joy of motorcycle riding (and a totally unexpected relationship between that hobby and pottery studies) and the challenge of painting realistic representations of pottery and other subjects that are interesting to me.

Since my retirement in September 2003 from Los Alamos National Laboratory, I've been assembling summaries of my eighty years of activity. The goal has been to compile them in a somewhat readable form, mostly for my family and me but also for the amusement of people a century from now. To them, these days will seem quite primitive, similar to my feelings about the world of my great-grandparents, whose writings about their day-to-day activities would be enormously treasured if they existed.

The earliest draft for this book was the unpublished "Harlow Memoirs," completed in 2009. We printed about twenty-five copies and distributed them to our family, some close friends, and several archival institutions in Los Alamos and Santa Fe. Some parts of this book are copied from the memoirs, while other parts are modified or completely rewritten.

I have been lucky in the opportunities that have come to me, over and over again; my life has been filled with enormous good fortune, being in the right places at the right times through all phases of my activities. Equally important have been the wonderful people who have surrounded me: my family, friends, and collaborators along the way, to whom I am overwhelmingly grateful.

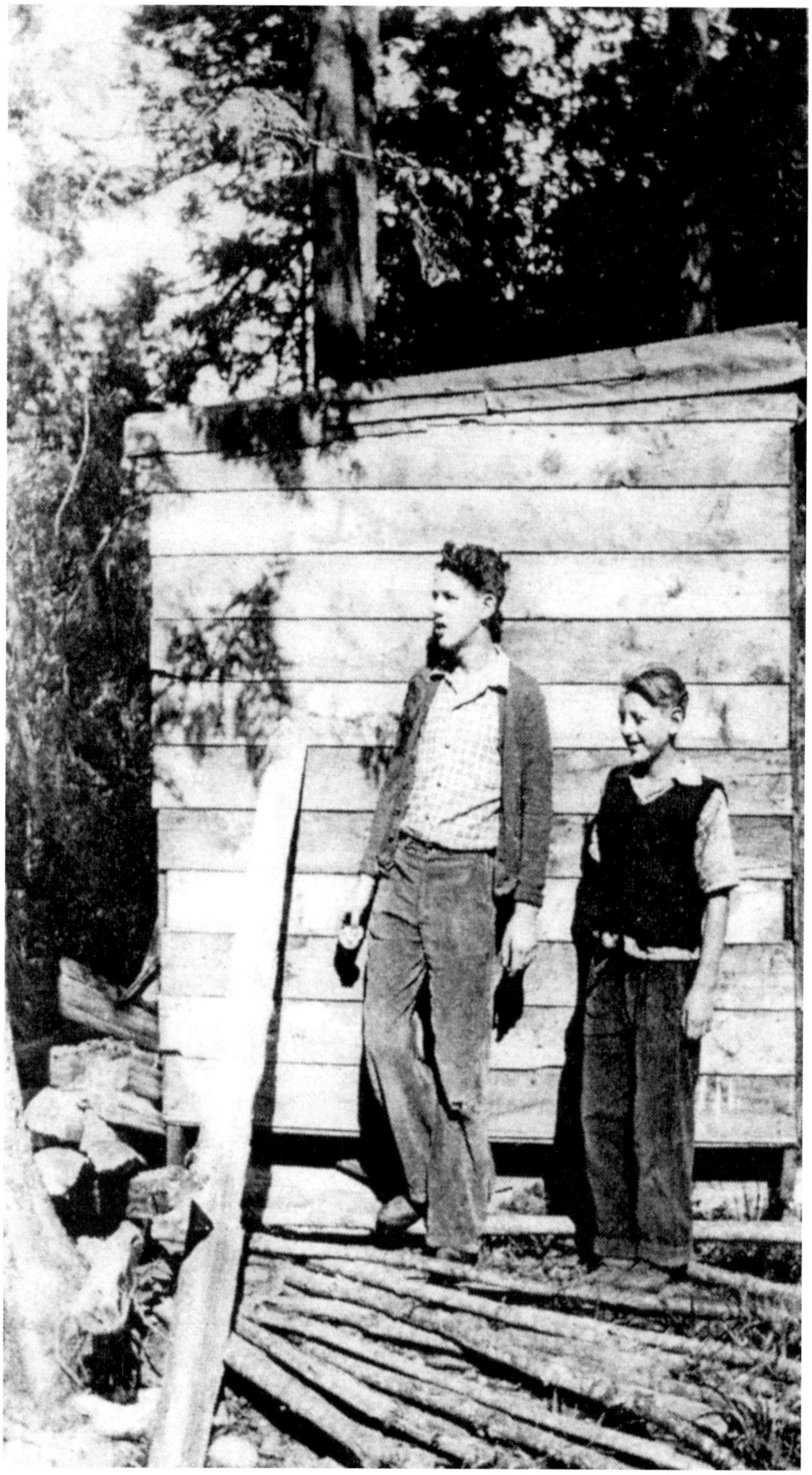

1

The Seattle and Bremerton Years

My life began in Seattle, Washington, January 22, 1928. I descend from a long line of hardworking but undistinguished ancestors who eventually settled in the Seattle area. My brother, Bruce, was born on March 18, 1932.

The Seattle years (1928–1941) were rather tough for our family, both financially and because of the poor health of my mother, Florence. My dad, Francis Harvey Sr., in contrast, was healthy and strong, but he was not home much of the time—working long hours at many different jobs to provide a very modest but acceptable living.

A special treat for me while I was living in Seattle was going with my dad to the annual engineering open house at the University of Washington. I remember being especially impressed by the great machines, which had huge wheels with belts connected to other huge wheels on nearby machines. I don't remember what the machines were supposed to do; it really didn't matter at the time. One especially fascinating exhibit featured chemicals that were poured together, and after a short time, the whole mixture would suddenly turn a different color (green, I think). There was also an electric display with a pair of large copper balls and flickering bolts of lightning jumping between them. I'm sure there was much more. The engineering open house had a profound effect in initiating my interests in science, especially physics.

Figure 1. My brother, Bruce (*right*), and I at the tool house Dad built near the shack on Kitsap Lake, about 1942. (Frank Harlow family photos.)

Another interest was kindled by a sixth-grade field trip to the University of Washington's Natural History Museum. The mineral and crystal displays were especially attractive, and I was also much impressed by the Northwest Indians displays: I can still visualize the totem poles, canoes, and fringed leather clothing on mannequins. These things formed the seeds for my much later interest in rocks (especially fossils) and Indian artifacts (especially pottery).

After my mother died in April 1941, my father, my brother, and I moved across Puget Sound to the much smaller town of Bremerton. Our father's sister, Aunt Bessie, generously opened her home to my brother and me, while our heartbroken father built a little shack for himself on the forested shore of nearby Kitsap Lake. (Eventually, my dad married again, to a very nice lady named Charlotte Randall.)

There was a little stream beside the shack, which emerged from a pipe that Dad installed; he got his water there. There he lived, except for visits to town to get groceries and to see us. He also built a big shed from native materials and planted a big garden. His money came from an estate left by his father to him, his sister Bessie, and his brother Bert, who lived in a little house a few hundred yards away from the shack.

Bruce and I lived in town with our Aunt Bessie, and we saw Dad on Wednesday and Saturday evenings and Sundays. He usually slept on the couch at our house on Wednesday and Saturday nights, but mostly he was out at the shack. Sometimes I stayed there with him, especially in the summer. (He had two single beds in the shack, plus a little woodstove.)

Dad paid Aunt Bessie something for our room and board, and after getting a job, I spent about five dollars on groceries each week to help pay my way, and I bought some of my clothes. Otherwise, there was little to buy, so I saved quite a bit of money. When I was not working and had no homework to do, I would go out on my bicycle—usually somewhere along the saltwater beach. I often went fishing, but I rarely caught much of value. I always made these excursions alone.

THE WAR YEARS (1941–1945)

I was still in school on December 7, 1941, when the Japanese bombed Pearl Harbor. Dad and I had gone out to get a load of alder wood for the fireplace at Aunt Bessie's house that Sunday morning. When we pulled into the neighbor's driveway to unload the wood, Bessie came out onto the front porch to tell us the news. She made it sound quite ominous, and the events of the next few years demonstrated just how ominous it really was. After unloading the wood, we listened through much of the day to the news reports on the radio. The most important news was of the terrible destruction to the ships in Pearl Harbor, followed by the call from President Roosevelt for all members of Congress to return immediately to Washington in response to his announced intention to ask for a declaration of war. Students were excused from classes on December 8 to hear the president's speech, which included a request to Congress for tremendous powers and money to fund an overwhelming effort by the United States to build up its fighting capabilities. The response from Congress was almost unanimous in granting all that was requested. (I think there was only one dissenting vote.)

Thus began a period in US history that profoundly affected everyone in the country, and throughout most of the rest of the world. For a thirteen-year-old kid in Bremerton, the manifestations were especially visible. Until 1941, the city was a navy yard town of about fifteen thousand people, mostly associated with the maintenance and repair of military ships. Almost immediately, it became evident that the Bremerton Navy Yard was going to play an important role in the war effort. A major expansion of navy yard activities quickly resulted in a Bremerton population growth, from fifteen thousand to ninety thousand. To house the workers and their families, two very large vacant areas were cleared. Barracks-like apartment buildings were erected and occupied with astonishing rapidity. Even so, there was not room close by for all the required workers, and thousands of them had to live as far away as Seattle and travel by ferryboat, which required an hour's commute each way.

Because of the special importance of the navy yard, considerable changes were made to increase security. Admission to the yard required a special pass, and there was a great deal of publicity regarding the necessity of maintaining secrecy about the coming and going of the ships. The slogan was "Loose Lips Sink Ships." Even more visible was the establishment of a network of barrage balloons. These were fish-shaped objects, perhaps twenty feet or more in length, which were tethered to the ground by strong steel cables. Any airplane that struck a cable would be torn apart. The balloons were arranged around Bremerton, in a pattern that was sufficiently dense to preclude penetration by virtually any airplane. (In those days, a hostile plane had to fly low to achieve sufficient accuracy for bomb placement.) The balloons were filled with helium (probably not hydrogen) whenever the practice drills called for them to be lofted. One of these balloons was stationed in a vacant lot almost directly across the street from Bessie's house.

We had blackout practices in the town, like some we had witnessed in Seattle, and there was anti-Japanese propaganda in the form of posters, newspaper articles, and radio reports. The depictions were vicious: Japanese faces were caricatures of human appearance, with evil eyes and mouths. No one objected to those pictures (except perhaps people of Japanese ancestry, who in any case were by then mostly interned in detention camps, even those who were US citizens).

Unlike the situations in later wars (Vietnam and Iraq, for example), everyone seemed universally supportive of our effort to defeat both Japan and Germany. No one liked or cared about the power of conquest; no antiwar rallies were staged; everyone deplored the killing and destruction; and virtually every person was touched by the loss of family members, friends, or well-known young people living nearby. I think it was universally accepted that we had to do, or endure, whatever was necessary to achieve victory.

At the same time, every person was affected by a variety of constraints on his or her personal life. Fuel for both vehicles and heating was rationed, and we used the fireplace in Bessie's house almost exclusively for our heating; the frequent woodcutting that Dad, Bruce, and I did became an essential activity. (I can remember in the winter going to bed at night with my feet intolerably cold.) Lots of other things were rationed, even foods like coffee and sugar, and also soap. (Bessie had anticipated the restrictions on soap and bought big cartons of soap bars, which she unwrapped so that they would dry out and last longer. She stored them in a little partial basement.)

The high school was forced to initiate a double-shift system, with classes from 8:00 to 12:00 for the morning shift and 12:30 to 4:30 for the afternoon shift. Classes were forty-five minutes in length. All the way through high school, I was always in the morning shift. Jobs for young people were plentiful, because many civilian workers had gone to the military services, having been drafted or diverted to war-effort jobs.

During my first two years of high school, I worked for the Olberg Drug Store in downtown Bremerton, delivering prescriptions and other items by bicycle, straightening up the storage shelves in the basement, operating the cash register, selling candy (five cents per candy bar) or cigarettes (twenty-five cents per pack), and receiving money from customers at the lunch counter and soda fountain. I enjoyed working the cash register most. It was fun meeting people, even briefly, and I enjoyed the challenge of quickly making change for each purchase.

For the deliveries, my bicycle had a basket on the front. I was able to get a special navy yard access pass for delivery to military housing within the yard itself. One of the deliveries that I remember especially well was Rae's Rooms, located just a few blocks from the store. The rooms were on the second floor, at the top of a long stairway. I would ring a bell, and the door would open just a little way to reveal a woman dressed in a flimsy nightgown. She would take the delivery and always give me a huge tip—as high as fifty cents. I soon realized what kind of establishment Rae's Rooms was, but I didn't mind. The streets of Bremerton had many sailors at almost any time of the day or evening, and they provided a lively business for the rooms.

Because of the steep and hilly terrain on which Bremerton was built, some delivery areas gave me strenuous workouts, especially because my bike had only a single speed. Going across the Port Washington Narrows Bridge to Manette was fun, but there weren't many calls for deliveries to the huge, hastily erected, barracks-like housing development there.

About that time, it became clear to Aunt Bessie that my teeth were in bad condition, with lots of cavities. She had known Dr. Bisson, a dentist, for many years, and she arranged for me to start a program of dental remediation, probably when I was almost sixteen years old. Dr. Bisson was about to lose his laboratory technician to military service. I didn't know who first suggested it, but they quickly developed a plan for me to work for him and learn the techniques for making dentures, for which he would pay me about as much as Olberg's did and give me dentistry for free. The plan seemed ideal. Sometimes I worked on a workbench in a room adjacent to the dentistry cubicles, and sometimes I worked in Dr. Bisson's laboratory, not far down the hallway. Plasterwork for mouth molds was done in the laboratory, along with using a pressure cooker for curing the acrylic material of the dentures. Workbench activities included using a centrifugal casting machine for making gold inlays and a Bunsen burner, where I built the dentures out of wax and inserted the teeth. I don't know if Dr. Bisson felt that he got his money's worth from my activities, but I certainly enjoyed the experience, which turned out later to have a major impact on my army career.

Other things that I recall include two of my favorite classes in Bremerton High School. They were physics and chemistry with Mr. Dogan. He actually was not a very good teacher, spending an excessive amount of time on moralizing. I was especially bored by his lectures and demonstrations on the evils of drinking alcohol. Nevertheless, those classes with him cemented my career inclination for the subject of physics. Mr. Dogan extolled the virtues of getting a PhD, and that became an almost unfailing goal for all of my university years.

The other class I recall fondly was music. Mr. Berg was the teacher of vocal music at Bremerton High School. His technique for determining the pitch of each piece was to produce a faint whistling sound, which he knew how to do with unfailing accuracy for the particular note that he wished to produce. From that he could construct the interval to whatever pitch the music required. We all were in awe of his ability to do this and also liked him very much.

I enjoyed being in both the a cappella choir and the operetta *In Old Vienna.* I was listed first in the cast of characters in the printed program, even though my part was minor. I was also listed on the back page as the "business manager," but I never really figured out what I was supposed to do, so I did essentially nothing. I had one brief solo, which was only four lines long; the first line was "How now you lazy vagabonds." I practiced it over and over again and had it completely memorized so that it was sure to be executed perfectly. Right? Wrong. After one of the performances, I asked Mr. Berg how he thought I had done. As gently as he could, he let me know that my pitch was off by one complete note. How embarrassing! But in most respects, I think that the presentations went quite well.

I was also in the senior play as an "old father," in a plot for which no memory remains, except for my discomfort with having to say "damn" at one point in the play. Being the prude and nerd I was in high school, neither that word nor any other cuss word had ever passed through my mouth. Well, the play was a success, with little thanks to my small part of it.

I finished high school during the war years and would leave home forever shortly after reaching my seventeenth birthday. My high school graduating class was enormous, with about 250 girls and 190 boys—440 students in all. As I scan the lists in the commencement program, almost none of the names are familiar to me. Geraldine (Gerry) Anderson and Elizabeth (Beth) Hawkins are two girls I remember, while Phillip (Phil) Capp is a vaguely familiar name.

My social life in high school was nil; I rarely went to parties or out with other kids my age. Gerry Anderson (who was about four feet ten) went out with me once on a date, mainly to show the contrast between her height and mine (6 feet 5¾ inches). Beth Hawkins went out with me once or twice; I don't remember what we did on any of those occasions. I was essentially a social misfit in high school, and I trained myself not to care. I was not well coordinated physically, and I did relatively poorly in typing class and phys ed. This physical incoordination partly contributed to my lack of ease in social circumstances, but I was a good student, with quite high grades, for which it was not necessary to study very hard.

In addition to school and work, there was plenty of time to just get off by myself, mainly to go bike riding or saltwater fishing. From the beach at Port Washington Narrows, I would throw out a line with some bait on it and rather easily catch a dogfish, but there was nothing useful to do with the poor critter, so

I didn't do that very often. More to my liking was visiting the old wooden docks near the ferry terminal. These docks and their floats were old and not much used. The logs were encrusted with sea anemones, barnacles, mussels, and various other types of sea life. As the tide rose and fell, the connection between the float and the dock had to vary in angle, following the motions of the float, which could slide up and down against the vertical guide logs. I loved to lie on my stomach and watch the movement of the various attached life forms and of the poggies, which were little fish to be seen in abundance, especially when some bits of food were dropped into the waters. The sought-after prize, however, was the rarely seen sea perch, larger than the poggies and very nice to eat if it could be caught (which I was almost never able to do).

Kitsap Lake, where my dad had built his shack, was also a fun body of water. It was warm enough for swimming, and we had a little rowboat for traveling to other parts of the lake, which was a mile or so in width. We liked especially to go where the water was shallow enough for abundant water lilies to grow. The water was murky and didn't smell very good, and while that didn't impede our swimming, it did make us reluctant to fish. When we did try fishing and caught something big enough to eat, we found the flavor of the fish was like the smell of the lake.

My dad had two special friends during the war years, Joe Stangler and Joe Walkinshaw. He seemed to like Stangler better, and we visited his little cabin in the woods fairly often. Both of them liked shooting guns, and both were fairly skillful in reloading ammunition. I never cared much for shooting, much to my dad's disappointment, but sometimes he insisted and I shot one of his guns a few times. I really couldn't see what the thrill was. Dad, however, never went hunting, and although he was a meat eater, it never appealed to him to shoot an animal. Until recently, I had a few of his guns, which he gave me much later in life. I displayed them in our pottery room, mostly in remembrance of that facet of Dad's life. They now belong to our son, Keith.

One thoroughly unexpected result of the cleaning of ground for wartime apartment housing in Bremerton was the prolific growth of shaggy mane mushrooms in the disturbed soil. I could bicycle to the area and in a few minutes gather a whole grocery sack full of them. Aunt Bessie would lightly sauté them, and they were delicious! Other wild things we ate included a variety of berries. Wild blackberries were our favorite. In addition, we sometimes went to areas where little blue huckleberries could be gathered in abundance. In the pies that Bessie made, they were very strongly flavorful and delicious, much better than the much larger huckleberries that can be bought frozen these days. About the only frozen foods I can remember from sixty years ago were strawberries—the small ones from before bioengineering, which we had on *very* special occasions and which were much more intensely flavorful than the huge ones available now. Other wild berries included orange huckleberries, which we enjoyed eating freshly picked from the bush. There were also salmonberries, which looked like shallow raspberries but actually were not very good. Black caps also looked like shallow raspberries but likewise didn't have a very appealing flavor. We also sometimes gathered hazelnuts, but I don't think we knew how to roast them properly. The closely related filberts tasted much better, but they didn't grow wild in the area and were quite expensive. Licorice ferns grew on the damp side of trees near the shack, but we didn't know how to process them into edible form. Two other wild ferns were the common bracken and the large sword ferns that grew prolifically in the damp forests of the Olympic Peninsula.

2
My Time in the Army (1945–1947)

It may be surprising now, but I was indeed a soldier in the US Army, and not only was it good for me, but I actually enjoyed the experience. It gave me the self-confidence that I could do all the things other guys my age could do. Well, not all of them.

Near the end of my high school years, the pressing question was, Where do I go from here? The war was still blazing, and most of the guys I knew were enlisting in the military. That was an obvious choice for me. Because I was only seventeen at high school graduation, it was not possible to go directly into active duty (the minimum age being eighteen). To recruit young men under the age of eighteen, the army had established a special program, the Army Specialized Training Reserve Program (ASTRP). This program offered university training in basic science and engineering, which would later count as credit hours whenever we returned to civilian life and went on with undergraduate studies. I signed up in March or April 1945 and was assigned to report to Oregon State College at Corvallis for a term commencing in June (or July) of that year.

To be eligible, it was also necessary to pass a medical examination. One had to be shorter than six feet six, with a weight greater than some amount that I have forgotten. For the height requirement, I was able to slouch down to 6 feet 5¾ inches. But the weight was a different matter. Seeing how eager I was to join the army, the doctor put the minimum weight on the chart, despite my actual weight of 154 pounds. He said that if anyone questioned the number and wanted to reweigh me, I should either eat lots of watermelon or drink lots of beer before stepping on the scales. Fortunately, my weight was never challenged. Entry into the program required a commitment to commence active duty as soon as I reached age eighteen (or, as it turned out, at the end of the quarter of study in which I turned eighteen).

When the day came for me to leave home to travel to Corvallis, I was very excited riding the train from Seattle to Portland; it was the first time I had used that form of transportation, and it was wonderful. I was farther from home than ever before in my life. The train went along the Puget Sound, then through forestlands, arriving in Portland, Oregon, and continuing along the Willamette River to Salem, where I got off and traveled the few miles to Corvallis.

I was surrounded by lots of guys my age who were going to participate in the program. We were all fitted with uniforms, which we had to wear at all times except at night; no one in the services at that time could have or use civilian clothing. We lived in a dormitory and slept in double-decker bunks. Some of our time

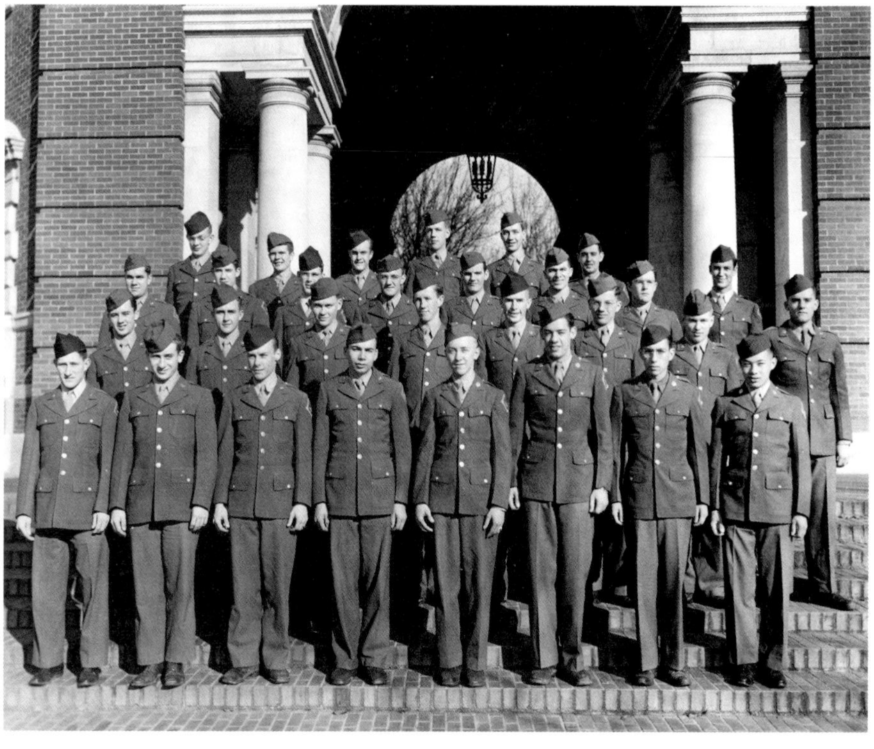

Figure 2. This is Section 18, Company B, SCV 3900, Oregon State College, Corvallis, summer 1945. I am in the back row. (Oregon State University Libraries Special Collections & Archives Research Center.)

was devoted to military matters, such as marching in formation, but most of it was spent in classroom studies of basic physics and mathematics, along with some nonscientific courses such as economics and history. We were dressed in army uniforms and received a small amount of pay. I remember enjoying virtually every bit of it.

During that first summer in the program, the war came to a halt, and the ASTRP program began to wind down. (Indeed, I think the whole ASTRP program ended during the first half of 1946.) In January 1946, I was reassigned to the program at Fort Douglas, in Salt Lake City, Utah, where I attended one semester at the University of Utah. By the end of March 1946, I had turned eighteen, so the term in Salt Lake City was my last.

I really don't remember very much about the six months in Corvallis. Images of marching in groups from class to class come to mind, but the classes themselves are a blur in my memory. The University of Utah classes are also not easily recalled, but I do remember some of the extracurricular activities: going on Sunday morning to hear the Mormon Tabernacle Choir and organ; taking a ski trip to Alta Ski Resort, paid for by the army; hiking through the foothills of the Wasatch Mountains east of town and crawling into some old mine shafts; attending a performance of Verdi's *Il Trovatore*; and staying with hundreds of guys in a big field house, with all the bathroom facilities lined up along the wall.

When the quarter at the University of Utah was over, I had about a week at home before being sworn into active duty. According to my enlistment contract, I became an active-duty soldier in the US Army, which seemed like a very special status at the time (taking advantage of the adulation for military personnel who had actually served in dangerous engagements during the war years). Basic training took me to Fort Lewis, Washington, where I entered a highly disciplined eight-week period that I actually enjoyed a lot (especially the close-order drill with our M-I rifles, in which I took lots of satisfaction for being able to do it quite well). We went to the shooting range to practice marksmanship, took hikes to learn about maps and compasses, had middle-of-the-night harassment by one or another of the company sergeants, and were busy every day with activities and classes.

There were two requirements that had to be met for graduation. They both involved a demonstration of physical prowess, in particular, arm strength. We were required to do ten overhead pull-ups and ten push-ups. Could I do them? No. As persists to the present time, my arms were weak, but my legs were powerful; I could do lots more squat jumps than the required minimum. (I can't do even one anymore.) When the day came when we had to show what we could do, we paired off, with each guy marking on some form exactly what his partner could accomplish. I cheated by persuading my partner to mark down the minimum for each of my arm exercises so that I could pass. I don't remember what I did to return the favor, but it was a relief to get the minimal counts for passing. (As I recall, I was able to do about eight of each before my arms turned to rubber.)

Just a few days before basic training ended, I was called into the captain's office. It had been discovered in my enlistment records that I had worked in a dental laboratory during high school, and there was a high-priority request for a position at the dental clinic at Brooke General Hospital at Fort Sam Houston in San Antonio, Texas. I was deemed to be ideally suited for the job.

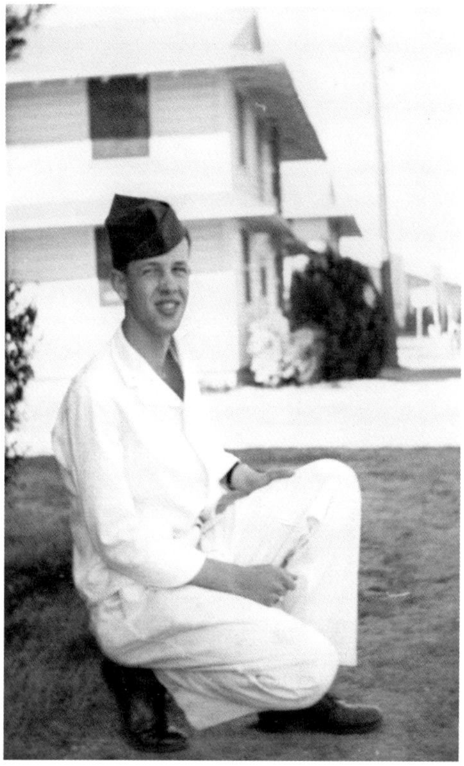

Figure 3. In my working uniform at the dental clinic at Brooke General Hospital, San Antonio, Texas, 1946. (Harlow family photos.)

Thus, the next trip was by train from Seattle to San Antonio, from July 9 to July 11, 1946. Several very memorable things occurred along the way. One took place in Fort Worth, Texas, where we had time to get out of the train and go into the station. There I was astonished to see side-by-side men's restrooms, one for whites and the other for blacks. Likewise, the water fountains in the building were segregated. Of course, I had heard of such segregation, but it was strange to actually see it. (In San Antonio, the buses had special seats for the blacks at the back and seats in the middle and forward sections for the whites.) The second memorable experience on the trip was stepping out of the train at Waco, Texas, into an "oven." It was *so* hot, especially in comparison to what I was familiar with in all the other places I had lived. I suppose it was around 100°F, but it seemed *much* hotter.

Arriving in San Antonio by train on July 11, 1946, I was again immediately aware of the intense heat. When I checked in, the major at the hospital told me that their oral hygienist had just left and I was to fill his position. "I've never cleaned teeth," I said to the major. "Never mind," he replied, "It's easy. Let me show you how, to get you started." He called a new young private who had never been to see a dentist in his life over to one of the dental chairs. "Open up," he commanded, and he said I should watch. "Hold your fingers like this," he said to me, as he showed how to pull off the deposits from the guy's teeth. "Here, now you try it. And don't worry if you cut him. His mouth will heal." At that point, I thought the private would faint, but he somehow kept his composure and let me try it.

And thus, with practice, I became an oral hygienist for the rest of my career in the active army. One time I cleaned the teeth of a general who was head of the entire Dental Corps of the US Army. A letter written by our clinic commander shows that my work was much appreciated. I was determined to be gentle and friendly to my patients, so as to make dentistry as comfortable as possible.

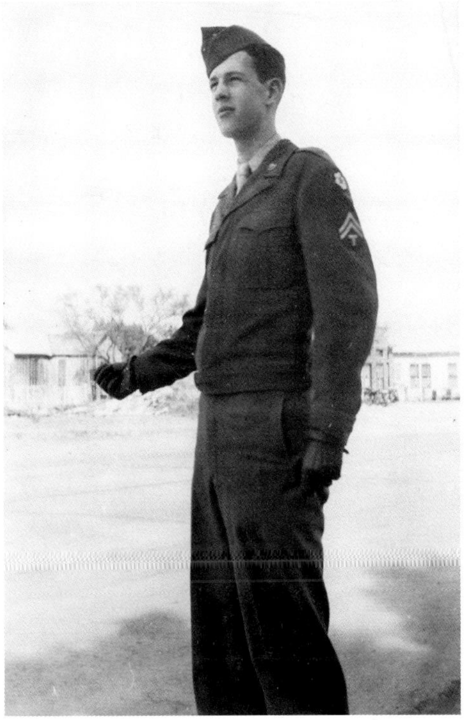

Figure 4. In my army uniform with corporal arm patch, December 1946. (Harlow family photos.)

I enjoyed San Antonio. It was fun to see fireflies for the first time, to visit the rattlesnake pit at Brackenridge Park, and to have Christmas dinner at the home of a family who sometimes befriended "lonesome" military people. While stationed there, I also took several trips around the area. It was easy for a man in uniform to hitchhike, and I went to Laredo and Nuevo Laredo once and beyond Nuevo Laredo to Monterrey, Mexico, another time. Walking across the bridge over the Rio Grande, we encountered military police (MPs) on the US side. They ordered us to take "pro-kits" (prophylactics) with us, which was a bit shocking to me, in that I had no intention of getting into a situation where the kit would be necessary. In Nuevo Laredo there was a lot to see that was interesting: a theater showing a John Wayne movie with Spanish subtitles; a huge marketplace with all sorts of fresh fruit (I bought some oranges, which I was forced to give up when returning to the United States); and little shops with guys standing in front saying, "Come on in and see my junk, shorty," in strong Mexican accents.

It was likewise easy to hitchhike in Mexico, and Monterrey was fascinating to see, but the transportation itself was completely forgettable. Not so, however, on the second of my two trips to Corpus Christi, which was also lots of fun, especially nearby Port Aransas, where there was a beach with seashells and lots of pelicans flying about. Returning to San Antonio during the second round-trip, I got a ride in a pickup truck carrying lots of grapefruit. Along a stretch of highway about halfway to our destination, there was an abrupt drop-off from the pavement (perhaps around four inches) to the dirt shoulder on the right side. You can probably guess what happened. The right front wheel went over the side, the driver overcorrected by turning too sharply to the left, and we plowed into an embankment on the left side of the highway. I broke the windshield with my head and whacked my left knee against something, while the driver got a broken nose and some other injuries that I didn't learn about (or have forgotten).

The driver of another car stopped to help us and gave me a ride to a nearby small town, where the local doctor sewed up a wicked gash on my forehead and another above my right ear. Someone called the hospital at Fort Sam Houston, and after a seemingly interminable time, an army ambulance showed up and took me on the rest of this memorable trip. At the emergency room of Brooke General Hospital, the doctor (a first lieutenant, I think) took one look at my head and mumbled something about the ineptitude of small-town doctors. "I have to completely redo this," he said as he got out a packet of appropriate instruments. "If I don't, you'll have a real hell of a scar for all the rest of your life!" "Yeah, OK, go ahead," I replied, as if I, a lowly private, had any alternative in the matter. And he did a good job. The scar is still visible, but I'm convinced it would be a lot worse if he hadn't taken the time to redo the job correctly.

Thirty years later, I started to develop an itchy lump in the scar tissue above my ear. Joe Martinez, the barber at Los Alamos who always cut my hair, brushed against the bump and out popped a little piece of that broken windshield, which had slowly been working its way out. I still have that fragment of glass in a little box at home. I was telling one of my companions at work about this incident, and he cracked me up with the remark, "I'll bet that this little piece of glass has all this time been the antenna to outer inspirational forces that have been feeding you good ideas ever since the accident."

Perhaps my most memorable trip in the army took place by train from San Antonio to New York City and back. The opportunity arose from the occasional necessity of escorting a patient (usually with a mental illness) to a special hospital somewhere else in the country. In this case, the young soldier was so ill that two of us were assigned as escorts to a mental hospital on Long Island. We were strictly ordered to have him handcuffed at all times to one or the other of us, and to the framework of his berth at nighttime. In exchange for taking this special-duty assignment, we were allowed to spend two or three days in New York City before returning. For the other escort, this was a fine opportunity to visit his nearby family, and I never saw him again after we delivered the patient to the receiving office of the mental hospital.

On the way to NYC, I remember waking up at night and looking out the window to see the capitol building of Arkansas at Little Rock. The trip across the Mississippi River was spectacular. I had never seen a river anywhere near its size! On arriving at Penn Station in NYC, we were met by a young soldier who was assigned to take us to the hospital. Even though this was by no means an emergency trip, the driver went very fast, with sirens blaring and lights flashing all the way. The drivers and passengers of other vehicles were no doubt wondering what kind of tragic drama was taking place in the ambulance. The highways formed a very tangled and complicated network, with beautifully arranged cloverleaf crossings to avoid direct intersection. The thing I noticed first about the city itself was the large number of huge apartment houses; thus, I understood how so many people could live in the city.

The driver took me back to Manhattan, where I got a small room in Hotel York, a moderately priced hotel about five blocks from Times Square and conveniently close to everything important. I had dinner every night at a clever place called an Automat, where the food was dispensed in slot-machine fashion.

I don't know which I looked at most on Times Square—the people or the signs (probably the signs). Row after row of huge electric signs flashed, blinked, moved, and dazzled the eyes of the spectator. One sign was a big movie screen with advertisements flashing on it like a movie in a theater. Another was a huge bank of little lightbulbs that flashed on and off at various times, producing moving figures in black and white. Advertisements for various beverages were huge glasses with bubbles rising in them. A giant man smoking a Camel blew huge smoke rings out over the street.

The people were equally interesting. They were one mad crowd, everyone going somewhere, anywhere. They didn't care when or where they crossed the street. A poor driver didn't have a chance unless he was in a mainstream of traffic. If a driver approached Broadway, he had to honk and fight to cross, even if the light was for him. The mobs of people formed a solid wall across the street and on the sidewalk, and one had to be in the stream of traffic going his way or he just went backward.

I was standing on the corner taking it all in when a man and woman walked up and said, "Here, take these. We can't use them." I found myself in possession of two tickets to a quiz show on one of the local radio stations, so I decided to go. It wasn't spectacular, and I did not get on it, but it was unusual and interesting. Worn out, I went back to the hotel and went right to sleep.

I learned how to use the subway (a fascinating experience), and the next morning I ended at the basement of Rockefeller Center, underneath the biggest building I had ever been in. Up, up, up I climbed, until I reached the street floor, where I was caught for several hours in the Museum of Science and Industry. Beautiful working displays of all the greatest modern inventions lined the rooms. What is more, a person had the freedom to work all the different displays himself. Besides the modern machines, there were all sorts of interesting gadgets demonstrating electrical, mechanical, and light principles. All of them "worked" or moved or otherwise were very interesting.

Knowing that there was so much to see and do in New York, I left the museum long before I wanted to. The next place I went was NBC Studios, to see if I could get a ticket to a broadcast, but there were hundreds of others clamoring for tickets, so I thought that I would be left out, particularly as all the tickets had been given out two hours before. But some beautiful angel was with me, for just as I was about to leave, a young man walked up and handed me a ticket that he could not use. Imagine my delight and happiness when I saw it was to the *Harvest of Stars* program with James Melton! It was the show I wanted to see more than any other. That program came from the largest radio station in the world. What is more, it was a floating studio, actually a room suspended within a room. The purpose of this was to eliminate all vibrations, particularly those of the subway beneath.

After the program, I went on a rather interesting tour of the NBC television and broadcasting studios. There were all sorts of things to see: studios, newsrooms, television sets that were in use, and sound effects rooms.

Desiring to crowd interest into every minute, I got on the subway, went to Thirty-fourth and Broadway, walked a block, and then began ascending the Empire State Building. I took two elevators to get to the top; the first one took passengers up fifty floors, at which point we transferred to another that took us up the rest of the way. I was electrified by the view, especially seeing the traffic so far below and buildings that had looked so big from street level but were so dwarfed from this dizzying height. I could see all of New York City, most of Jersey City, far into the Atlantic and up the Hudson, the Statue of Liberty enlarged through a telescope, a forest of huge buildings, and also Central Park.

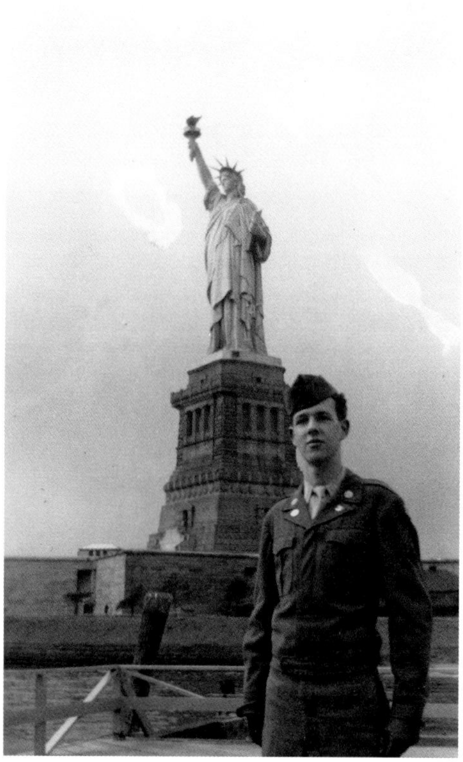

Figure 5. At the Statue of Liberty, March 1947. (Harlow family photos.)

I also went to the southern tip of the island and took the ferry out to see the Statue of Liberty. Unfortunately, the interior was closed to climbing because of some sort of internal maintenance. To prove that I was there, I asked someone to take a photo of me with the statue in the background. I also went to the Metropolitan Museum of Art, where I explored the Egyptian room with particular interest but didn't see any other exhibits because of closing time.

I went to the box office of the Metropolitan Opera and had a choice between two operas: *Lucia di Lammermoor* or *Tristan und Isolde.* I decided on the latter because it was surely "grand opera" at its most impressive. *Big mistake!* It's not that the seat was so bad (it was in the topmost balcony, from which the stage and singers looked tiny). The problem was that the opera is *long* and excruciatingly *boring!* Nothing happens; no beautiful music is heard (probably because the "Liebestod" comes near the end, by which time I felt petrified in the seat). But it was nevertheless an experience among many that made my stay in New York thoroughly memorable.

In our army barracks at Fort Sam Houston, one of the country-western songs that the guys played over and over again included the following lyrics:

> Detour: There's a rocky road ahead,
> Detour: Paid no mind to what it said,
> Detour: All these bitter things I find,
> Should have read that detour sign.

Otherwise, there wasn't much music in my army life until the winter of 1946–1947, when I learned that the San Antonio Opera Company was looking for people to sing in the chorus of three productions: *Aida, Faust,* and *Madame Butterfly.* It was a big deal for San Antonio; the company had engaged big-name soloists from the Metropolitan Opera in New York City. Because my army assignment left evenings and weekends free, I decided to try out for a part. Indeed, I made it, being classed as a bass. I was cast as a high priest in *Aida* and as a soldier in *Faust.* For *Madame Butterfly,* only a small chorus is required, and I was not in that opera.

We had frequent rehearsals with Mr. Griffin, who had the job of training the chorus. One problem in that regard was that while Griffin loved *Aida,* and concentrated our energies in learning that opera, he didn't care much for *Faust,* and he alarmed the production manager by neglecting to rehearse us for that opera. Finally, he was ordered in no uncertain terms to pay attention to the *Faust* chorale parts, and we worked hard to get caught up with the necessary schedule.

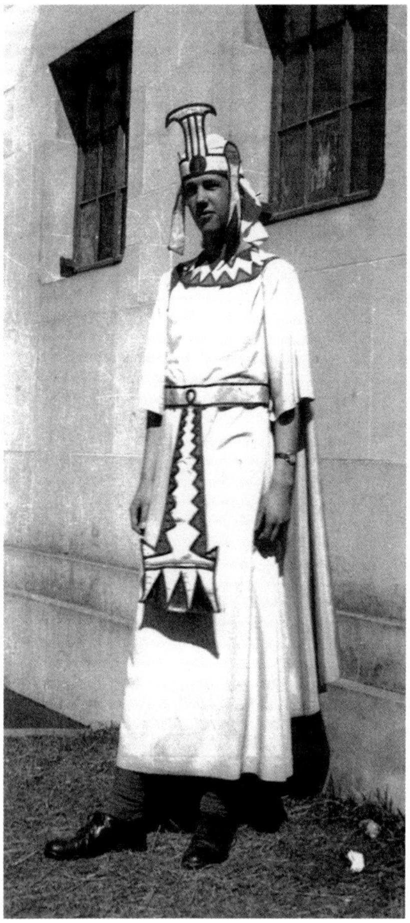

Figure 6. Dressed as an Egyptian priest for a performance in *Aida* during the Third Grand Opera Festival in San Antonio, Texas, March 1947. Before each performance, I removed my watch, shoes, and stockings and put on Egyptian sandals and makeup. (Harlow family photos.)

I had a scare as we approached the opening weekend. As a result of some infraction (I don't remember by whom or what), it was announced that we were to be restricted to our barracks and to the immediate area for the entire weekend. Fortunately, the US Army took compassion for my circumstance, and I was allowed to perform. There was a lot of fun and excitement in taking part, with fancy costumes, crowds of singers and dancers, an impressive orchestra, and a huge audience.

In early 1947, the army was eager to cut its size. World War II had been won, and there was no need for such large masses of people in the armed forces, so I was given the opportunity to be discharged. I took it, leaving the active army in April 1947, but I remained in the Army Reserve—first as an enlisted soldier and later, after getting my bachelor's degree at the University of Washington, as an officer, starting as a second lieutenant. I was later promoted to first lieutenant. These positions required my attending monthly meetings and going on active duty for two weeks each summer. Although the pay was not high, it was a good supplement to my rather meager budget.

3
The University Years

THE UNDERGRADUATE PERIOD (1945–1949)

I had finished three quarters of university credit, two at Oregon State College and one at the University of Utah at Salt Lake City, in the ASTRP program. World War II had ended the previous summer, and I think ASTRP ended during the first half of 1946.

After leaving active army service in April 1947, I resumed academic studies at the University of Washington. I entered in the summer term in 1947 and registered in the Physics Department, of which Professor Utterbach was the chairman. That first term was a disaster for me. My mind had been so firmly set on other activities and thoughts during my army days that I found it hard to concentrate. My grades were low: a C in physics and a C in mathematics. It was enough to make me contemplate changing majors, and I took an introductory botany course on the assumption that my capabilities (whatever those were) might blossom more easily in that direction of study. This digression was interesting, albeit short-lived, and I returned to the study of physics with better results in the following terms.

I also enjoyed other courses. Astronomy was fun, but I don't think I learned much. I especially enjoyed our night sessions when the sky was clear and we could see planets through the big university telescope. But the intensely exciting era of the Hubble telescope and the exploration of the moon, Mars, and even Titan were still years away. Quantum mechanics was fascinating, and my physics course finally got off on a good start with this and other branches of that field.

I also took cello lessons as a university course, and I enjoyed them, but my abilities were quite limited and my interests didn't lie in struggling with the necessary discipline of practice and more practice. Physical education courses were required for undergraduates, and they were mostly a burden for me because I was not sufficiently coordinated to perform any better than just marginally well. Swimming was a fortunate exception; it came rather naturally to me, and I did very well in the course, except for one setback: I caught a miserable fungus infection on my feet (athlete's foot), which landed me in the university infirmary and kept me out of the pool for the rest of that term.

Recreation during the undergraduate years consisted of going to an old-time silent-movie series and taking the bus to downtown Seattle for browsing around in the stores and along the waterfront. I was completely a loner—no social life, no dates (until graduate school days), and no bumming around with the guys.

During my first term at the university, I lived in a boarding house a short distance north of the campus. At first, I was paired with an older guy with a German accent in a double room on the second floor. But it soon was clear that the arrangement was not going to work for me—not because of the other guy but because I needed privacy. So, knowing there was an unoccupied corner in the basement, I asked to be moved down there. Here again the arrangement was not satisfactory, so I went to the university housing office to see if any other places might be available. After a little exploration, I found a situation that proved to be excellent until my marriage in 1952. Mrs. Sophronia Kalin and her son John lived in a little house perhaps a half-mile northwest of the campus, and they were looking for a student to live with them. Rent was $25 per month and meals were $35 per month. I could afford that: my GI Bill credits from the army paid $75 per month, plus tuition, books, and supplies, and I soon learned that it was easy to find students wanting some tutoring in math and physics at $1 per hour, for which I generally earned about $30 per month. That was plenty for my needs.

I never got to know John Kalin very well. He lived in a basement room and was gone (working somewhere?) for much of the time; he rarely ate meals with Mrs. Kalin and me. Mrs. Kalin was gone all day, Monday through Friday, at a job as a church secretary. Within a year or so, John moved away, and Mrs. Kalin was a little bit uncertain about my living with her. But the uncertainty disappeared when she and I finally realized that we were related! Her sister's daughter was married to Frank Randall, the brother of Charlotte Randall, who had become my stepmother when she and Dad were married, so that made it OK for Mrs. Kalin and me to live in the same house.

One summer when the term was over, I spent a month building a new concrete retaining wall and front steps for Mrs. Kalin's house. It was a hard project, for which I had no assistance. Constructing forms for the wall, steps, and walkway took several weeks. Then I contacted a concrete company, which sent a delivery truck with soft concrete. For the next several hours, I worked harder than at any other time I can remember, tamping down the concrete in the retaining wall, forming the steps, and smoothing the walkway. It was an exhausting experience, but it all turned out very well, even better than I had anticipated. (I thought that the wall would last forever, but that turned out not to be the case. A few years later, after my wife and I moved to Los Alamos, I learned that Sixth Street, including Mrs. Kalin's house, had become a new raised freeway and that all the houses in its path had been torn down. My concrete triumph had been destroyed.)

By going to school four terms a year (fall, winter, and spring quarters consisted of three months each, while the summer quarter was concentrated into two months), I was able to get my bachelor of science degree in 1949. My grade-point average (3.5 out of 4) just barely made me eligible for Phi Beta Kappa, and my science record resulted in my getting elected to Sigma Xi.

THE GRADUATE SCHOOL PERIOD (1949–1953)

Things changed for me after I earned my BS degree. I entered graduate school in the Physics Department at the University of Washington, but my GI Bill funding had run out at the end of my undergraduate period and it was necessary to seek other means of financial support. For a couple of years, I was a teaching assistant ($110 per month), working about twenty hours per week, guiding younger students in laboratory classes and in "quiz sections." The latter were devoted to supplementing the more formal lectures presented by the faculty, answering questions, explaining difficulties, and giving informal tests. I also spent a year as a research assistant ($175 per month), working at the university's sixty-inch cyclotron, doing various odd jobs required to bring the machine into active usage, and writing an analytical paper on the expected beam behavior. I applied for and received a National Science Foundation predoctoral scholarship ($250 per month).

I taught a course called Physics for Music Majors, which was required for students in the Music Department. I was completely in charge of choosing the topics, administering examinations, and grading students. The class taught me a very important lesson: classroom teaching was a profession that I *never* again wished to engage in. On the other hand, one-on-one teaching turned out to be a major activity for me at Los Alamos, and for fifty years I enjoyed working with high school seniors (about ten of them), undergraduates (about 120 of them),

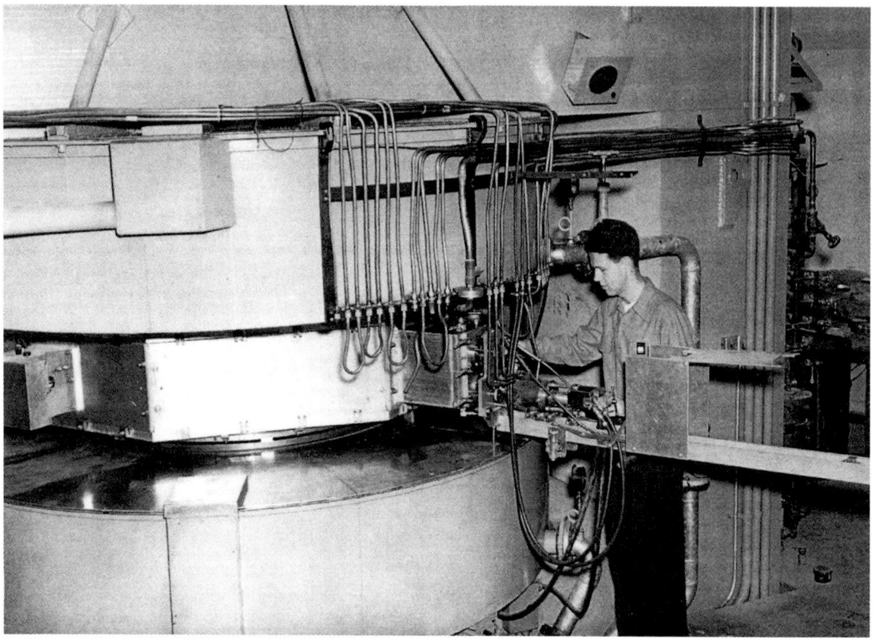

Figure 7. Adjusting the sixty-inch cyclotron at the University of Washington. (Harlow family photos.)

graduate students (about fifty of them), and service academy summer-program students (about ten of them). I was the PhD research and dissertation adviser for sixteen of the graduate students. I also continued tutoring students, although less frequently than when I was an undergraduate.

Courses in graduate school were enjoyable and fascinating, and I did better than during my undergraduate days. Perhaps the most interesting were the courses on analytical dynamics, electrostatics and electrodynamics, quantum mechanics, and modern analysis—taught in the Mathematics Department by Professor Zukerman, a super teacher who made the difficult subject very clear and comprehensible. I did so well in these courses that the department gave me the Sebastien Karrar Prize for top graduate student. The prize was $50—a lot of money in those days.

Achieving a PhD became more and more firmly established as my goal, but two foreign languages were required for the degree. German came to me quite easily and naturally; I did well and sort of enjoyed it. (The poem "Du bist wie eine Blume" is still imprinted in my memory; I can spout out both verses with little effort.) French was another matter. German was taught analytically, emphasizing vocabulary, grammar, and the reading of technical literature. The approach used for French was for me much more nebulous, emphasizing the pronunciation of words and phrases but never focusing on basic structure. I soon began to detest French classes, but being driven by necessity, I learned enough to pass the scientific reading test required for the graduate degree.

I also started getting more sociable in graduate school. For one thing, I met lots of students as a teaching assistant in the laboratory classes. In late August 1951, I finished my report on the cyclotron beam and asked Professor George Farwell if there was someone who could type the paper for me. He replied that the Physics Department had just hired a new secretary and because school was not in session until September, she likely would have time to work on it. So I went with him to the department office, and he introduced me to Patricia Jean Nystuen. What followed was one of the most important things in my life—we were married on June 21, 1952. (My life with Pat is discussed more fully in chapter 4.)

EMPLOYMENT INTERVIEWS (1953)

For the next year, there were no recreational trips as I was concentrating on finishing school and Pat was working as a medical secretary to help pay the bills. In the spring of 1953, however, I did take two trips to interview for jobs, with the anticipation of finishing school by the end of August. One trip was to the Bell Laboratory in Murray Hill, New Jersey; the other was to the Sandia and Los Alamos Laboratories in New Mexico (see chapter 5).

COMPLETING MY PHD

Dr. Boris Jacobsohn was a specialist in theoretical physics in our department, so he became my adviser for PhD research, dissertation writing, and guidance through the oral examinations that were required for completing the degree. Our work together had both positive and negative aspects. The positive ones were his pleasant personality and sharp mind. The principal negative one was his absolutely dictatorial insistence on my following exactly the research steps that he prescribed in detail. Whenever I suggested an alternative idea about how I planned to achieve my goal, he would say, "OK, Frank, you can follow that path if you wish, but remember that if you don't finish by the end of August [1953], I won't be around for a whole year." I knew what he meant: on the first of September he would be leaving Seattle for a year at the Institute of Advanced Studies at Princeton, so I

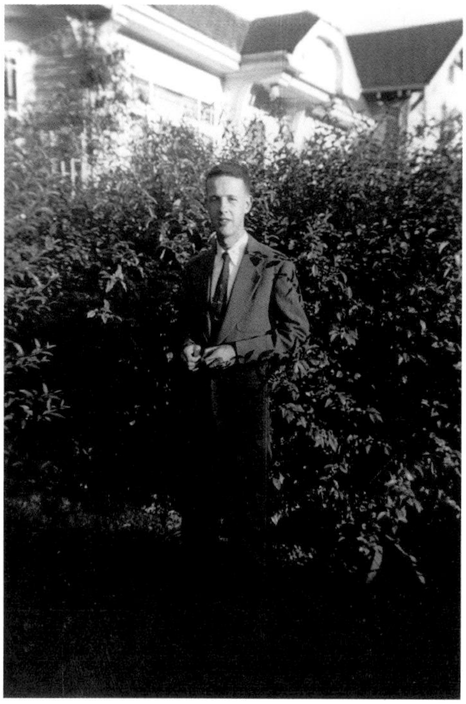

Figure 8. I have just successfully finished the oral defense of my PhD dissertation, thereby completing all my university work, August 14, 1953. (Photo by Patricia Harlow.)

was faced with a terrible dilemma. I wanted experience in independent thinking, but I was also eager to finish in time, so I followed his ideas completely, and by working very hard every day, I was able to take my final defense-of-dissertation exam on August 14, 1953. I published my dissertation, "Nuclear Isobars in Intermediate Coupling," in the *Physical Review* in 1954.

Jacobsohn's other PhD student, Cheng Hsiu Chang, still had a couple of weeks of work to do when Jacobsohn left. Cheng ended up having to spend an entire year waiting for him to return. The price I paid for simply doing what I was told, however, was that for several years at my new job in Los Alamos, I had very poor self-confidence. The consequences are described in chapter 5.

My wife, Pat, took a picture of me a few hours after the last papers were signed for the PhD degree. I look exhausted, which is certainly how I felt. We had two or three days to relax before leaving for work in Los Alamos on the first day of September 1953.

4
Family and Homes

In my late teenage years, I began to realize that a major life goal was to have a wife and children and a home that would be an anchor for living. I wasn't very sociable in those years, and indeed the label "nerd" was very appropriate during my time in high school. It wasn't until I was twenty-three years old and a graduate student at the University of Washington that everything changed. When Professor Farwell introduced me to the Physics Department's new secretary, Patty Nystuen, I remember vividly the feelings that led me instantly to think, "This is the person I want to marry." After we finished discussing the paper she would type for me, I left the Physics Department office, but my sense of exhilaration was incredible. "What should I do to make further contact? Soon! Hey, I've got it. I'll wait at the front door at five o'clock and see which way she's going and pretend I'm going that way also." But I didn't have to pretend, at least not as far as the direction was concerned.

Shortly after five, she came out the door. "Oh, hi," I said, trying to sound nonchalant, despite the butterflies in my stomach. "I was just heading home. Which way are you going?" She pointed toward the northwest. "Hey, that's my direction too." So we walked along together, and my head was in such a spin that none of the words can be recalled as I write this many years later. In fact, we lived just a few blocks from each other.

I visited Patty often, as much as our busy schedules would allow, and our first "date" was at Woodland Park, where there was a little lake and a zoo. One day in early October, after we had known each other for about six weeks, I couldn't keep my thoughts to myself. "Will you marry me?" I asked. She seemed very surprised and indicated that she would think about it. Two days later she said yes. "But let's wait until next June, when I'm done with school," she added. I wanted to get married right away but could see that she was correct, so we eventually settled on the first day of summer, June 21, 1952. The faculty and graduate students in the Physics Department professed not being surprised at our plans to get married. Professor Henderson said it was obvious what was happening.

During my frequent visits to her apartment, we would sit close to each other on the couch and talk about our lives and dreams for the future. We often played a recording of Rachmaninoff's "Rhapsody on a Theme of Paganini," which thereafter became a memory piece for those wonderful evening visits. But we really couldn't spend large amounts of time together; we both were consumed with schoolwork. Patty was in the last, intense stages of finishing her bachelor's degree in geography, and I had more than a year's work to do on my dissertation.

The wedding at the little Episcopal church near the university was to be fairly small, to be followed by a banquet at the Meany Hotel and a honeymoon in Vancouver, British Columbia. We visited with Mr. Cochran, the minister, to talk about our religious convictions and plans for the future. (He later became a bishop in the Episcopal Church.) I had rarely attended the Episcopal church in Bremerton with my Aunt Bessie, and I had not developed any formal religious affiliation. Mr. Cochran didn't try to influence me in that regard. After we were married, Patty and I went together every Sunday to St. Mark's Episcopal Cathedral, and after moving to Los Alamos, we went every week to the little meeting room on Trinity Drive where a small Episcopal congregation shared space with other meetings. Mr. Kenneth Shook was the priest at that time. Throughout these various exposures, I never formed a desire for any formal church affiliation.

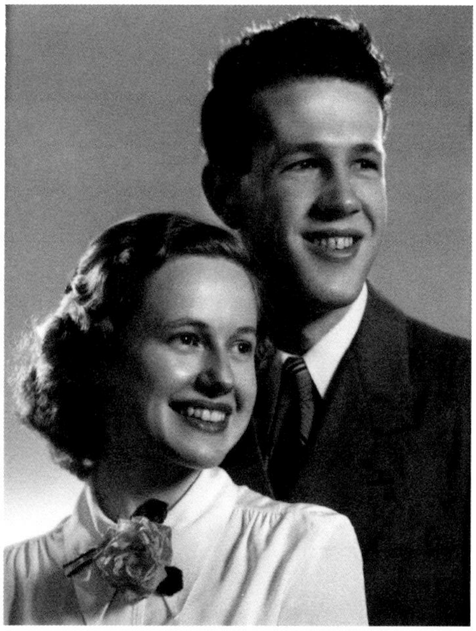

Figure 9. Our wedding photograph, June 21, 1952. (Photo by Maxine and Reinard Studio, Seattle.)

We invited only close family members to our wedding and reception: Patty's parents (Mary and Oscar), her brother and sister (Carol and John), her aunt Clara from Minnesota, my father (Harvey), my brother (Bruce), and Aunt Bessie. Carol was maid of honor, and Bruce was best man. It rained the day of the wedding, and Dad claimed that he could hear thunder at the crucial moment of the service when we became husband and wife. But the rain was not hard, and we managed everything without getting soaked.

We explored the neighborhood around the university to find a nice place to live. One of them was ideal—a very nice apartment, close to school and nicely furnished—but at a cost of more than $100 per month, it was beyond our budget. We settled instead for a converted double garage behind a house owned by Mr. and Mrs. Tustin. The rent for the double garage was about $65 per month.

It was interesting to see the interior of Mrs. Tustin's house. She had connections with the owners of Ringling Bros. and Barnum & Bailey Circus and had the means for acquiring a dramatic collection of furniture and other rare articles, mostly Oriental, which she stored in every part of her house. From her front door to the back of the house was a single narrow passageway with artifacts stacked high on both sides. My impression was that all of this material was rare and valuable, and she told us stories associated with many of the pieces.

The living room of our apartment had a wood-burning stove that was the source of heat for the entire structure, but we soon noticed that it was very hot around our heads and very cold around our feet and legs. We invested in a fan, which helped even out the vertical variations in temperature. The humidity in the place was always quite high, which had both good and bad effects. The good part was that we could grow orchids on the south-facing windowsill. (My favorite was and still is a beautiful plant called *Coelogyne cristata,* which grew and bloomed nicely for us.) The bad part became distressingly apparent when I stored a beautiful leather cello case and a pair of shoes on the floor behind the couch. It didn't take long before they were covered with mold and were damaged beyond repair.

The desk in the living room was used a lot during evenings and weekends, when my dissertation work was pursued at home. The kitchen refrigerator was so noisy that it would immediately destroy any quiet mood. We called it Mr. Mood Breaker, or Mr. MB for short. Because of our tight budget, we ate frugally. At the Pike Place Market, we could buy colt meat and squid at very low prices, and they both were very edible.

Patty got a job as a medical secretary, and I managed to get a National Science Foundation scholarship, so our finances were not too bad. We treated ourselves to an occasional movie at the Varsity Theater and to supper at Lun Ting's Chinese Restaurant, both within walking distance. My brother, Bruce, sometimes lent us his car—we didn't own a vehicle until we moved to Los Alamos.

Mrs. Tustin did not want us to have a dog or cat, but a hamster was OK. We made a cage for it, and it was lots of fun to have around. It learned to open the peanut butter jar holding hamster food by grabbing the lid in its teeth and walking around to unscrew it. It then jumped in and rapidly filled both cheeks with as much food as possible. One time the little critter managed to escape, and it climbed into a hole in the upholstery of the couch. I had a terrible time getting it out. I would reach in as far as I could and feel his whiskers tickle my fingers. So I figured that putting my hand only partway to where he was sitting, feeling his whiskers, and then lunging as rapidly as possible would allow me to catch him. As I recall, that strategy actually worked. We were sorry to have to find a home for both him and the orchids when we left for Los Alamos, but in both cases we felt good about the people who took them.

Besides the dissertation, my main activities away from home were playing the cello and going to Army Reserve meetings once a month at Fort Lawton. Shortly after our wedding, I had to go for two weeks of training at Fort Lewis, which was a real drag. At least by then I was a commissioned officer, so the pay was higher than in my corporal days, and the money came in handy.

In the summer of 1953, my dissertation work became a frantic race with time. I was very tired of it all, but Patty was a tremendous support for me, as has been the case many times thereafter. Finally, it was all done. Pat had done the typing, I had inked in the equations, and the result was approved and defended, all at the last possible moment. It was almost impossible to believe that she and I were free from that phase of our lives. We had two or three days to decompress, and we spent the time looking around town, including an elevator ride to the top of the Smith Tower, the tallest building in Seattle at that time but now completely dwarfed by dozens of newer buildings.

Then it was on to work, flying from Seattle to Denver and thereafter to Santa Fe.

When we arrived in Los Alamos, the people who met us and took us to lunch at Fuller Lodge were amused because Patty was still carrying the umbrella that had been necessary on the damp day when we left Seattle. That afternoon, we went to our new home, 3784 Gold Street, Apartment 3, upstairs on the north side of a four-apartment building. The Zia Company had moved in some furniture (wicker, I think) and some dishes, pots and pans, and so on.

We met Harry and Vilma Ballance, who lived in the other upstairs apartment in our building, and also soon met Stretch (James) and Pat Fretwell, who lived in another, nearby building in the Gold Street Apartments. (Stretch was nearly as tall as I.) We bought a small amount of furniture at a garage sale: a little table (which I still use in our pottery room) and a few chairs. I signed in as a Lab employee on September 2, 1953, and found where the Theoretical Division was located (about 0.7 miles from our apartment, easy walking distance for two round-trips per day).

Early September in Los Alamos is almost always beautiful, with crystal-clear blue skies, stunning mountain views, and numerous wildflowers; Michaelmas daisies and Indian paintbrush are among the most spectacular, complemented by abundant wild sunflowers and numerous smaller plants, mostly with warm yellow flowers. We were enchanted and took numerous walks together to enjoy the beauty of our new home.

We had no car with which to explore beyond our walking range, and there was no public transportation. Thus, we were delighted when the Fretwells came to our rescue. In chapter 6 on fossils, you can read about one of the earliest trips they arranged, to the little town of Jemez Springs. The thirty-mile trip took up to three hours each way over the narrow, one-lane dirt road that wound its way up into the Jemez Mountains, across the side of the huge Valles Caldera, and then down into the deep canyon cut by the Jemez River. We also went with them to Cochiti Pueblo to a ceremonial dance, which was fascinating to see, hear, and feel. Patty and I felt more enchanted by these and other excursions than we had ever anticipated.

Stretch lent me an acetylene torch and a few silver-working tools, and I bought some silver (at eighty-five cents per ounce) and pieces of turquoise and soon was delighted to see that I could actually make some nice jewelry. I worked in our little utility room, which was cramped but adequate. Patty especially was eager for me to make a set of napkin rings, which I did, and we continue to use them.

Some months after we arrived, Stretch asked us if we would like to buy his car, which was a 1937 LaSalle. I found it comfortable to sit in, as compared with the cramped quarters that many cars had. Patty liked it too. So at last we had wheels! The old car was reliable, although its one fault was a tendency to shimmy at speeds above forty miles per hour. But that didn't bother us; there was no need for speed during our trips to Santa Fe or even, occasionally, Albuquerque.

One of our trips to Santa Fe was specifically for the purpose of getting some furniture so that we could return the rather ugly pieces provided by the Zia Company. We shopped around but didn't see what we liked (or could afford) until we looked in the Sears & Roebuck store on Lincoln Avenue, a couple hundred yards from the Plaza. Up on the balcony, in the back of the store, we saw exactly what we both wanted. It was solid oak furniture from a company called Ranch Mode. (Later the company changed to making furniture that was much more flimsy and not as attractive.) To purchase a few pieces, we borrowed $600 from the bank. As time went by, we bought a couch, two stationary rocking chairs and a matching chair that didn't rock, a dining room table and chairs, a nice bed, and a sturdy four-drawer bureau, all of which—except for the couch—are still in service.

The trips to Albuquerque were tedious. The highway had two lanes that passed through the center of Bernalillo and entered Albuquerque on Fourth Street, on the west side of the railroad tracks. In the fifteen or so miles between those two cities, the roadbed consisted of concrete slabs, each perhaps fifty feet in length. When Patty was carrying our first child, driving over the concrete slabs (ca-thlunk, ca-thlunk, ca-thlunk) was almost impossible for Patty to tolerate.

We missed our hamster in those early days at Los Alamos, and Patty got two kittens, which she named Hepsibah and Mahitable, but we didn't have them for long. We also got a middle-aged cocker spaniel named Skippy, who turned out not to be house-trained, so we took the dog back to its previous owner. The next dog was a little black cocker spaniel that we called Tristram (named after a distant relative who was a whaler on Nantucket Island), but our luck with pets continued to be bad—Tristram became very sick and sort of hysterical, so we couldn't keep him either. We didn't try again until a few years later, when Patty found a little dog (part basenji) at the Santa Fe Animal Shelter. She had gone alone to Santa Fe between Christmas and New Year's Day while I stayed home with our children. I remember Patty calling from the shelter to see how I felt about her bringing home the dog, and of course I was delighted. Taffy was a wonderful member of our family for sixteen years. After she died, I buried her in a deep hole that I had dug in the garden by the west fence. I put a pile of volcanic lava rocks on top, which are still there. Altogether, we had three very special dogs—Taffy, Lindy, and Shag. There have also been other fun pets along the way. Our daughter Celia had an iguana, our son, Keith, had various snakes, and Patty had a canary named Paisano.

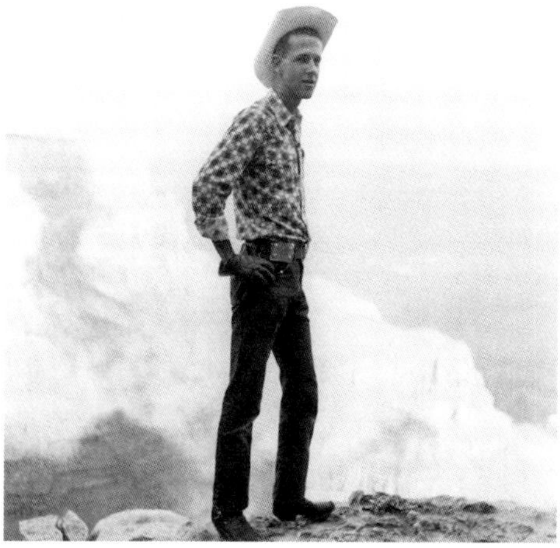

Figure 10. Patty took this picture of me during our vacation trip to the Grand Canyon in October 1955. (Photo by Patricia Harlow.)

Before our first daughter, Catherine, was born, I taught Patty to drive a car. She was an enthusiastic and talented learner. At that time, the nearby town of White Rock was essentially abandoned. It had been a place for Manhattan Project workers to live, and it consisted of numerous little "wing-foot" houses, where people could temporarily live until better places could be built, so it was an ideal locality for driving lessons and practice.

Shortly thereafter, I got my first motorcycle from Alan Netz. The deal between Patty and me was that if I got a motorcycle, Patty would get a piano; that sounded fine to both of us. The beautiful little piano is still a nice part of our home. Although it is seldom played anymore, it is a nice reminder of the piano-lesson days of Catherine.

When Catherine was born, on March 3, 1955, we were still living in the Gold Street apartment, only a few hundred yards from the Los Alamos Medical Center. Just as with all the rest of our children, I was there watching as Katie (as she is now called) first saw the lights of this complex world.

In those days, all housing in Los Alamos was rented from the US government. Eligibility for a particular apartment, duplex, or house was based on the number of children in the family and on the number of "housing points" the employee had earned. The points were figured on the basis of two attributes: the length of service and the salary of the family member working for the Lab. With Katie's birth, we became eligible for a two-bedroom place. We moved to a duplex on the north side of town, on Thirty-fourth Street, a few months after Katie's birth; we stayed there for about two years. It was a pretty place, down in "Skunk Hollow." Behind the duplex was a wooded area in a shallow canyon. We planted giant sunflowers by the back door; they were enormously successful.

Our most famous visitor at the duplex was Subrahmanyan Chandrasekhar, with whom I worked during the summer of 1956 and who later won a Nobel Prize. Chandra was an avid observer of the political scene in this country and was a very dedicated Democrat (or Republican—I don't remember which), and politics dominated much of the evening's discussion.

Our second daughter, Carol, was born on November 3, 1956, while we lived in the duplex. It's interesting that she was noticeably different from Katie from the day she was born. She was more easily startled, but at the same time, she was somewhat less lively.

With Carol's birth, we qualified for a place with one more bedroom and were able to get a single-family house on Piñon Loop, close to where we are now. This was a Group 16 government house, well-constructed and very nice to live in. We were in the Piñon Loop house from 1958 to 1960. Interesting visitors included my brother, Bruce, whom I had not seen since our wedding in 1952, and Patrick Sutherland (see chapter 6 on fossils), who came to see us frequently at first and then once every other year until he died. Dad visited while we were living at Piñon Loop, and he much enjoyed playing with Katie and Carol. I always attribute our having more children to a comment he made to Patty, something like, "These kids are really fun, but don't you miss having babies around the house?"

At Piñon Loop, we saw the Soviet *Sputnik* going over our house. Although neither Katie nor Carol realized what they were seeing, they nevertheless witnessed that historic event, because Patty and I pointed their faces upward as the space vehicle passed by. We planted apple trees in the backyard and erected a swing set, which was subsequently moved to each of our two following houses. We also planted a piñon tree in the front yard—the only one on Piñon Loop—but it was cut down some years after we left.

Our third daughter, Celia, was born on June 30, 1959, while we lived at Piñon Loop, and once again we were eligible for a house with one more bedroom. In 1960 we moved a couple hundred yards to a four-bedroom Group 16 house on Sage Loop. The advantage of going to the same style house was that everything could be transferred to the new place without having to worry about where things would fit. (The floor plans of all Group 16 houses were the same, except for the layout of bedrooms in the back parts of the buildings.)

We missed the sense of pride of ownership of a house, or even just a piece of property. Patty and I began exploring the area, especially around Santa Fe, to see what was available and how much it would cost. I told people around the Lab that we were looking, and a resonant chord was struck with one of the staff members, Robert Wagner. He was building a home in Nambé and needed some money. He also owned fifteen acres (actually 14.6 acres) of land in the Tano Road district just north of Santa Fe. The land was beautifully situated on a ridge, with fabulous views to the west, north, and east. Land in that area was selling for $750 per acre, but he said he would take $300 per acre—that is, $4,500 for the land. This amount would essentially deplete our savings, but Patty and I thought it was a fabulous investment and decided to make the purchase. That was about 1964. Later, the adjoining land on the same ridge was purchased by Mrs. Maytag of the Maytag Washing Machine Company, and she had a fabulous mansion built on the property. Not only that, but there was a gated entrance controlled by a family living in a very nice, separate house by the gate. At the present time, beautifully situated land in that area has been selling for between $50,000 and $100,000 per acre, and the value continues to go up and up. We don't plan to build a home there; we simply keep it for financial security in our old age or to will to our children for them to sell.

Our son, Keith, was born October 24, 1960, while we were living in the Sage Loop house. There were no original government houses with more than four bedrooms and only a few enlarged four-bedroom Group 16 houses that had additions built by the government for special people. One that was modified to have six bedrooms and two and a half baths was occupied by Russ Duff and his family. He had further modified the interior in several very nice ways and seemed content to stay there forever. We knew the Duffs; Tony Hirt and I had published a paper with Russ on the instability of a diffusing interface between two fluids. We decided to be thoroughly content with the Sage Loop house and never move again, unless for some unexpected reason the Duff house was vacated and we had enough priority points to qualify for it.

In 1962 the Duffs decided to move to California, and we immediately applied for the place. On Friday we were told that our position was second on the list; the Cowans were ahead of us. We had a tense weekend waiting to see if the Cowans would actually take it. On Monday they declined, and it was ours!

Again, the move was easy. The house, located on Eleventh Street, was only about 250 yards away from the Sage Loop place. An even luckier part of the situation was the announcement that the government was about to sell the houses in Los Alamos, with first refusal given to the current tenants. We eagerly accepted the offer to buy and signed for a twenty-five-year mortgage to pay off the $11,500 debt for house and land. We're still here, just Patty and I; all the children have left home. A Los Alamos insurance agent told us last year that he would give us $250,000 for the place, sight unseen, but we declined.

Music was a significant part of our children's lives. There were lessons, recitals, orchestra concerts, and summer music camps. Katie played the piano for a while, taking lessons from Rosalie Heller. Katie later switched to cello, taking lessons from the high school orchestra director, Don Beene. Carol also studied cello, at first with my instructions on the tenor viola, then with Don Beene on a regular cello. Celia studied viola; Charmaine Weber was her teacher, but Celia quit at the end of her sophomore high school year. Keith studied cello for a while also. He had wanted to play the French horn, but the high school band director, Jan MacDonald, advised him not to go in that direction because his mouth was not shaped right for the instrument. Keith also tried playing the double bass in the high school orchestra for a while. I enjoyed hearing them playing in the high school orchestra. Mr. Beene did a great job in bringing out the best in all the kids.

Katie went several times to the Hummingbird Music Camp not far from Jemez Springs. One thing that bugged her (literally) was the mosquitoes. Their bites caused her a lot more discomfort than most people experience, but she enjoyed the camp's program of activities. I think Carol went there for one summer session, but the next year she went to a two-week music camp in Nebraska, which she thoroughly enjoyed.

Recitals were stressful for our kids, and perhaps even more so for Patty and me, but at the same time, they were sort of fun. One year, Carol played "Kol

Nidre," accompanied by Gusti Kalmus, and did an especially good job. Katie is the only one of our four kids who has made music a lifelong profession. She continues to be a delight to hear, especially in her string quartette.

In the 1950s, I also continued my music, playing cello with the little Los Alamos Orchestra, led by Gusti Kalmus's husband, Ernie. We played pieces like "Eine Kleine Nachtmusik" by Mozart; the Bach double violin concerto, with Mr. and Mrs. Tom Weber playing the solo instruments; and Barber's "Adagio for Strings."

Music was not the only thing our kids did outside of school. We encouraged them to produce "summer books" containing text and drawings describing their summer activities. All four of them did an excellent job every year, and at the end of the summer, we gave each of them some money to spend as they wished. I kept the summer books in my office for many years, but not long ago we turned them over to the kids. Swimming was also popular with all four kids. They much enjoyed going to East Park Pool, where we had a multiyear membership. I filmed home movies when they showed how they could swim and dive.

Those were busy years for Patty and me. She did a great job keeping our home together while I struggled to make a good reputation at the Lab. We both attended the kids' activities, agonized over some of the things they did, and tried to figure out how to help them during various problematic times (which I won't enumerate).

We liked to take family trips to Santa Fe and made a game out of identifying landmarks along the way: the Rio Grande, Black Mesa, Camel Rock, and others. In Santa Fe, we walked around town, looked at people during Indian Market each Labor Day weekend, and shopped for everyday things we couldn't get in Los Alamos. On one occasion, Carol tripped on the sidewalk of San Francisco Street about one block west of the Plaza. She bumped her head on a low brick wall and cut it rather badly. I carried her to the car while Patty attended to the other kids, and we went to the emergency room of nearby St. Vincent Hospital to get the wound stitched. More fun in Santa Fe were the trips to the Laboratory of Anthropology, where I took one kid at a time.

Patty and I were not very sociable when the kids were still home, and that pattern has continued to the present time. We rarely got a sitter to watch the kids while we went out. The visitors who came to see us were mostly family: Patty's mother, brother, and sister, and my dad.

Starting in 1973, things changed a lot for us. Katie graduated from high school and left home to attend the University of New Mexico in Albuquerque. Carol left the same year to accept a Rotary Exchange adventure that took her to Sydney,

Australia, for her senior year of high school. In 1975 Celia left home at the end of her sophomore year to go with friends to live in Denver. Patty and I were very distressed. Keith continued his high school courses, graduating in 1978. Then he immediately went into the US Coast Guard for a four-year enlistment.

THE EMPTY NEST

After 1978, our six-bedroom house was empty except for Patty and me, but we made good use of every room: a pottery room, Patty's workroom, my painting room, our master bedroom, plus the two and a half bathrooms, kitchen, dining room, and living room.

As Patty puts it, she and I tend to lead separate lives. Not absolutely, of course, but to a large extent our activities have been somewhat different. For her, there is the Episcopal church, where she has been active for many years in Altar Guild work; the Museum of International Folk Art in Santa Fe, where she went every week as a volunteer in the Textile Department for about twenty-five years; the American Association of University Women; the Embroiderer's Guild; Scottish country dance lessons and performances; plus all the things she does to keep the house nice and give us good meals. My main activities included going to the office, working on studies of Pueblo Indian pottery, and painting pictures.

Throughout the 1980s and 1990s, one of my favorite evening recreations was to drive to the eastern end of Los Alamos Mesa, just before the highway plunges down toward the White Rock turnoff and the Rio Grande Valley. From the parking area, I could walk eastward along what had been a one-lane dirt road that was now blocked by a big pile of dirt and a fence—mainly, I suppose, to keep people from pushing their old cars off the very steep and high cliffs. Less than a half-mile farther, the old road reached the tip of the mesa, where someone or some organization had installed a bench and a waterproof box on a stake, where it was possible to read a brief description of the sights across the valley and the name of the place, Meditation Point.

With the noisy highway a couple hundred feet below my perch, I didn't really meditate out there. I much preferred to sit on a rock rather than the bench. My thoughts were then mostly devoted to pondering technical research problems at work, and I often got ideas that proved useful.

As the sun sank lower and lower toward the Jemez Mountains behind me in the west, its light was reflected from windows of houses on the Sangre de Cristo foothills. They would shine as brilliant points of light; I called them my Valley

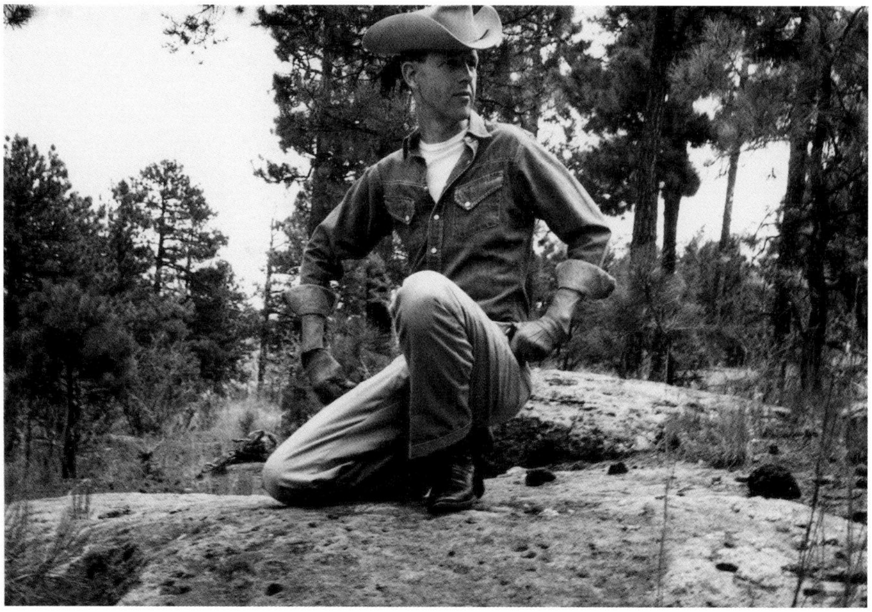

Figure 11. I took this picture of myself using a time-lapse camera in 1965. (Photo by Francis Harlow.)

Stars. Typically, I would be able to count as many as fourteen, but they would gradually disappear one after another as the sun sank lower and the world around me darkened into twilight, then to the blackness of night, when the true stars would shine brightly in the sky and perhaps the moon would be visible.

On one such night, I went back from Meditation Point a few hundred yards, where the mesa widened, and guided by my flashlight, I moved southward through the piñons and junipers toward another place where a very old road climbed the steep cliffs. I saw deep ruts from wagon wheels where the road reached the top of the mesa, but that night something *very* memorable occurred. I first saw it as a sudden brightening of the trees and ground, as intense as daylight, and my first thought was that an airplane had lost its motor and was silently gliding toward me. But then I looked up and saw the brightest meteor I have ever seen, streaking across the sky from north to south over the valley. Suddenly it shattered, and all that remained was a cloud of smoke lit by the half-moon in the southern sky. The smoke (debris) was actually clearly visible for a minute or so, until it disappeared in the upper atmosphere.

For every twenty or so times I went out to the end of the mesa in the evening, only one would be to Meditation Point. The others would be to my absolutely favorite spot at the tip of a shorter mesa just to the north, which sprang as a spur from the Los Alamos Mesa. It commenced about a mile before the Meditation Point parking area, behind a cluster of industrial buildings located immediately to the west of the boundary between Los Alamos County and Santa Fe County. Stepping through a gap between two of the buildings, I crossed the county line, which lies about five feet behind the buildings. From there it was less than a quarter of a mile to the tip, where there was a rock made of solidified volcanic ash. On its top was a shallow depression that was very comfortable for sitting. Although most of my visits were in the evening, I also enjoyed going to that same spot in the rare circumstance of a dense morning fog filling the air. I could hear the cars on the distant highway, perhaps three-quarters of a mile to the south, but it was impossible to see them through the morning fog. In fact, it was almost impossible to see the bottom of the canyon nearly straight below my resting point. It felt like looking into Puget Sound from the Bremerton docks, which I had liked visiting when I was a teenager. In both cases, one could sometimes see the shadowy features of some indeterminate objects lying on the bottom.

Since 1964, I have not been farther from Los Alamos than Albuquerque, but Patty has loved traveling to Australia to visit Carol and her family, to India to visit her old college roommate (Carolyn Parpia), to Japan, China, and Italy (with Carol Bronson), and two times to Norway to visit the town of Nystuen and to cruise the west coast to above the Arctic Circle.

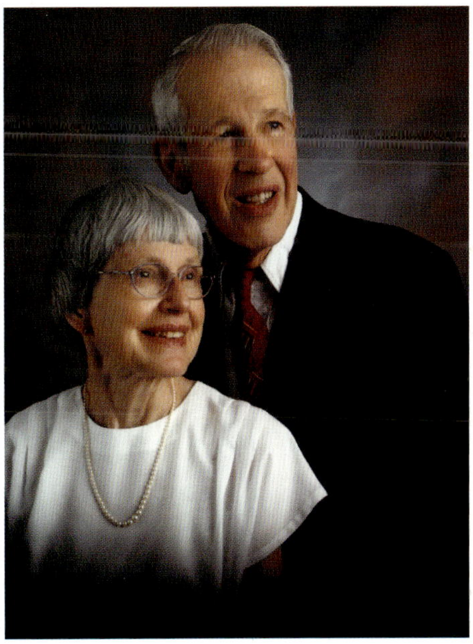

Figure 12. Our fiftieth wedding anniversary photograph, June 21, 2002. (Photo by Don Taylor Studio, Los Alamos.)

Patty has been a wonderful partner to care for me during various bouts of illness requiring surgery (six occasions), chemotherapy, radiation, and two cardioversions. Her main physical problem is osteoporosis, and I worry when she does things like climbing ladders and carrying heavy loads. Taken altogether, Patty and I have much to be proud of in our four children and certainly for fulfilling admirably the expectations and hopes that I felt even before meeting my wonderful wife.

Patty and I celebrated our fiftieth wedding anniversary on June 21, 2002. The kids gave us a nice party and a present that is a real treasure. Katie, Celia, and Keith spent many hours working on a giant, four-page collage with photographs of Patty and me and our families from as early as the 1930s.

Every year in early May, we go together to buy petunias. It's fun to walk around the greenhouse in Pajarito Acres, where the Foxes have a huge selection of plants each spring. I'll have prepared the garden in front of the kitchen window by digging in some potting soil, and we work together in the planting. Each year, we have a wonderfully attractive mass of color from those petunias. One of Patty's particular skills is to get bulbs to produce beautiful flowers: tulips, daffodils, narcissus, and others. On the south side of the north wing of the house, we have a miniature rosebush that we got in a little pot when we were still in the Gold Street apartment, and we've taken it along with us during every move. It has occupied its current spot for forty-two years, and we both enjoy it a lot. We also have a couple of peach trees (Jubilee), an apricot tree (whose blossoms freeze about four years out of five), and two apple trees that have very nice fruit, which Patty turns into applesauce to be canned in jars for wintertime enjoyment. Our bird feeders are lots of fun to watch as the birds compete with one another for the best spot to stand while eating. Two thistle-seed feeders also hang outside the kitchen window. They attract pine siskins, who grasp the wire net or coarse-woven fabric sock and wrestle the seeds through the little gaps, often hanging upside down while they eat. Patty can identify the kinds of birds better than I, and it's fun to consult with her.

One amusing incident happened to Patty and me in Santa Fe many years ago. We were sitting in a restaurant with two older ladies who remembered a lot of things that went on in Santa Fe during the 1920s. Somehow the conversation turned to the subject of household help. They both expressed considerable disgust at the effects Los Alamos had had on salaries paid to Indian women who cleaned or washed and ironed clothes for families of the scientists. "We could hire an Indian for one dollar a day, and Los Alamos people spoiled that by paying ten dollars per day," said one of the ladies with sincere disdain. That one issue seemed paramount in her mind regarding Los Alamos. Patty and I have laughed about that ever since.

As we gradually accumulated Pueblo Indian pottery in the 1960s and early 1970s, our kids would tell their teachers and classes about our little museum. As a result, we were asked again and again to allow students to come for a tour. Often they came by school bus, and typically, they stayed for forty-five minutes to one hour. Patty would manage the goings-on in the living room while I entertained the kids in the pottery room. I don't know how many sessions we had, but I would not be surprised if it were as many as fifty.

Other visitors also came to see our pottery collection and to discuss authentication of their pieces. That way we met some very interesting people, mostly dealers and collectors. Dennis and Janis Lyon from Phoenix came often while they were building their collection of early historic pottery. Bob Gallegos from Albuquerque has also been a very welcome visitor.

We've also had students living at our house for weeks or even months at a time while they were working with me at the Lab. Of all of them, I think Patty and I most enjoyed Didier Besnard from France and Murray Rudman from Australia.

Patty was usually a part of the conversations, although she would excuse herself if the visitors were not to her liking. Other pottery-related visitors were my book coauthors: Duane Anderson and Dwight Lanmon. Patty and I are very fond of both of them. Whenever we had book-signing sessions in our dining room, Patty was an enthusiastic presence, conversing, unwrapping books, and putting the signed copies into boxes.

Through all of my years in Los Alamos, the one constant that has kept me going is having Patty as a major part of my life. My appreciation for all that she has done and been is unbounded.

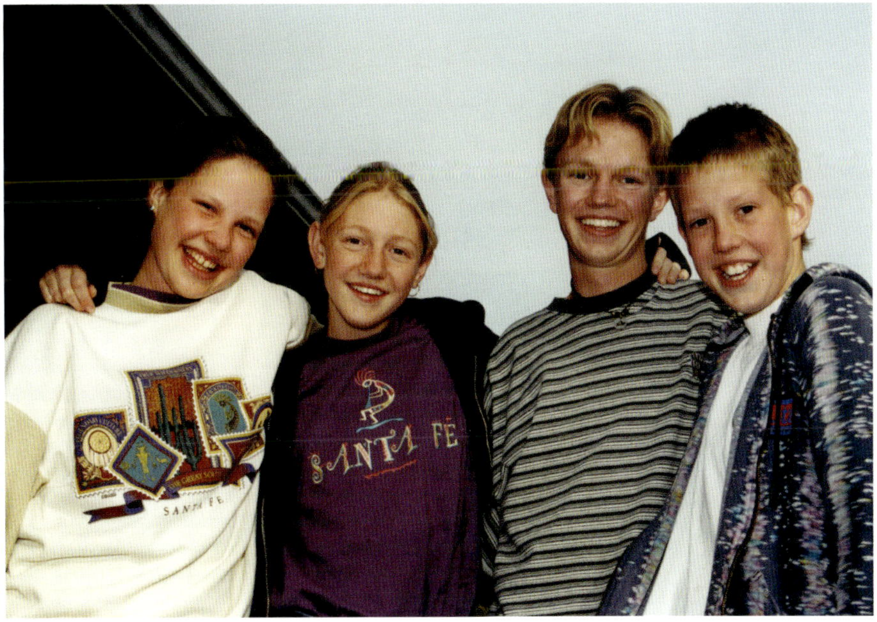

Figure 13. Our four grandchildren: Lisa Muiznieks, Haely Harlow, Clinton Harlow, and Adam Muiznieks, September 4, 1997. (Photo by Patricia Harlow.)

5

Los Alamos National Laboratory

COMING TO LOS ALAMOS

Los Alamos National Laboratory (called Los Alamos Scientific Laboratory when I joined the staff), the town of Los Alamos, and north-central New Mexico have been fabulous surroundings in which I have lived the majority of my life. The Laboratory has given me a remarkable amount of freedom to pursue research directions of importance to me and, I think, to the rest of the technological world. The final section of a paper I wrote in 2003 points out the feeling that I continue to maintain, namely, that I've been extremely lucky throughout my life to be in the right place at the right time. (The paper, "Fluid Dynamics in Group T-3 Los Alamos National Laboratory," was published in the *Journal of Computational Physics*, 195 [2004], pp. 414–33.) Significant collaborators and supporters have all played crucial roles in our success over the past fifty years of my employment at the Lab.

Why did we come to Los Alamos? Well, of course, after finishing school, to find a job to support Patricia and me and our anticipated children was a logical step. The organization had to be scientific to a significant degree and would preferably be located in an interesting and comfortable part of the country. ("Comfortable" refers to climate.)

At the university, I had discussed my possible future directions with various members of the Physics Department staff. In particular, John Manley (department chairman), George Farwell (who first introduced Patty and me), and Seth Nedermeyer (a former Los Alamos expert on explosives) had all been here in the early days of the Laboratory, and they encouraged me at least to consider the idea of coming here. On the other hand, my PhD adviser, Boris Jacobsohn, wanted very much for me to go to a university and pointed out several possibilities to explore. I figured that it was prudent to get information on both types of places: the universities and the well-established laboratories. For the former, Boris knew of several possible openings at the University of Wyoming and the University of Kansas. For the latter, there were the famous Bell Laboratory at Murray Hill, New Jersey; Sandia National Laboratories in Albuquerque; Livermore Laboratory near San Francisco; Geophysical Institute in Fairbanks, Alaska; and Los Alamos National Laboratory in its little town near Santa Fe.

Boris based his suggestions on the assumption that my further research directions would continue to lie in the field of nuclear physics. I didn't tell Boris that quantum mechanics and the associated mathematical formulations were really outside the scope of my anticipated conceptual abilities and that for me a career in classical physics held a lot more promise for success. In particular, the field of fluid dynamics and turbulence seemed especially attractive, despite the paucity of my academic exposure to the subjects (consisting of only a week or two in one of my mechanics courses) and even though, years before, the eminent physicist Richard P. Feynman had warned that describing turbulence was the hardest unsolved problem in classical physics.

Years later, I gave examples of the sorts of problems that had attracted me to this field of research. At a conference in Los Alamos in 2003, I played videotapes of the explosion of Mount Saint Helens in 1980, videotapes of the twisting failure of the Tacoma Narrows Bridge in 1974, and vintage films of tornados. I asked myself, Can such a thing be calculated, really meaningfully calculated? That sort of problem became the focus of my life's endeavors.

JOB INTERVIEWS

While I was finishing my dissertation, I interviewed for positions at Bell Laboratory, Sandia Laboratories, and Los Alamos Scientific Laboratory. The Los Alamos interview was the most difficult to arrange. The first setback was that they lost my carefully prepared employment application. My inclination was to wipe Los Alamos off my list, but John Manley and George Farwell strongly encouraged me to persist. "Fill out the application again and send it in," they insisted. "If you can get past the Personnel Department, you'll find that the rest of the Lab is great." So I sent another copy and eagerly awaited an invitation to come for an interview. About that time, I got an invitation from Sandia Laboratories, and it seemed efficient to visit both places in one trip. I called the Los Alamos Personnel Department, which said that no arrangements had yet been made for me to come (the second setback). I'm sure that my voice sounded impatient when I insisted they make arrangements for coordinating an interview with my trip to Sandia; after all, it wasn't going to cost the Lab more than my round-trip flight (on Carco Airlines) from Albuquerque to Los Alamos. They grudgingly agreed to see what they could do and finally said it was OK to come and see the place and talk to a few people. "Seeing the place" turned out to mean that they mentioned a few places to go but had no one available to drive me around town.

I packed my nice clothes for the interview and flew from Seattle to Albuquerque, but on arrival I discovered that my baggage had not arrived with me (the third setback)! "We'll try to locate it and get it to you as fast as we can," said the clerk with an expression that indicated that he couldn't care less about the matter. I went to the Alvarado Hotel (a beautiful old landmark that subsequently was torn down, much to the chagrin of history-minded people in the state). The baggage had not appeared by later in the evening, so I went to bed and immediately learned something about the effects of dry, semi-desert air in New Mexico. When I slid into bed, bright flashes of static electricity were generated between the sheets and my hairy body. They didn't hurt, of course, but were a real novelty that I had never seen before. Likewise, in the morning when I reached for the light switch: zap! But still no baggage. No electric shaver. No nice suit to wear. So I went to Sandia unshaven, wearing jeans and a scruffy leather jacket. The interviewers were genuinely sympathetic, and the interview and tours went well.

Later that day, my baggage arrived, so for the trip to Los Alamos the next day, I was properly shaven and attired. The interview with Carson Mark and Bob Richtmyer, the leader of the Theoretical Division and his deputy, also went well. I expressed an interest in working with hydrodynamics, and they seemed to think that was OK. Afterward it hit me like a bolt of static electricity: Los Alamos is surely the place for us to go!

I received offers from Bell, Sandia, and Los Alamos; in addition, I had a verbal commitment for a job in Fairbanks at about $750 per month. I remember that the Bell job was $570 per month. In contrast, Los Alamos offered $520 per month, but by then I had already decided that if Los Alamos made a reasonable offer, that's where we would go. Patty, bless her heart, was willing to accept whatever decision I made.

EARLY DAYS AT THE LAB (1950s)

We arrived in Santa Fe on Labor Day, September 1953, and we spent the night at La Fonda Hotel. The next morning, a taxi arrived to take us to Los Alamos, and north-central New Mexico became our home for (so far) more than sixty years.

I was assigned to a group of scientists working on various projects in the Theoretical Division office, which was housed in the Laboratory Technical Area, an old barracks building alongside Ashley Pond. My "boss" was Rolf Landshoff, the leader of Group T-3, a small group of people with various interests and projects. Rolf assigned me to work with Al Peaslee on a computer code designed to solve problems of material motion in the presence of appreciable radiation transport of energy—that is, a nuclear explosion.

I was fascinated with the new machine called a computer. Los Alamos had received an IBM Model 701 computer earlier that year. It was the world's first commercially built computer, and it enabled me to get in at the beginning of a new technological era, which has evolved at an astonishing rate in the subsequent

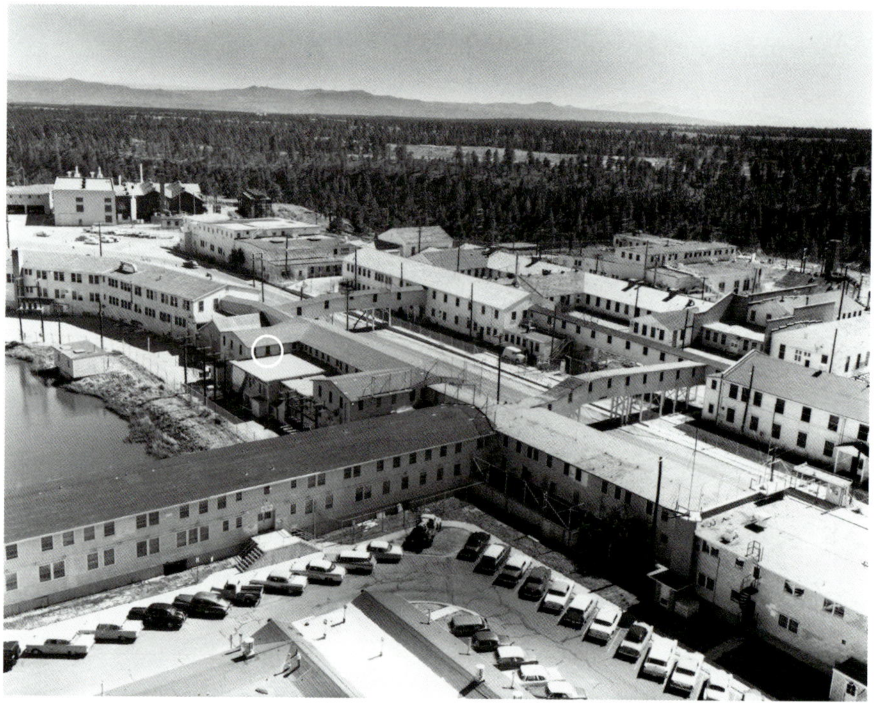

Figure 14. A Laboratory technical area by Ashley Pond, about 1953. The small white circle to the left of center marks where my office was located. (Courtesy Los Alamos Historical Society Photo Archives.)

half-century. That first machine had a console where we loaded our IBM cards, pushed various buttons, and received printouts of the results. The guts of the machine were in a large adjoining room, where the most visible manifestation of its presence consisted of rows of shelves on which were numerous cathode-ray tubes, each with a memory for the storage of discretized information. Running calculations was a hands-on process for each user, who was assigned blocks of time on a 24/7 schedule. If my assigned time was 2:30 to 3:00 a.m., I would set my alarm clock accordingly and hope I didn't stumble and spill my box of IBM cards during the sleepy trek from my office to the computer on the floor below.

With luck, we could solve a radiation-hydrodynamics behavior study with a finite-difference mesh of twenty-five cells in a period of about an hour. Today that sounds incredibly slow and primitive, but at that time it was an enormous improvement over what we could previously accomplish. We never dreamed of the power that would become available during the following years. For example, the little laptop computer on the table in front of where I'm writing now is vastly more powerful than the old 701, capable of solving the twenty-five-cell problem in less than a millisecond.

WITNESSING A NUCLEAR TEST

A remarkable event for me occurred in April 1954. The Laboratory had a policy that newcomers should witness a nuclear explosion and observe all the experimental equipment required for monitoring the physical processes that took place. Accordingly, I was offered and accepted the opportunity to go to the Marshall Islands, in particular, Eniwetok and Bikini Atolls, for a two-week observational excursion. Along the way, numerous associated experiences helped make the whole trip memorable.

Bob Frank was my traveling companion. We flew to Los Angeles, and there we caught a first-class flight to Honolulu. First class meant that there was a lot of personal service during the flight, including special meals and drinks. It also meant that when we got off the plane, there was a special arrival ceremony in which hula girls put strings of orchids around our necks and a group of musicians played Hawaiian songs. We were taken to the Edgewater Hotel at the southwest end of Waikiki Beach, where we were surrounded by lush tropical plants and were a stone's throw from the beach. We stayed there for three days before continuing our long journey. Bob had a cousin there who managed a Hawaiian shirt manufacturing company, which we visited. Fancy flowery fabrics were imported from the mainland United States and then assembled into garments. (The purpose was to legitimatize the "Made in Hawaii" label.) Bob's cousin was very generous with his time and transportation and took us all over Oahu Island, through tropical jungles, to pineapple plantations and orchid farms, and past some of the world's most famous surfing beaches. He took us to Ishii Gardens, a very fancy Japanese restaurant, where we could pretend to sit on the floor at a low table that had a hidden well underneath for our legs. The waiter cooked our food at the table, and it was delicious! I spent time also wandering through some of the tourist trinket shops along the street that paralleled the fabulous (and expensive) resort hotels along Waikiki Beach.

Soon, however, it was time to leave, and we went to Pearl Harbor to catch a C-47 military transport plane. Talk about a contrast with the first flight! The C-47 had hard benches along the sides of a big open space in the body of the plane. Also, to our dismay, it was subject to various types of malfunctioning. Indeed, something (unknown to the passengers) distressed the pilot after we had been in the air for about an hour, and he decided that it was necessary to return to Pearl Harbor for repairs (which actually didn't take very long). But by then it was evening, and soon we were flying in the dark, seemingly thousands of miles from the nearest land. Our journey took us somewhat south to Johnson Island, where we got off and went into the nearly deserted airport terminal to warm ourselves and stretch our legs after the cold and cramped flight. But soon we were on our way again, reaching Kwajalein Atoll as the sun was rising. We waited several hours there while approval for continuing to Eniwetok was being verified and the next flight was being prepared for takeoff. (I should comment that all the flights on this trip—from Los Alamos to and around the Marshall Islands and back—were on old-fashioned propeller planes; jet planes were not in use at that time, and indeed I've never flown on a jet plane.) Finally, in the late afternoon, we arrived at Parry Island on the Eniwetok Atoll.

Parry Island is the main inhabited place in the atoll. We combined visits to the experimental facilities and laboratories with helicopter flights around the atoll and adjusted ourselves to the high temperatures and humidity during the following days. Regarding the latter, each of our living spaces included a locker with a continuously burning lightbulb to prevent mildew and mold. Food was exceptional, consisting of the best steaks, vegetables, and desserts prepared by skilled chefs. (Good food was considered one of the chief perks for people who had to stay there for long periods. This was Operation Castle, which took most of the first half of 1954.)

Our days were not completely filled with work, however, and we spent some time snorkeling around the coral heads in the lagoon. The atoll was formed by a huge mountain rising sharply from the otherwise deep surrounding ocean. Over long stretches of geologic time, the mountaintop was covered with countless lifetimes of coral, which could not grow above sea level, so the whole atoll is no more than a few feet above sea level. There is essentially no tide at an atoll. (Tides are formed by water piling up or pulling away from continents and are driven by gravitational forces of the moon and sun.)

The lagoon floor consisted of intensely white sand made from ground coral. Here and there in the lagoon were coral heads—roughly circular masses of living coral and other marine life—perhaps five or ten meters in diameter and four or five meters tall, extending to within a meter below sea level. These coral heads had vast numbers of marine species in and closely around them. Some of them were very dangerous, and we were given special instructions as to what we should avoid. Eels and stonefish were among the worst of the movable animals, while the stationary *Tridacna* clams were potentially lethal in their ability to trap a person under water until he drowned. Those clams were spectacular to see, being nearly a meter across and possessing brilliantly colored lips that quivered over the edges of the open shells. If something got too close, such as a hand or a foot, the shells would snap shut with remarkable speed, and nothing could be done if a body part was trapped by the shell. We swam out to the coral heads and snorkeled around on the surface of the water or duck-dived down for even closer looks. All around us were huge numbers of little fish, brilliantly colored, trying to satisfy their curiosity by swimming very close to the strange intruders. I can't imagine that any other coral heads or reefs in the world could be more beautiful and exciting to see.

Sharks were quite rare in the lagoon, but we saw lots of them from a ship near Bikini, where they were eating garbage that was thrown overboard. On the shores of the lagoon were fascinating seashells and chunks of red coral, and I still have several of the most interesting specimens.

On the outer parts of the atoll, between the islands and the deep, steep plunge to the ocean floor, is a shelf that was also fascinating to explore. The shelf has a maze of little channels, perhaps five to ten centimeters deep, with little islands between them, each perhaps thirty to seventy centimeters across. (The entire width of the shelf must have been about one hundred meters.) We had been advised to bring a pair of old tennis shoes before we left Los Alamos; they were absolutely essential for walking on the shelf. Any cut from the sharp shells or corals was very likely to get infected with any of several very mean germs. So

I wore shorts, a T-shirt, and tennis shoes and went exploring. The little channels were always filled with water, which often lapped over the tops of the little islands, driven by the free-ocean waves hitting the outer edge of the shelf. The fauna on the shelf was quite different from that of the coral heads in the lagoon. There were many different kinds of sea slugs, anemones, urchins, and I don't remember what else. After a while, the effects of the intense tropical sun, direct or reflected from the water, began to draw my attention. I got one whale of a sunburn on my legs and felt it, especially in bed at night, for several days. But I was determined not to let that get me down—there was still so much to be seen and done.

Another of the fascinating places to explore was Japtan Island, to the right of Parry Island when facing the lagoon. Between the two islands was a channel through which small ships could pass from the ocean into the lagoon and back. To get from Parry to Japtan, we had to use a small boat to go the distance (perhaps three hundred to five hundred meters). Japtan had come out of World War II unscathed. It still had large coconut palms and areas of virgin jungle. The whole island was not very large, perhaps five hundred by three hundred meters, which was distinctly smaller than Parry Island. Fresh coconuts lying on the ground were delicious. (Later I heard that people were advised not to eat them because of radioactivity imparted by some of the nuclear explosions on the farther island of Eniwetok.) We also explored the jungle areas, with dense vegetation and huge lizards. On the ocean side was the rusting hull of a ship that had run aground, which was not deemed worth removing.

After about a week on Eniwetok Atoll, we got word that it was time to go to Bikini to see the installations there and to witness a nuclear explosion. At Bikini, our quarters were on the command ship, which was moored in the ocean. From it we went by helicopter to visit several islands and especially to see the barge holding the device. Afterward, we returned to the ship to watch the shot at a distance of twenty-seven miles, through very heavy, dark goggles. It's difficult to find the words for how awesome the experience was. The explosion we saw transformed a peaceful island to a raging column of infinite complexity, and it demonstrated the incredible intricacy of material behaviors that combine so many aspects of the physics involved in turbulent material phase transitions.

The explosion we saw was the "Union" shot, fired on April 25, 1954. With a yield equivalent to 6.9 million tons of high explosives, it was about five hundred times as powerful as the bombs dropped on Hiroshima and Nagasaki. (These descriptions are taken from the unclassified report *Announced United States Nuclear Tests*, NVO-209, Rev. 3, released in January 1983 by the Office of Public Affairs, US Department of Energy.)

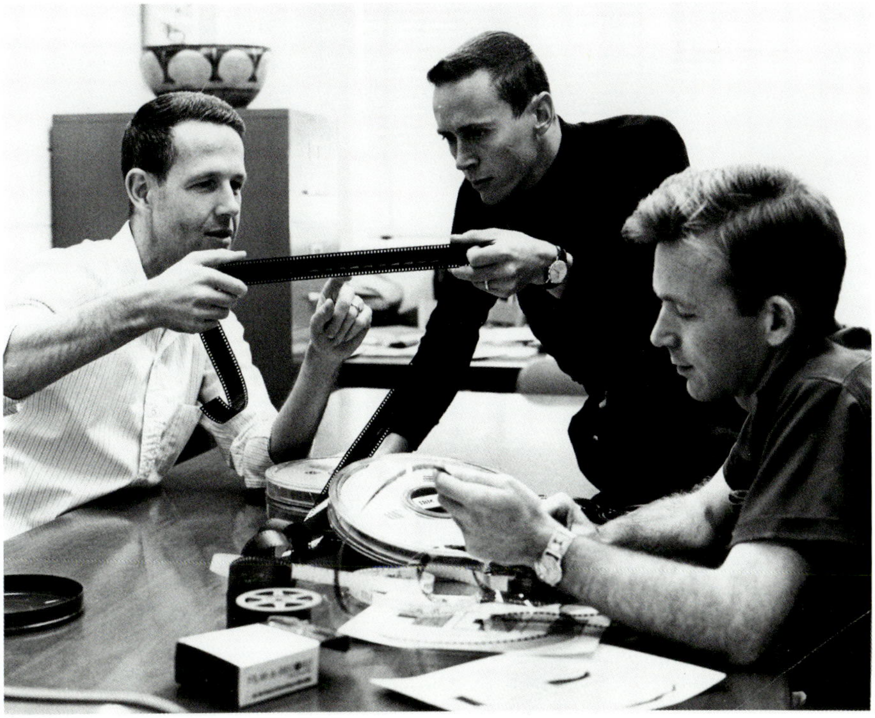

Figure 15. Frank Harlow, Eddie Welch, and John Shannon of Group T-3, examining computer tapes at LANL, about 1965. We are looking at the results of a computer calculation printed on 35mm film. (Harlow family photos.)

The ship steamed back to Eniwetok through the night. Treated as VIPs, we each had a private stateroom. We had seen so much of the experimental and engineering facilities and the equipment for processing the data that the observational instruments had recorded. Those data were the challenges that our computer codes had to be able to describe.

Having fulfilled our purposes for the trip, we soon retraced our steps to Los Alamos in an uneventful journey. The whole experience had a tremendous effect on my emotions.

CHANGING CAREER DIRECTIONS

After that trip, I slowly began to realize that I had a dilemma insofar as my career directions were concerned. It would have been fine for my boss (and for my annual pay raises) for me to continue working with existing solutions techniques, continually updated for each new computer that came along, and solving a never-ending array of specific problems. Alternatively, I could depart from that "applications" route and think about a variety of completely new techniques for solving problems that at that time were beyond the capability of any existing mathematical methodologies. I chose the latter path, even though my raises in pay each year would be minimal because of my abandonment of the problem-solving assignments that were expected of me. (No one was fired in those days except for "extreme cause.") My disfavor was intensified by my back-row silence in the mandatory Theoretical Megaton Group meetings, where people like Carl Walske, Al Petschek, and Bob Thorne were very vocal in their contributions to the discussions.

After five years of obscurity, however, the particle-in-cell (PIC) method that we developed began to show significant power for solving a field of problems of large contortions of materials that had previously defied solution by any other existing technique. Conrad Longmire and Stan Ulam both recognized the value of this new technique and ultimately persuaded Carson Mark to give me a huge (for that time) raise in pay and to appoint me to the position of T-3 group leader. (Rolf Landshoff had left Los Alamos, and T-3 had no leader at the time of my appointment in 1959.) By that time, the Theoretical Division had moved (in 1956) from the old barracks around Ashley Pond to the newly built Administration Building across the bridge.

SOME PERSONAL MATTERS

In 2003 I described the immensely wide-ranging topics on which we worked during my fifty years with Group T-3 in a paper published in the *Journal of Computational Physics* ("Fluid Dynamics in Group T-3 Los Alamos National Laboratory"), which also includes a complete list of my publications before 2003. The topics we studied ranged from issues related to national defense in the early years to a much broader array of issues, including social problems and natural cataclysmic events.

While the article refers to many of the technical issues addressed by our group, it doesn't say much about some of my personal internal dynamics, which seem appropriate to mention here in terms of my Lab activities. Various periods were especially stressful to me. The first was in the middle 1960s. Our technical work in Group T-3 was progressing very well, but there was a lot of pressure on me to be as nearly infallible as possible in knowing the right answers to numerous questions about how each project should be proceeding. The group members were not aware of the state of my nervousness, which threatened to overwhelm me for several years.

Later in the 1960s, we learned of a forthcoming budget crunch at the Lab, and by 1968 it was clear that some people were going to lose their jobs. The cause of all of this was public reaction to the expenditure of large sums of money on the space program. John F. Kennedy's dream of getting people to the moon and back during the 1960s had been achieved, but the euphoria of national pride was soon overwhelmed by concern for the cost. Yes, NASA proved that the adventure could be accomplished, but what did we really get from it? The answer was perceived to be a little basket of rocks and nothing more. So the popular backlash became a tremendous pressure on Congress to cut federal spending for "science." Los Alamos was not the only place that suffered: universities lost large amounts of federal support, and governmental agencies like the National Science Foundation received only a small fraction of their previous yearly allocations for distribution. The Lab faced the prospect of a large RIF (reduction in force—that is, in numbers of employees). In the Theoretical Division, the leader of each group was required to identify candidates for termination. I protested that designating specific people would be disastrous if the names were made public before decisions were finalized. I was assured that the names would be kept absolutely secret, so I reluctantly furnished the three names that T-3 was required to produce. So what happened? You've already guessed it: within a few days the names were leaked by someone whom I was never able to identify, and the effect on morale was horrible! In the end, several good people in T-3 volunteered either to retire or to move to a job somewhere else, but for the people on the RIF list, the pain and scars from that incident remained for years.

During that dark period, Carson Mark, who had been badly injured in an automobile accident, was staying home in a special hospital bed rented for the duration of his recovery period. I visited Carson quite often, usually to discuss the future for the T Division groups, and especially T-3. We eventually agreed that there were two choices for our future. One was to join the nuclear weapons program, which had been somewhat protected from the RIF, and the other was to get funding from sources outside the Laboratory. The first choice would have destroyed forever the goals and dreams that T-3 had envisioned and proved its capability for achieving. The second would place us in direct competition for funding with groups across the whole of US science and technology.

I brought the question to the group members, and after much discussion, we decided to take the very risky path of achieving external self-support. Our confidence at succeeding came from the fact that we had developed powerful national recognition for being able to solve problems that no one else was able to do until they got the techniques from us. While this seemed immodest and boastful of us, subsequent developments proved overwhelmingly that we were correct. I won't list our funding sources, but an interesting historical tidbit is that the Lab had so little involvement with outside funding that the external-contracts office of the Lab consisted of just Mac McGuire and his secretary. It was not long before the management of outside Lab contracts grew to be a large organization. As a postscript, it has been reported that the budgetary crunch and RIF were so stressful to Norris Bradbury, who served as director of the Lab for twenty-five years, succeeding Robert Oppenheimer, that he resigned his position in 1970 as a direct consequence.

Another stressful time for me arose in 1973. Within that single year, both positive and negative things occurred in a bewildering sequence:

- My first book on fossil brachiopods was published.
- My landmark book on matte-paint pottery was published.
- I had my first major one-man show of paintings (at the Jamison Galleries in Santa Fe), where twenty-five paintings were sold during the opening afternoon.
- Byron Thompson of our group died of brain cancer.
- Two of our children left home to begin the next phase of their lives.
- I ceased to be group leader of T-3 (after fourteen years) and had to ponder the choice of becoming associate T Division leader or returning to science. (Fortunately, I chose the latter.)

The late 1970s and early 1980s were times of professional confusion for me. Perhaps it was a midlife crisis associated with turning fifty in 1978. In any case, the period 1978–1982 seemed very unproductive to me, and I worried about whether I'd have any more good ideas in my life. Fortunately, Didier Besnard came from France to Los Alamos, and we worked together through most of 1983 on problems of fluid turbulence and multi-field flow. I felt revitalized and thereafter easily found wonderful challenges to keep me happily busy.

Marvelous people in our group contributed in many essential ways to the success of our technological explorations. These people had come from various places. Some were chosen from the numerous employment applications that came to the Personnel Department. (It was always strange to sort through a pile of applications, putting some of them into a "maybe" pile and most of them in a "rejection" pile.) These sorting decisions were made after only brief deliberation, and in every case, I felt that in one short moment the applicant was being deflected into one or another pathway of life.

I also shamelessly "stole" some of the people who came to T-3 from other Laboratory groups. Carson Mark kept insisting that I hire only PhDs, but I was convinced that a mixture of talents and experiences was crucial to a healthy group. I remember his once remarking that it was amazing how I could get such great and important work from people without PhDs. I think the validity of my choices was a direct result of getting to know people from other parts of the Laboratory and then convincing the best of them that T-3 would be a place for the development of their careers. I can think of at least five people who came to T-3 in the 1960s who were "stolen." All of them turned out to be fabulous contributors to our activities.

Students also came to T-3 over the years. They ranged in level from high school seniors (usually around five of them) to advanced graduate students, usually in one or another field of engineering. In addition, we used to have a US service academy student each summer. Typically, each spent around six weeks between his or her junior and senior years. They came from the army, navy, and air force academies, with a total of about ten in as many years. Altogether, I think that our students were very good to outstanding

I was the most likely staff member in our group to take responsibility for the students each summer. (In some cases, they remained for several years.) The long-term students were almost always here to conduct PhD research and dissertation writing, mostly with me. I was the research adviser for fifteen of them, in collaboration with academic advisers from various universities. As a best-guess estimate, the total number of students who worked with me from 1959 to 2005 was probably in the range of 130 to 150.

One thing that contributed appreciably to the success of our people (staff and students) was the idea of working together in two- or three-person collaborations. Computer programming and elaborate mathematics are areas in which I have relatively little talent. Thus, because most things I've accomplished have involved the generation of large and complex computer programs or sometimes the accomplishment of long and arduous mathematical manipulations, it was always necessary to have someone with a high level of capability in one or the other of those skills in a project. It was quite rare for T-3 to have someone working alone on a project.

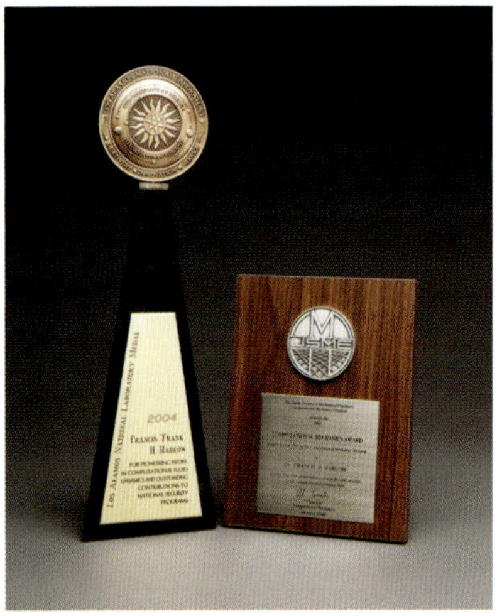

Figure 16. My Los Alamos National Laboratory Medal (*left*) and my 2001 Japan Society of Mechanical Engineers Computational Mechanics Award (*right*). (Photo by Addison Doty.)

In my fifty years at the Lab, I have been honored with several awards, including being named a lifetime fellow of Los Alamos National Laboratory (1981), receiving the Japan Society of Mechanical Engineers Computational Mechanics Award (2001), and being named a lifetime fellow of the American Physical Society (2003). In 2004 I received the Los Alamos National Laboratory Medal, which has been awarded to thirteen people since it was established in 2001. The award "recognizes individuals who have made a contribution that changed the course of science, a major enhancement of LANL's ability to accomplish its mission, a significant impact on sustainability and/or established a major direction for the lab and the nation."

INTERESTING PEOPLE AT THE LABORATORY

One of the great advantages of working at Los Alamos has been the opportunity to interact with some remarkable people who came here as visitors or collaborators. Some are very famous in the scientific world; others may be less well-known but were very important to me.

Indeed, a book could be written about the outstanding scientists of the Los Alamos National Laboratory. In this section, I mention only a few who have been very special to me. There is no intended significance to the order of these comments.

Enrico Fermi

I met Enrico Fermi once, and it was not in scientific circumstances. He was here for a brief visit, and I was not involved with those discussions. What happened, however, is that by pure coincidence, we found ourselves standing side by side at adjacent urinals in the men's washroom. He looked at me and said, "You sure are tall," or words to that effect. And I, with my usual level of social composure, replied "Ah, yes, I guess so." And that was the sum total of my interactions with the famous Fermi.

Fred Reines

Fred Reines was somewhat familiar to me when he was a staff member of T Division. After his famous neutrino work here, he took a position at one of the University of California campuses. Whenever he came back to Los Alamos for a visit, he would stop by my office and we would have a nice conversation about the earlier days of the division and about some of the administrative activities he had become involved with. On one of those occasions, we got to talking about his delight in creating little poems. "I'll write one for you," he said. Then after a few minutes of thought, he wrote three lines on the subject of thermodynamics:

> There is delight in the illusion
> That given wild enough confusion
> There follows such precise conclusion.

During another visit more than a decade later, he quoted to me a two-line verse (The Sun and Earth conspire / To dress the moon in gay attire), which I copied onto the same page. I think that was our last visit together. Later, when he won the Nobel Prize, he was quite ill. He never came to Los Alamos again.

P. Y. Chou

After commencing my own work on the theory of turbulence transport, I became familiar with the pioneering work in that field conducted by J. C. Rotta in Germany and by P. Y. Chou in China. I never met Rotta, but in 1987 Chou came to Los Alamos to meet with a former student of his, who was here doing postdoctoral work in the T Division. By remarkable coincidence, Chou's daughter (who was traveling with him) turned out to be the second wife of a longtime friend of mine, John Chu from Columbia University in New York. It was great having the opportunity to meet Chou and to discuss the current status of turbulent transport theory. I still keep in touch with John Chu, whose age is close to mine.

Oleg Belotserkovskii

Oleg is a widely known member of the Russian Academy of Science, specializing in numerical techniques for the solution of complex problems in the flow of fluids. He and I corresponded for years, and he has sent me copies of books that he has written. About a decade ago, he proposed coming to Los Alamos for two or three months to give a series of lectures on his work. John Hopson, at that time the group leader of T-3, thought that the visit was a great idea and arranged for the travel and finances for both Oleg and his wife. On the day of their arrival at the Los Alamos Airport, John and I went to meet them and help with their luggage. When we got to the prearranged Gold Street apartment, we all sat down for a few minutes to get acquainted. Soon he became very agitated and said pointedly that he was "very eager to meet the famous Frank Harlow as soon as possible." I sat there and almost burst out laughing. John quickly repeated the introductions that had been given at the airport (but obviously had not been heard in the excitement of the arrival). Oleg looked dumbfounded. He blushed a little as he got up and walked over to me and bowed, explaining that he thought I was just someone that John had brought along to help with the luggage (which is likely what would have happened in Russia).

In preparation for each of his lectures, Oleg constructed numerous transparencies for the overhead projector by hand, using various colors to draw the words and pictures onto the blank sheets. I went to his office in the T-11 building every workday, and we talked about his next lecture, Russian life and politics, physics problems that had not yet been solved, and various other topics. He was always interested in describing his activities and showed very little desire to discuss anything going on in Los Alamos or north-central New Mexico. It was an interesting three months.

Whenever he sent me a book thereafter, he always inscribed it with personal and sentimental words in a manner that is apparently standard in his circle of colleagues and friends.

Hans Bethe

Hans Bethe was a very special person in the scientific activities of the world. We first met when he gave a summer series of lectures on the theory of the deuteron while I was a graduate student at the University of Washington. Some years later, when he was here at Los Alamos for an extended visit, I met him again. He was interested in a technical discussion on the current status of knowledge about turbulence in fluids, and the first time we met for these discussions, he made it very clear from the start that he wanted to talk about *physics* and *not* about computers or numerical solutions to problems. That was fine with me, and we got along very well in our interactions

Alan Bishop, a former T Division leader, told me several times about Hans referring to me as "Young Frank"; there were not very many people old enough to call me that. When Hans died, the Lab had a memorial get-together of his friends and collaborators, which his wife and sons also attended. Those of us who had worked with Hans were invited to write a short paragraph about him to be assembled in a memorial book for his family.

Murray Gell-Mann

Like Fred Reines and Hans Bethe, Murray Gell-Mann won the Nobel Prize in Physics. Murray and I spent considerable time together. Besides physics, he is very knowledgeable about tropical birds, ancient coins, and ancient Pueblo Indian pottery; he bought from our collection some examples mainly dating from about 1000 to 1400. Murray is a fun guy, a strong contrast to Hans Bethe, who was very serious but nevertheless a delight to be around.

Sometimes Murray and I would sit up until well past my bedtime, and the conversation would often turn to the topic of quarks and other esoteric aspects of quantum physics. He would solicit my questions and always claimed that they were useful and made him think hard. He never teased me about the stupid things I would bring up, and he would try to explain to me what he knew about each issue and also about the mysteries that still surrounded the field. One time, with wistful sincerity, he said that age was creeping up on him and that it was likely he would never achieve his dream of winning a second Nobel Prize. I never confessed to him that there had been times, much earlier in my life, when I thought that someday I might win my *first* Nobel Prize, but of course that never happened.

Don Pettit

Don Pettit is a nice guy—smart, hardworking, and very friendly. I knew Don when he was working in the Explosives Division at the Laboratory. We were both members of a team formed to study specific problems regarding the interaction of a strong explosion and a piece of metal. Without my knowing it, Don made two things that he thought would be of interest to me. One was a cylinder filled with water containing numerous tiny planar particles, which were capable of showing the flow patterns after the cylinder had been rotated about its axis for enough time to produce essentially uniform radial velocity. When the rotation of the cylinder was suddenly stopped, the flow then exhibited strong patterns of dynamic instability, which changed with time in a very interesting fashion.

The second thing he made involved the interaction of an explosive shock wave and a little flat piece of metal, with a branch of foliage placed between the plate and the explosive. The result was a permanent imprint of the plant structure, which we explained in terms of shock diffraction processes. The cylinder was apparently discarded during moving among the T-3 offices, but I still have the metal plate with the plant imprint.

Don often told me about his dream of becoming an astronaut and being weightless in space. He applied for the job and was accepted into the training program. A newspaper article reporting that he had arrived safely at the space station also mentioned that, among other duties, he was going to perform some fluid dynamics experiments. I commenced an investigation into how I might communicate with him by e-mail while he was in space. Yes, it was possible, based on our knowing each other and because we would have a significant basis for meaningful discussion of his activities. I sent him a message and quickly received his reply, and we continued the correspondence as he performed his weightlessness experiments.

RETIREMENT DAY

I retired from the Los Alamos National Laboratory on September 4, 2003, after fifty years and two days of continuous employment—the first person ever to reach that milestone at Los Alamos. Retirement day celebrations consisted of an all-day symposium of reminiscences about the early days of Group T-3. Of the

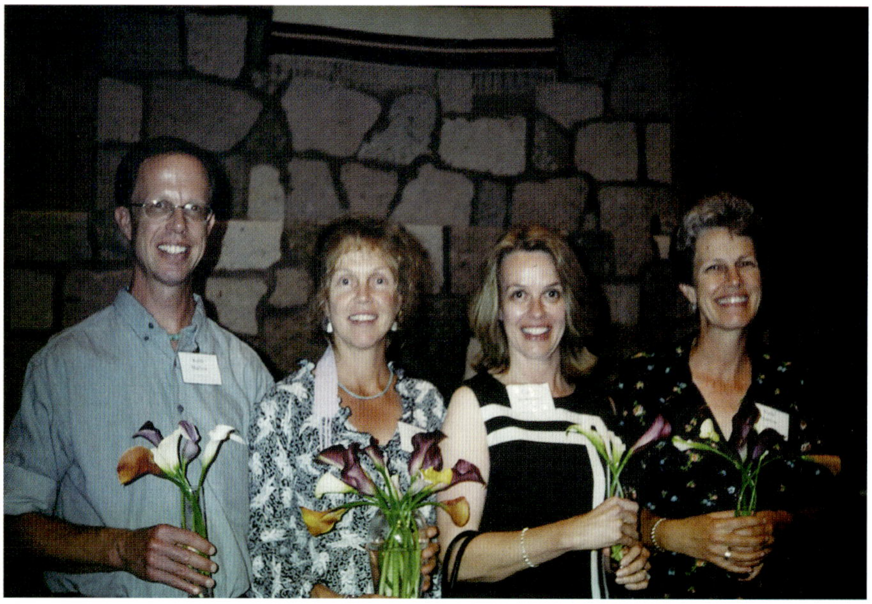

Figure 17. Our four children: Keith Harlow, Celia Harlow, Carol Muiznieks, and Catherine Harlow, September 4, 2003, the evening of my retirement banquet at Fuller Lodge, Los Alamos. (Photo by Patricia Harlow.)

ten of us who worked together in the 1960s, seven were present, having come from many parts of the country, and Didier Besnard came from France. There was an evening banquet at Fuller Lodge (my choice because of many sentimental memories of that place), followed by speeches and presentations. Our four children attended. (Our daughter Carol and her husband, Juris, traveled from Australia.) Our son, Keith, asked to speak and pulled from his pocket a long poem he had written about various facets of my life, which he delivered in syncopated rapper style:

> It was 1953, arriving with his wife,
> Settling up here on the hill, starting a new life.
>
> He joined up at the Lab with a group they called T-3,
> New ideas flowing strongly like ten rivers to the sea.
>
> Together with the others who made up that new think tank,
> The comments that he made were mostly very frank.
>
> He went to the Pacific, where his eyes they must be goggled,
> Two suns came up again that day, he found his mind was boggled.
>
> Back home again he started with something called Particle-in-Cell,
> And many people around the world said it was really swell.
>
> Sometimes those physics questions approached the edge of the insane,
> Stretching every corner of his hardworking, curious brain.
>
> Realizing that just thinking didn't bring answers every day,
> Hearing, following his feeling was often a better way.
>
> The answer then for many a tricky computation,
> Was to listen closely for what he heard in his imagination.
>
> But even when T-3 was struggling, working under the gun,
> No doubt they all endured many a goofy pun.
>
> Working and creating the first computer-generated movie,
> When all the chores were said and done, the results were pretty groovy.

Somewhere along the way with personal style he took a chance,
Blue jeans seemed a better fit than those early ironing-board pants.

And in the colder months when there was rainy, cloudy weather,
Soon you'd find him stepping out, wearing that black leather.

He picked up various hobbies to relax and get away,
Discovering the people and customs in places like Santa Fe.

Sometimes rumbling down the road over the speed limit on his Harley,
Bugs and grit lodged in his teeth, looking, crunching, gnarly.

He wrote about the pottery made by people in the state,
Then started creating paintings that turned out really great.

Back at the Lab he moved on, doing his part with the study of motion,
And could probably even create a formula for a concrete ocean.

So at a time when the world was growing, changing, moving fast,
In the right place at the right time, his discoveries will last.

So now's the day our hearts are one, together with three cheers,
To celebrate the man of the hour, who dedicated fifty years.

The audience liked it a lot, and for me it was the high point of the day. The day was a resounding success thanks to the hard work of many people, especially Mike Steinkamp, Mike Steinzig, Jody Shepard, and Rod Linn—to whom I am deeply grateful.

At the end of the evening, I introduced many of the people who had come to the banquet: my family; T-3 Group and T Division personnel; group pioneers, both technical and administrative; and special guests (including Duane Anderson and Dwight Lanmon from my "Santa Fe life"). My talk ended with the following heartfelt salute to everyone who had worked with me: "All of you made history, setting the course for computer fluid dynamics in the world, with results that have been translated to many languages and used in many laboratories. I salute you and thank you for giving me a really exciting and fulfilling career."

AFTER RETIREMENT

Things didn't change very quickly as a result of retirement. I became a "guest scientist" in Group T-3 of the Theoretical Division and was allowed to keep my office and security clearance. For a while I went to the office about four days a week, working on my memoirs and also on Lab projects.

Gradually, things changed. After a couple of years, I quit going to the Laboratory and devoted my time to painting, to working with Dwight Lanmon on four pottery books, and to thinking and writing about philosophical topics. My Laboratory years had come to an end, and I finally felt completely retired.

6
Fossils

One of the first excursions we made after arriving at Los Alamos in 1953 was to the Jemez State Monument, close to Jemez Springs, deep in San Diego Canyon. The canyon had been cut so deeply by the Jemez River that limestone and shale of the Pennsylvanian period (nearly 300 million years old) had been exposed.

The Fretwells took us there because we had no car at that time, and we enjoyed a very pleasant picnic in nice September weather. We hiked up a little tributary canyon that drains into the Jemez River during summer rainstorms, and there I began to notice seashells (!) that had washed down from the cliffs above us. That moment had a profound impact on my activities for the next few years. I had no idea what kinds of shells we were finding or how old they might be. We gathered a few of them to take home and ponder.

At the Los Alamos Mesa Public Library, I looked at an encyclopedia and several books on geology. It didn't take long to realize that these shells were brachiopods, not clams, which they had appeared to be at first glance, and that there was a vast difference between these two kinds of animals. (One reference compared it to the difference between fish and birds.) Twice as old as most of the dinosaurs, these little critters lived in abundance in the shallow branches of the ocean that once covered this area of New Mexico.

Altogether, three main incursions of ocean waters covered this place I call home, occurring in the Mississippian period (about 360 to 325 million years ago), the Pennsylvanian period (about 325 to 299 million years ago), and the much later Cretaceous period (about 145 to 65 million years ago). During the last period, huge dinosaurs prowled around the ocean bays of north-central New Mexico. Great thicknesses of river sediments also covered this area during the periods called Permian (about 299 to 252 million years ago), Triassic (about 250 to 200 million years ago), and Jurassic (about 200 to 145 million years ago), which lie between the Pennsylvanian and Cretaceous periods. A variety of animal skeletons have been found in those rocks, but I've not been involved in seeking specimens or learning about those strange animals.

For too many years, my evenings and weekends had been devoted to studies and homework, and I was determined not to give the Lab more than its due, instead spending the rest of my time with family and on other fascinating activities. From 1953 to about 1959, I focused my free time on fossils, especially brachiopods.

JEMEZ SPRINGS

The cliffs at the Jemez State Monument are only a fraction of a mile north of the town of Jemez Springs. I've gone back there many times to explore every layer of limestone and shale, finding fossils in many of them but especially in the uppermost gray shale, just below the transition to the Permian red beds. The topmost layers at Jemez Springs are from the latest parts of the Pennsylvanian period. In those layers, the brachiopods are especially abundant, very well preserved, and beautiful. They range in size from smaller than a fingernail to as large as three inches across. One very unusual species is even tinier; it's a rather rare species that builds its home on the outside of larger brachiopods, where it looks like a little scab with whiskers clutching the host shell.

Sitting there and carefully scratching through the loose, dark gray shale, I found the world to be so very calm and peaceful. Towering to great heights above me on the other side of the river were the spectacular cliffs of early Mesozoic sediments. The feelings I had were always wonderful and refreshing. Every fifteen minutes, the bell at the Catholic home for retired priests, far below me by the river, would chime the time.

NAMBÉ FALLS

One of the beautiful outdoor attractions of northern New Mexico is the waterfall east of Nambé Pueblo. It's not a grand place like Niagara Falls or Victoria Falls in Africa. In contrast, Nambé Falls are in an intimate setting—cool, damp, and secluded—near Nambé Pueblo. This interesting little village has a nearby site (long abandoned) that flourished around AD 950 to 1000. A narrow dirt road took me through the pueblo, past the sacred meeting place (kiva), and out into the countryside (which may be a big housing development now; I haven't been to the falls since around 1960, and a lot could have changed since then). In a couple of miles, I reached the little home of Mrs. Leon, who, for twenty-five cents, opened a rustic wire gate and let me through.

Continuing east, I arrived at an open space that was sometimes used for sacred dances and other celebrations by the Nambé Indians. The stream was south of me, emerging onto the flat fields from a constricted passageway that led me to the falls. Proceeding along the stream, I saw the fossil beds that were my attraction. Beyond that are the massive cliffs of even older limestone, and I had to wade in the stream to get through the narrow passageway. Then, there I was at the falls, perhaps four hundred yards east of my car. The geological structure is awesome, with the falls cascading down the steep cliff of ancient pink granite; the saltwater ocean spread over its bedrock for the first time in north-central New Mexico around 300 million years ago. I climbed up a narrow, slippery trail through lush foliage on the south side to see the falls in their full glory. (I say "falls," plural, because the water drops in two tiers, with a total height of perhaps one hundred feet.)

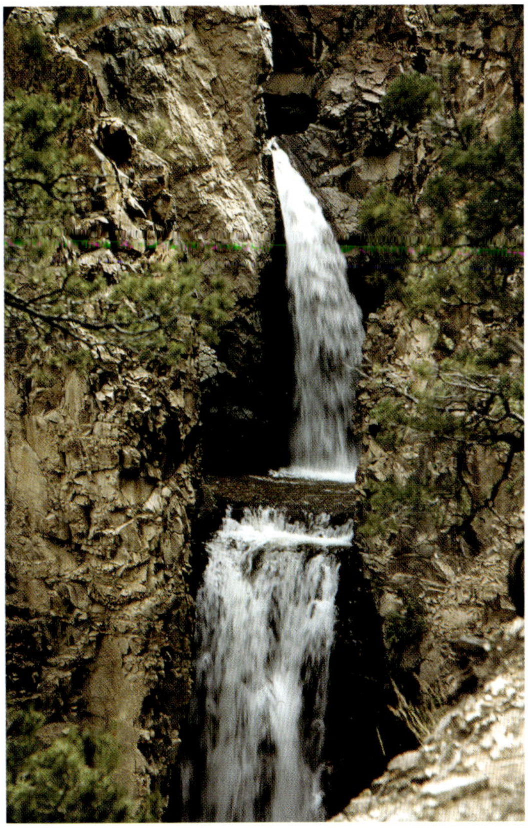

Figure 18. Nambé Falls. (Photo by Francis Harlow.)

Returning back through the narrow passageway, my principal goal for the day lay on the north side of the stream. There, I never ceased to gaze with humility at the ancient ocean beds, now tipped and folded by the intrusion of the pink granite, which poked farther and farther through the beds to form the nearby Sangre de Cristo Mountains, which reach their summits about ten miles east of here. These ocean beds and the sediments piled on top of them lay there as peaceful and flat as on the days they were formed, until the heaving earth squeezed up the mountains around 14 million years ago.

Besides building the mountains and tipping and folding the seabed, the powerful forces of nature also opened cracks and fissures for many miles in all directions, resulting in much volcanic

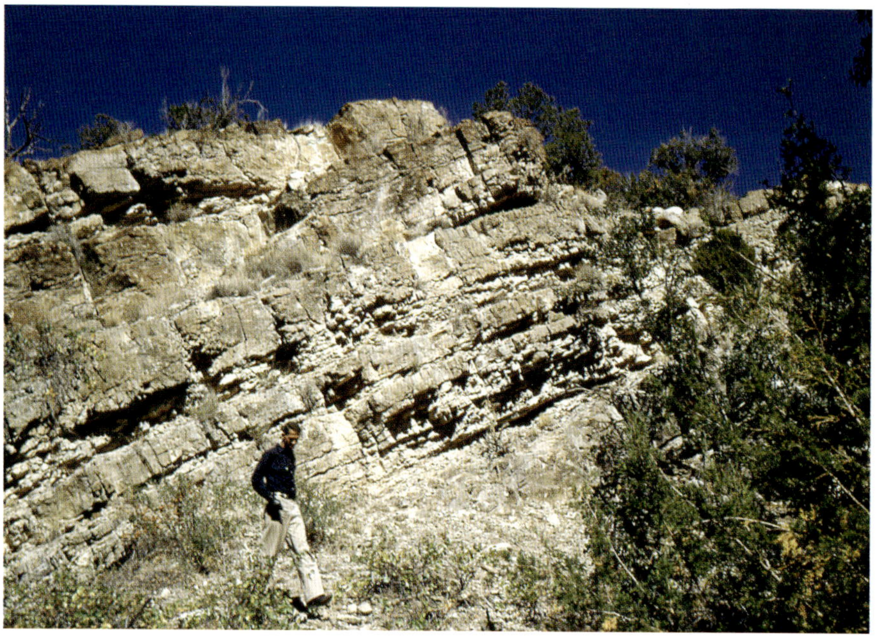

Figure 19. Patrick Sutherland took this photograph of me at the Pennsylvanian period layers at Nambé Falls, September 1956. (Harlow family photos.)

activity for many millions of years thereafter, culminating in powerful volcanic eruptions that produced the lava fields and thick beds of volcanic ash on which Los Alamos is situated.

Here at Nambé Falls, the only evidence of this intense activity is the tipping of layers formed from gentle deposits of minerals in calm lagoons. Here the waters swarmed with little creatures that lived and died and were buried in deposits that were compressed into the beds of limestone and shale that we see today. These beds are not very thick; some of the limestone layers are as much as four or five feet in thickness, while others are no more than a few inches. Between the layers of hard limestone are beds of much softer material called shale. There is even a bed of sandstone, formed on the beaches as the ocean receded for some hundreds or thousands of years before returning to produce more marine deposits. The sandstones have long since been permeated with minerals to form layers that are as hard as rock. In some places, one finds remnants of trees that grew in the lush forests. Some have been petrified, with complete fidelity for their fibrous structure. Others left impressions of their forms, with the surrounding sand making a mold.

Perhaps the most intriguing aspect of the ocean deposits at Nambé Falls is the great difference in animal life from one layer to the next. Most of the species I found were brachiopods, rarely more than a few inches across and often smaller. These seashells are beautiful to my eyes, with much variation among them sometimes preserved to perfection but often seen only as fragments that tease the mind as to how the whole critter looked. Usually, the interiors of the shells are inaccessible, except by using very sophisticated machinery for sectioning through the hard interior rock to reveal traces of interior structure. In contrast to clams (very rare in the Nambé marine beds), brachiopods often have a very delicate, interior skeleton made of the same material as the surrounding shell. Also in contrast to clams, each individual animal was often attached by means of a fleshy finger (pedicle) to the sea bottom or perhaps to another shell. Some kinds also have impressive arrays of external spines, ranging from very fine (almost like hairs) to as coarse as a hefty darning needle. Sometimes these spines served for attachment, and the pedicle is missing.

A fascinating thing about the seabed at Nambé Falls is that it was deposited at times when the sea was very restricted in its extent. These were the earliest days of the Pennsylvanian period, when much of North America was above sea level. As a result, I found lots of species that had never before been discovered and described in the paleontological journals.

THE QUARRIES AT SANTA FE

East of central Santa Fe, where houses were once sparse, lay the quarries from which limestone had been extracted for building the older houses in town. The quarries were never dug out to form awesome pits like those in some eastern marble quarries or in the copper mines in southern Arizona. The quarries in Santa Fe consisted of tilted rock shelves of limestone interspersed with layers of shale.

From the quarries one had a fine view of most of Santa Fe, the city's cathedral, capital buildings, business areas, and housing. The contrast with Nambé Falls could scarcely have been more striking. Nevertheless, the quarries had a charm of their own, including a feeling of isolation (despite the presence of a few nearby houses and buildings). Here I found many of the brachiopod species that also occur at Nambé Falls, but there were others, equally strange. Adding these to our collections gave a major enhancement to the scope of our studies. (I feel sadness thinking and writing about the Santa Fe quarries because they no longer exist, having been scraped over and converted into a fancy gated community of houses.)

PATRICK SUTHERLAND

I enjoyed visiting with Walt and Alma Wright at their rock and mineral shop on Cerrillos Road/Highway 14, south of Santa Fe, and later at the Original Trading Post on San Francisco Street a few blocks west of the Santa Fe Plaza. They seemed genuinely interested in my brachiopod studies, and I liked to hear from them about all the other geological sites they had visited in New Mexico. During one visit, they asked me if I had met Patrick Sutherland from the Geology Department of the University of Oklahoma. "No," I said, adding that I had never even heard of him. They urged me to get acquainted. The year was about 1955, and I had written the first draft of a manuscript describing the types of Pennsylvanian brachiopods I was finding.

It turned out that Patrick had been studying the Pennsylvanian layers in many of the more remote parts of the Sangre de Cristo Mountains. He, Art Montgomery (owner of the famous Harding Mine near Dixon, New Mexico), and John Miller were studying the geological structure of the mountains and the sediments that washed down from them. Art was the hard-rock specialist, working on pre-Cambrian granites and associated minerals; John was the specialist in sedimentary rocks; and Patrick concentrated on Pennsylvanian marine deposits, all under the auspices of the New Mexico Bureau of Mines and Mineral Resources. As a result of our combined efforts, we were able to recognize and give scientific names to twenty-nine new species and three new genera of early Pennsylvanian brachiopods in our report published in 1973.

Patrick was a very fussy perfectionist, and he had the rigorous background in paleontological training that I lacked, which suited our work together very well. Before we met, I had already worked out a lot of the taxonomy of Pennsylvanian brachiopods from this area and had a first-draft manuscript for an article. Patrick had also collected numerous specimens but had made no attempt at classifying them. It was soon obvious to both of us that we should join forces and publish the report together.

We also recognized that the brachiopods from the uppermost Pennsylvanian layers at Jemez Springs were so different from the rest of our material (from earlier in the Pennsylvanian period) that it would be appropriate to write a separate paper to describe them. That paper, "Late Pennsylvanian Brachiopods from North-Central New Mexico," in which we named a couple of new species, was published in the *Journal of Paleontology* in 1967.

The larger report, however, dragged in its progress. By about 1958, most of my part was done, but Patrick became distracted by other projects, and I started nee-

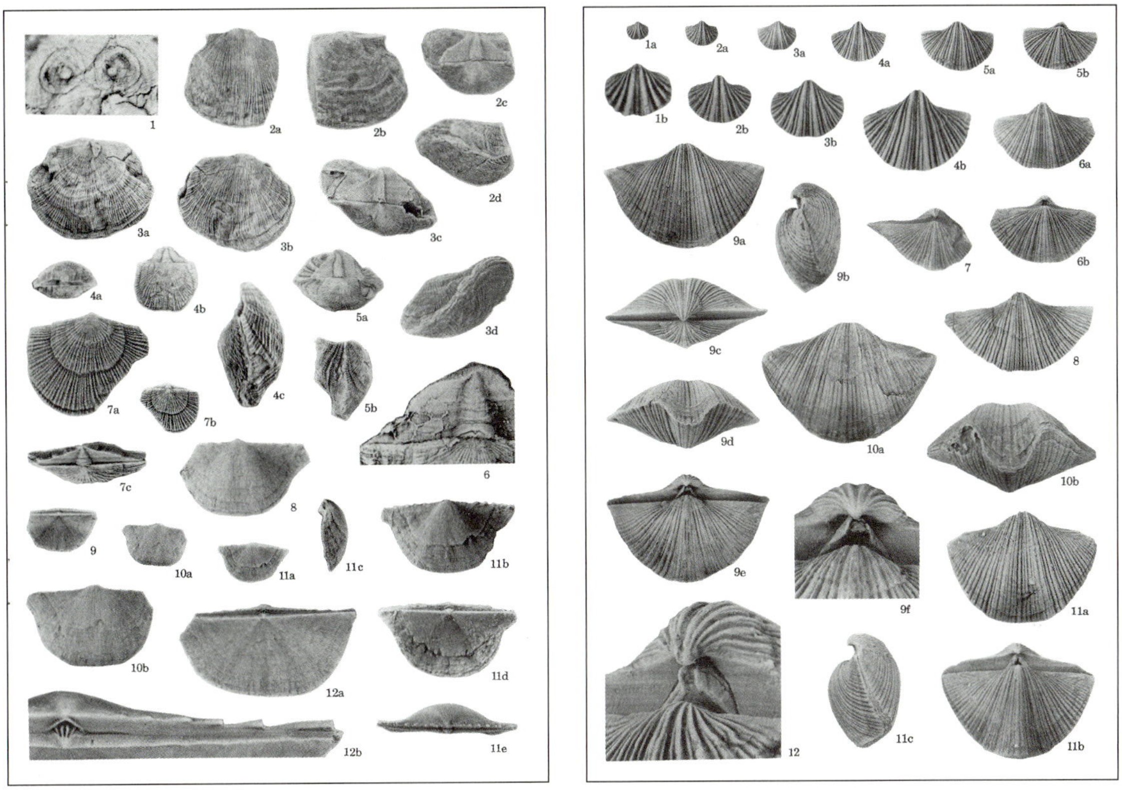

Figure 20. Fossil brachiopods found at Jemez Springs, New Mexico. (Photos by Patrick K. Sutherland. Reproduced from Sutherland, Patrick K., and Francis H. Harlow, "Late Pennsylvanian Brachiopods from North-Central New Mexico.")

dling him in the 1960s—at first gently and then more firmly. My arguments were, (1) he had put so much time and effort into the work that it would be a shame to see it wasted; (2) there was much good new material to report that would be useful to both geologists and paleontologists; (3) the publication would give a great boost to his professional career; and (4) he was obligated to prepare a final report for the New Mexico Bureau of Mines. Patrick later told me that without my continued pressure, he probably would never have gotten his part of the work done. In this regard, his perfectionism perhaps worked to his disadvantage. Numerous drawings of the stratigraphic sections needed precise drafting, and every fossil specimen had to be painstakingly cleaned and then coated with India ink (yuck!) for obtaining perfect photographs. (I've always been disturbed by his insistence on the ink, which will surely perturb future generations that may wish to make detailed observation on these specimens.)

Our report, *Pennsylvanian Brachiopods and Biostratigraphy*, published by the New Mexico Bureau of Mines and Mineral Resources in 1973, includes illustrations of rocks, brachiopods, and measured stratigraphic sections from Jemez Springs, Nambé Falls, and the Santa Fe quarries. In the opinion of J. T. Dutro Jr., who reviewed the publication in the *Journal of Paleontology*, the final report is a masterpiece—thanks in large part to Patrick's perfectionism.

FOSSIL EXCURSION VIGNETTES

The thrill of finding a new species or an especially revealing specimen of a known species never waned. Sometimes the preservation was so perfect that the brachiopod shell looked almost exactly as it had appeared when living in these shallow seas. Sometimes the discovery was of a single valve showing the muscle scars and other structures of the inner surface. These were always special moments that made an expedition worthwhile, even if nothing else of note emerged. Often such discoveries would mean very little to anyone else, like the example of *Rhynchopora* that had been waiting there for 300 million years for me to notice. In all my visits to Nambé Falls, I found only one example of that genus, a well-preserved, dull gray shell the size of the end of my little finger. It made such an impression that I remember lying on my right side on the steep outcropped layer, a soft shale not more than about six inches thick, gently running my fingers through the loose material in the hope of finding something. The layer was very close to the bottom of the Pennsylvanian sequence, and I felt it was sure to contain something special. What a thrill to see that little guy suddenly emerging into the first sunlight that had shone on it since it lived on the ocean floor. Having found one of them, I was optimistic that more must surely be nearby—but no; after much patient searching, no other example emerged. Indeed, that single *Rhynchopora* is the only one of this genus that I ever found in any of my numerous fossil-hunting trips.

Another thrill occurred on a hillside about a mile east of Taos, where I went to check out the scene a few times. The whole hillside is dark gray, crumbled shale, with most of the fossils rather poorly preserved and not very interesting. But there I found a virtually perfect trilobite that seemed to be a completely new species. Trilobites were abundant during the first half of the Paleozoic era but were approaching extinction by the time of the Pennsylvanian period, so it was a major discovery to find one in such good condition. I decided to send it to Professor Carl Branson of the Department of Geology at the University of Oklahoma for study, but I heard nothing back to indicate he had received the package. I asked

Patrick Sutherland (from the same department) to look into the matter, but his investigations revealed nothing. The specimen has never turned up.

Apache Canyon near Lamy (southeast of Santa Fe) cuts through somewhat later layers of Pennsylvanian marine shales, and I liked going there to find some very handsome, silicified brachiopod specimens. As one approaches Lamy (just before the turnoff along the railroad right-of-way), a little dirt road turns off the highway toward the east, directly under some high-voltage power lines where the fossil beds are located.

Another time I went to see Cretaceous rocks, this time Mancos shale deposited about 65 million years ago by a major incursion of the ocean. Walt Wright told me that just before La Bajada escarpment, about twenty miles south of Santa Fe, there was a turnoff to the east on a little dirt road leading to the old town of Waldo. "After a few miles, you'll come to some beautiful and colorful shales that are well worth seeing," he said with a glint in his eye. "There's one place there," he continued, "where a rather flat field is pierced by some spectacular, long volcanic dikes that have penetrated through fissures in the ground." The ground he described was the top layer of a thick marine deposit in which one can see huge ammonite shells. He told me the mileage, and I found the place with no difficulty. Both the dikes and the ammonite shells were spectacular to see, although the latter were not well preserved and would be impossible to remove without heavy equipment.

A TRIP TO ILLINOIS, IOWA, AND OHIO

A long trip to the country's heartland was also very important for me, but in several very different respects. The goal was twofold. Insofar as the Laboratory was concerned, I was to give a technical paper at a University of Chicago meeting and then travel to various universities in Illinois, Indiana, and Ohio for the purpose of recruiting new employees for the Laboratory. For me, however, there was a third important attraction—namely, to visit several early Paleozoic (Ordovician and Silurian) fossil sites in Indiana and Ohio.

The trip to Chicago was by train, departing from Lamy, New Mexico, and arriving at Chicago the next day. It was a peaceful trip, with lots to see out the windows, from Apache Canyon to the plains of Kansas and Missouri and on to the sprawling metropolis that was my destination. The train depot was downtown, and I remember being impressed with the big (but old) buildings and the elevated platforms of the urban transportation system. I headed to the Windermere

Hotel, across a large park from the Museum of Science and Industry (which I didn't visit). After getting settled in my room, suppertime became central to my thoughts. The Windermere had a large dining room, so I decided to check it out.

"I'm sorry sir, but we request that our patrons dress more formally," said the receptionist at the dining room. I was wearing only a shirt with nothing over it and also jeans and cowboy boots. "Perhaps you have a jacket you can wear. We can furnish you with a tie." So I went back to my room and put on the only jacket I had brought, a classic black leather motorcycle jacket. The receptionist eyed me suspiciously when I returned to the dining room. "Right this way, sir," he said, and he escorted me to one of the most prominent tables in the room, where I had a delicious supper.

A follow-up to that incident occurred a couple days later when I was checking out. The young man operating the elevator said to me rather timidly, "It's been an honor to have you here, sir. We didn't know that you're one of the star performers at the big rodeo this week, until the manager told us." I gave him a rather generous tip and hoped he didn't notice that I was blushing. I certainly didn't want to spoil his illusion of an encounter with a world-famous cowboy!

From Chicago, my recruiting activities took me to the University of Illinois at Urbana-Champaign. There I met students and faculty and tried to impart my genuine enthusiasm for a career at Los Alamos. After that I traveled east to Columbus, Indiana.

While I was in Columbus, I realized that the little town of Hartsville, where the famous Silurian Waldron shale outcroppings are located, was only about twenty miles east. I had no map or idea where the site was, relative to the town, but with a free day, I decided to explore the area. I splurged on a taxi ride from Columbus to Hartsville and on the way questioned the driver about the location of nearby geological outcroppings. He said he didn't know but that there was a field just before Hartsville that I might check out. I figured it was not likely what I was looking for, but lacking any better leads, I decided to stop and hike around. The highway had a little rise toward town, and the "field" was directly north of where he pulled to the side. I paid him and got out. "Good luck," he called out as he turned around to head back to Columbus.

The day was overcast but not wet or cold. I crossed the highway and climbed a short embankment to the field, which turned out to have a lot of hummocks overgrown with weeds, now dead for the winter. But in some places there were little open spots of dirt, so I bent down to look and discovered A RICH ASSORTMENT OF BEAUTIFUL FOSSILS! I was ecstatic. This was, beyond any doubt, a major outcropping of the famous Waldron shale! I don't know if it was the only one around the town, because there was no point in looking anywhere else. I was like a kid in the proverbial candy store. It was as if no one else had collected fossils there for many years. I could have gathered bucketsful of specimens, but there was no way I could carry more than a sampling. Besides, it would not have been fair to future collectors if I took lots of material.

In the middle of the afternoon, with plenty of time for the bus, I decided to see what the town of Hartsville looked like and perhaps buy something to eat. The center of town was not far away, perhaps a quarter of a mile. Like so many towns, it had a central plaza. I noticed a bus on the other side and decided to confirm the schedule for my bus an hour later. But it turned out that *this* was my bus! I had not realized that there was a time-zone change between Columbus and Hartsville, so, luckily, I was able to get on the return-trip bus just a short time before it left.

Later, in Ohio, I met Mr. Kercher, with whom I had corresponded concerning Ordovician fossils in his area. In this case, the adventure was not the same as at Hartsville. Mr. Kercher already knew exactly where to look and was generous in giving me a day of his time to drive me around and point out the outcroppings. The place with Ordovician fossils turned out to be a high embankment (a railroad cut) of dark gray shale that was loaded with beautiful fossil specimens of the classic Ordovician species that I had seen in geology books. Again I gathered only a small number of examples.

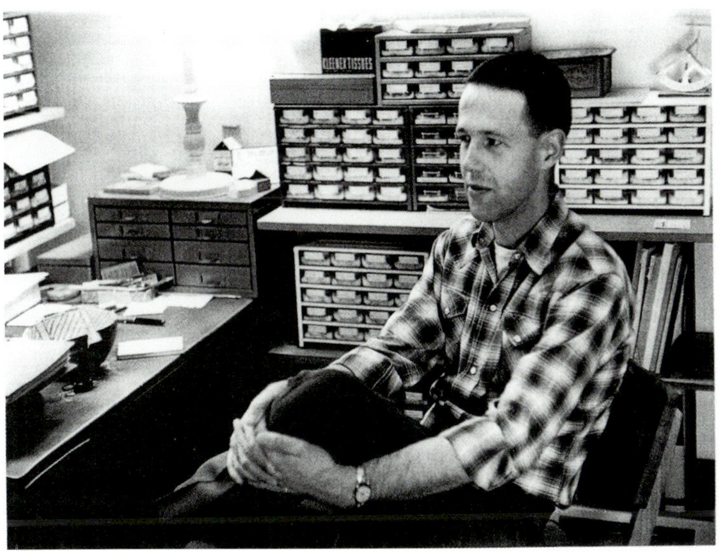

Figure 21. My cabinets of fossils, December 1961. (Photo by Al Lowry, LANL.)

SOME BEAUTIFUL FOSSILS FROM THE WORLD'S OCEANS

The study of fossil brachiopods from north-central New Mexico came to an end for me in about 1960. There simply was nothing more to be discovered, except perhaps by means of sectioning tools and careful analysis of skeletal parts through a series of cross sections, but that would have been a long and laborious study.

Through additional purchases and trading with collectors in many parts of the United States, I had obtained several thousand specimens of brachiopods, mainly from the Paleozoic era, and I thereby enjoyed numerous contacts with very interesting people. (Alan Graffam, of Ardmore, Oklahoma, became an especially good friend through correspondence.) Eventually, it became evident that this extensive reference collection should go elsewhere, and Patrick suggested the University of Oklahoma Geology Department. I painstakingly packed all but a few specimens into the drawers of my storage cabinets and shipped them to the university in Norman. My "babies" had found a good home, and I had gained enormous pleasure and satisfaction in the studies.

Trilobites were among the most attractive of ancient animals living in the world's oceans. Their overall existence extended from about 540 mya (million years ago) until about 300 mya, when they became forever extinct. The anatomy of almost all trilobites is characterized by a body with three longitudinal lobes and numerous narrow ridges extending between the left and right edges. The other main feature is the head, with various structures, especially primitive eyes, one on each side. A few examples from my collection are shown in figure 22. The black one on one corner of the gray slab is from the ancient Cambrian rocks of Utah, from which numerous examples have been extracted. Below are three other handsome trilobites that date a bit closer to our time. In the middle is the curled body of an even more recent type. Especially prominent in the photograph is a brown trilobite on the brownish-gray slab at the right. This is a modern sculpture of an earlier and rare type. The originals are very expensive, while the sculpture is very accurate and quite cheap to purchase. That slab is about eight inches long.

A crinoid looks at first sight like a flower on a long stem. Crinoids are actually animals living on stems that are firmly attached to solid bases. The upper body consists of a cuplike structure with numerous little stems sprouting from the upper rim. Like corals, brachiopods, and other sea animals that are firmly attached throughout their whole life span, these critters have no eyes. What they possess is longevity, having lasted from the Cambrian period to the present. The slab shown in figure 23 was given to me by Alan Graffam, my good friend living in Oklahoma. When he sent it, the crinoids were not visible, having been buried in a soft shale.

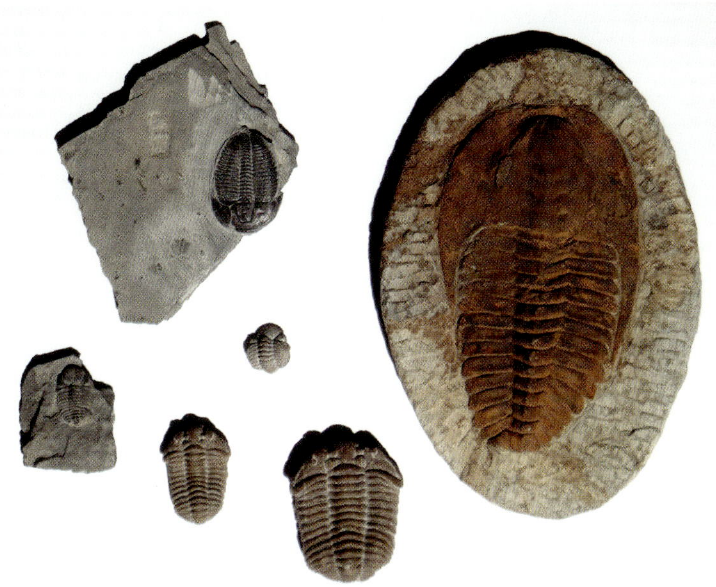

Figure 22. Trilobite specimens, Harlow collection. (Photo by Dwight Lanmon.)

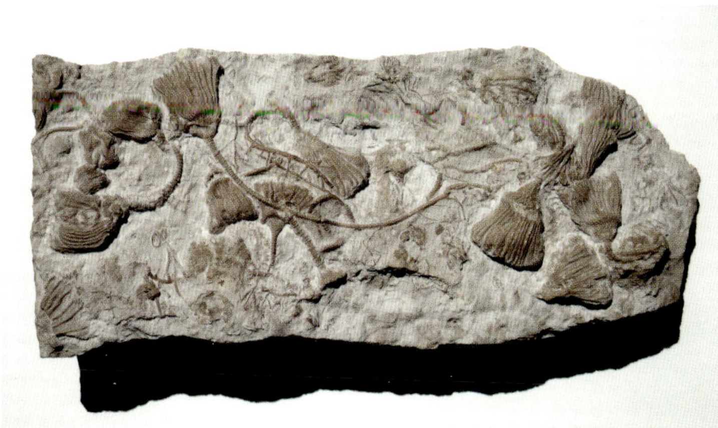

Figure 23. Crinoid specimens, Harlow collection. (Photo by Dwight Lanmon.)

He said, "Scrape gently on the soft side and see what emerges." I did, and as you can observe, the results are spectacular. The hard rock base is about twenty inches long and very heavy. After being buried approximately 350 million years, it has now become a real treasure of my fossil collection.

7
Motorcycles

SOME INTRODUCTORY THOUGHTS

Gymnastics, ice-skating, skiing—what grand and glorious feelings activities like these produce. There's a kind of genius involved that is quite different from science and mathematics. It's an intrinsic skill, a talent for the instantaneous and spontaneous processing of data and reacting without studied analysis. A good musician has it. The spontaneous processing that comes from combined talent and years of self-discipline becomes so ingrained in a performer that all of his or her intentions can be focused on interpretation. An athlete likewise responds instantaneously to the rapidly changing circumstances of a game.

With envy in my heart, I must confess that none of these things lies within my capabilities. I tried skiing twice and ice-skating once. I played cello for around ten years, played tennis for some years (and always lost), and struggled to learn somersaulting and completely failed with cartwheels. But surprisingly, I turned out to be a pretty good swimmer. Despite my lack of physical ability for fast and spontaneous activities, another type of activity works moderately well for me. It's the type that relies on studied processing of data and slow muscular reaction to circumstances. Science and art (painting) are two areas in which I have succeeded—not famously but well enough to take much joy in explorations and discussions in both fields.

All of which leads me to motorcycles. Certainly, the best motorcyclist ("biker") must be able to respond instantaneously and spontaneously to rapidly changing circumstances. But there is another very pleasurable skill in biking that exploits the ability for the studied processing of data and reaching a conclusion with precision. With some degree of success in this type of biking, I captured something that felt (to me) like the thrill experienced by the gymnast, ice-skater, or musician. Instead of relying on bodily power, however, I relied on the power of the engine between my legs.

For example, East Jemez Road, exiting Los Alamos from the south side of the bridge, goes downhill, with many back-and-forth curves. There's no challenge in biking along that road with the goal of simply arriving at a destination. More challenging is maneuvering the machine with precision. The centerline is clearly marked all the way, and a common goal for me was to follow an imaginary path exactly one foot to the right of the line—not only that, but to do so with the (imagined) perception of projecting to (imagined) observers an image of perfect posture and control. When I watch Mike Steinzig ride his motorcycle, I see the control of a machine—which I imagine being able to achieve myself—on the curving highways that I loved to explore.

Even more exciting were rides at night in the dark, along Trinity Avenue. The streetlights created ever-changing shadows that jumped ahead and then faded; drivers in cars had no awareness of this beautiful ballet of illusive forms. I would go west, cross Los Alamos Canyon Bridge, and head up toward West Jemez Road. My headlights kept exploring the dark bushes and trees beside the road, jumping eagerly from one to another in ways that seemed both capricious and merry but also rather scary and even malicious in their surreal meanderings. I loved it. I would park the bike in a lonely spot and, when I turned off the headlights, become enchanted with the sudden contrasting blackness of night.

That brings me to another facet of the joy (for me) of biking: the possibility of transforming myself into a completely different person—the sort of macho male superhero who inhabits comics and movies. Dressed in black leather pants, boots, jacket, and gloves and wearing a helmet of either fancy or sinister design and decoration, I become transformed. No one can see who really lies within the outer covering, and that frees my imagination. I can become that superhero for an hour or so along mountain roads or the highway.

Sometimes the exercise of precision riding was replaced by the exhilaration of speed. Along the road to Española, with no one visible in front or behind, I would feel my right hand gunning the throttle. Suspending my studied analysis, I would let the glove move my hand with a mind of its own. Actually, I never went faster than about ninety-seven miles per hour, and then only on my very reliable

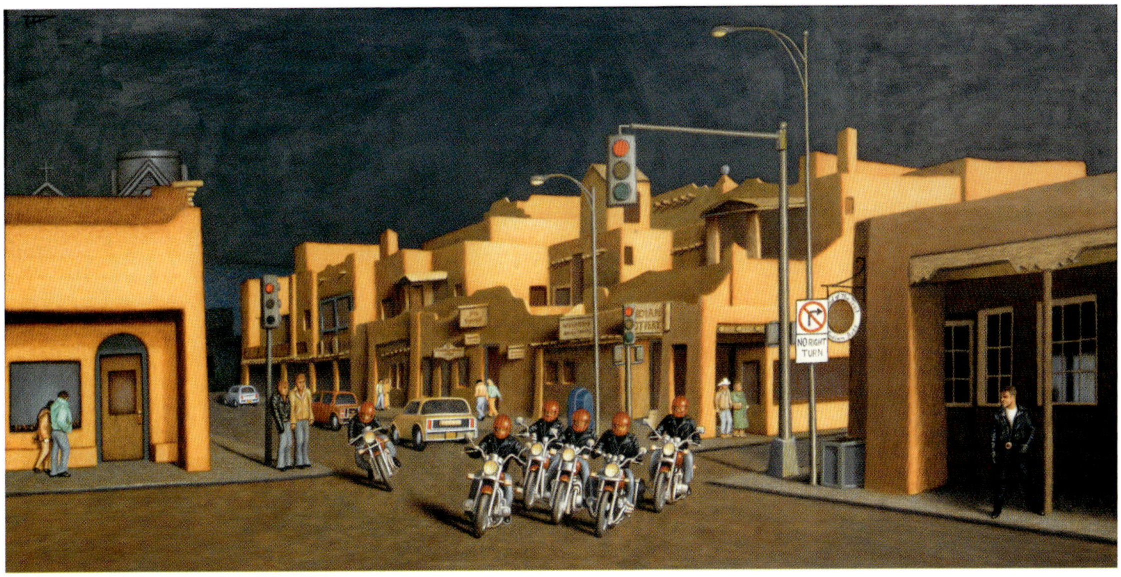

Figure 24. *Bikers at La Fonda Hotel, Santa Fe*, July 1997. Acrylic painting, 24 x 48 in. (Photo by Mike O'Keefe. Los Alamos County Collection [LACC], FH-1165.)

Honda. Sometimes, while climbing the front hill to Los Alamos, there would be a car ahead going the speed limit for that steep and winding highway. Again I would suspend caution and let my right glove take control, squeezing out the power of the engine to take me flying past the automobile, filled with passengers who admired the freedom of this unknown superhero on the bike.

Now that I'm older, my balance and reflexes are not as keen as they were in earlier days, so I don't ride a motorcycle anymore. Instead, my biking is vicariously experienced through my paintings. I've depicted my fine old 1940 Harley-Davidson bike in half a dozen or so pictures and other bikes in as many more. (See figs. 24, 79, 81, and 82.) Usually I depict a biker guy nearby, and although the person has a face out of my imagination, people sometimes ask if it's a self-portrait. In a real and important sense, the answer is yes, although I have no interest in trying to represent myself accurately in any painting. I try instead to depict the spiritual image of the superhero dude described above. It's a depiction of the person I used to become whenever I hid my true image from the world. Even if the face and stance don't look like what I see (or saw) in the mirror, the guy is nevertheless me—that is, the me created by my feelings and imagination when I'm roaring down the highway, the me I become when everything is right.

THE FIRST MOTORCYCLE (APRIL 1955–JUNE 1956)

With my new job at Los Alamos Scientific Laboratory, it soon felt possible to indulge my long-held dream of owning a motorcycle. I don't remember how I learned about the bike that Alan Netz wanted to sell, but we struck a deal. It was a 1952 Harley-Davidson 45 side-valve flathead. The number 45 corresponds to the displacement, forty-five cubic inches, which converts to 737 cubic centimeters, a medium-sized vehicle among modern bikes. I was incredibly excited to drive it to our duplex on Thirty-fourth Street. In those days, we didn't have to pass a Motor Vehicle Department test to get a driver's license for riding a bike, and there were no requirements for wearing a helmet. Indeed, I think that helmets were not available at all. Alan gave me a few pointers on how to ride, and the rest was up to me. (Incidentally, the deal between Patty and me was that if I bought a motorcycle, she would get a piano, which I thought was a fine exchange. We still have the piano, while I've had three motorcycles through the years.)

The gearshift was on the left side of the gas tank, which to most bikers was very awkward. To change gears, the rider had to take his left hand off the handle, a potentially dangerous action. The clutch was activated by the left foot. This

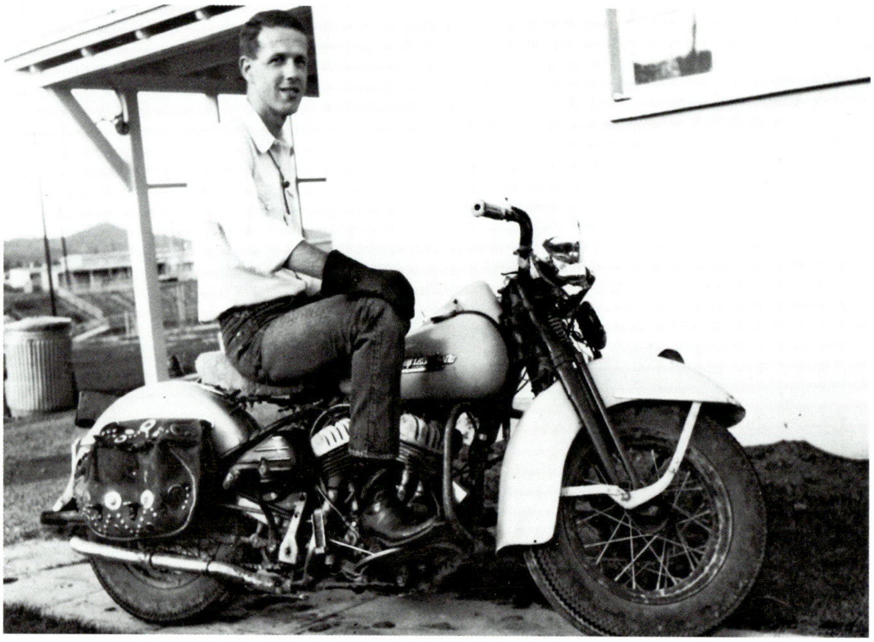

Figure 25. My first motorcycle, a 1952 Harley-Davidson 45 side-valve flathead. (Photo by Patricia Harlow.)

transmission arrangement was affectionately known as a suicide clutch, but I didn't consider it troublesome, having never used the later foot clutch. (The clutch has been attached to the left handle on all Harley motorcycles since 1953, while gears are shifted with the left foot.) I had also been warned about the kick start, which could snap back with great force if the biker was not careful (it has been known to break a rider's leg), but I never had any trouble with it.

One thing that Alan talked me into was hill climbing. I was embarrassed to say no, and thus I yielded to his insistence that we go to a rather steep dirt hillside where bikers dared each other to climb the hill. Of course, I failed miserably, with the bike falling onto its side about halfway up, and I had to suffer the indignity of Alan and another guy helping me right the machine and get it back down the hill. I don't remember how many times I tried, but it was always with the same result. I eventually chickened out and never went back.

One time I was riding north of town, and the chain broke. I was able to get hold of Alan, who drove out to where I was stranded. We hooked a chain from the front of the bike to the rear of his pickup, and he drove while I rode on the bike. At one rather sharp turn, there was some gravel on the road, which he may not have seen, because he kept going without slackening his speed, and of course klutzy Frank lost control and the bike was on its side in the street, with me miraculously unhurt. For that I was glad for the heavy leather jacket, which got noticeably scuffed on the right arm and shoulder. Dick Moore, who lived in the Sundt Apartments on Trinity Avenue, fixed the chain for me and subsequently helped keep the bike running with various and sundry repairs and adjustments. (I met Dick Moore when we were living in the Gold Street Apartments. Whenever he noticed me walking home for lunch, he gave me a ride on his powerful Harley.)

The bike was great for riding to work, although my cutoff air temperature for the trip was 35°F—below that I took the car. (I noticed that 35°F at our duplex translated to a lot colder whenever I had to cross a canyon or dip down into one.) After a while, I was told by the neighbors up the street that whenever I went roaring by, their TV would flicker, but they were good-natured about the matter and didn't ask me to stop going that way.

That first Harley was a great adventure for me, but the following year, I succumbed to the pleading of a young guy to sell him the bike. He worked at Los Alamos and stayed with his uncle while his family lived in Texas. He wanted the motorcycle to go visit them. I don't remember how he paid me for the bike, but we made the transaction and I got Edward Jones (the boy or his uncle—I don't remember which) to sign acceptance of responsibility. As a fascinating example of the casualness of the day, the document of title assignment was a little piece of paper on which the notary public impressed her seal.

The kid rode the bike on several round-trips. Then one day I read in the *New Mexican* newspaper that he was rear-ended by a vehicle while waiting for a light to change and was killed! That had a terrible effect on me, and it was fifteen years before I got another bike.

THE SECOND MOTORCYCLE (1976–1977)

My second bike was a Honda 550-four. It was much peppier and more robust than the Harley, and it was a very reliable vehicle. I never had any trouble with it except the one time a car ran me off the road, just beyond the Los Alamos Canyon Bridge, where a two-lane turnoff onto West Jemez Road took people to some of the more remote areas of the Lab. I was in the left lane, and a car in the right

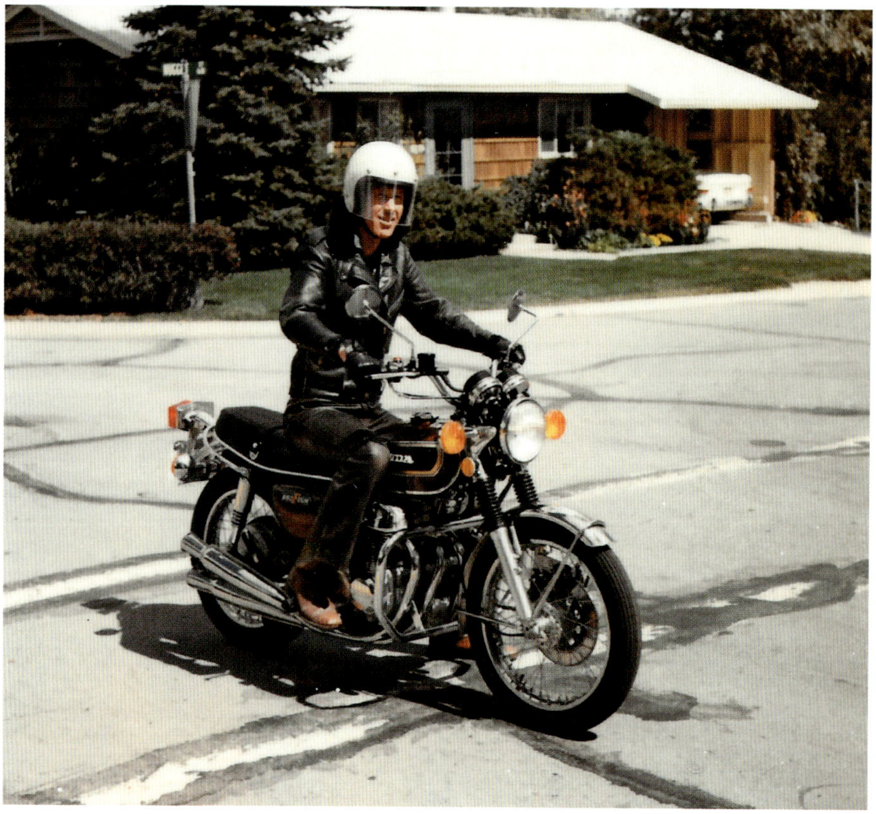

Figure 26. My second motorcycle, a Honda 550-four. (Photo by Patricia Harlow.)

lane was close beside me. Suddenly he decided he wanted my lane, and he rapidly negotiated the change. I had no time to pull ahead or lag behind and thus had no choice but to go off to the left. Fortunately there was no embankment there or any appreciable drop-off, but I couldn't maintain control and ended up laying it over onto its right side about ten yards from the road. The driver of the other vehicle either didn't notice or didn't care; he just continued on his way. Fortunately I wasn't hurt, but I added a few more scuff marks to my trusty old leather jacket. The right-turn signal was bent out of shape, and there were a few other scrape marks, but nothing was serious. The bike still ran fine, and after a quick trip to the Honda shop in Santa Fe, it was essentially as good as new.

After getting the Honda in September 1976, I was eager to accumulate some miles on it, to get the five-hundred-mile tune-up that would release me from the recommended speed constraints of the break-in period. Getting the mileage was easy, and a few weeks later I made an appointment for the checkup. That morning the outdoor thermometer registered 19°F. Brrrr! I decided to go nevertheless, putting on flannel pants under my heavy leather pants and as many layers of shirts and sweaters as would fit under the leather jacket. My hands were covered with the most insulated of my gloves, and I wore my boots with heavy socks and my helmet, which I couldn't figure out how to stuff with extra insulation. It was still rather dark at the beginning of this frigid journey of about thirty-five miles. At Pojoaque, there was a trucker's eating place, where I stopped to warm up, and then I proceeded on my way. Everything turned out OK, and by early afternoon the trip back to Los Alamos was not nearly as frigid.

I remember one especially embarrassing incident with that Honda. My office was in the Laboratory Administration Building, in front of which were a large parking lot for cars and a smaller one dedicated to motorcycles. I pulled into the latter with a flourish and gracefully dismounted, feeling that all the nearby people were bursting with envy to see this handsome dude with the gorgeous bike. I turned with disdainful insouciance to head in for a day's work, only to have the image shattered a few seconds later by a heartrending CRASH. Can you believe it? I had forgotten to put down the kickstand. The bike simply responded to the pull of gravity and awkwardly lay on its side. Immediately, there was a crowd of people there to gawk and to offer help in righting the vehicle, which fortunately was not hurt. The only damage was the enormous blow to my ego. What a KLUTZ! The thought haunted me for weeks.

This time it was Darryl Holm who persuaded me to sell him my motorcycle. I don't know if he still has it; I've never seen him riding around town on the bike.

THE THIRD MOTORCYCLE (1981–2001)

The acquisition of my third motorcycle came about because of my interest in collecting early historic Pueblo pottery. Many years ago, before Pueblo pottery became well-known (because of my books, Forrest Fenn claims), I became fascinated with the evolution and intertribal influence in styles of pottery made in the period 1550 to 1850. Before about 1970, examples could be purchased in Santa Fe "curio" stores for prices that we could just barely afford but that were bargains compared with prices today. We were soon sending \$5 to \$10 per month to Mrs. Julius Gans, Rex Arrowsmith, Bob Ward, Jim Riley, and other dealers to purchase pots that were then for sale at \$35 to \$75—which later became as much as a thousand times more expensive. One large storage jar made at Zia Pueblo around 1780 especially attracted my attention. It was so beautiful and in such perfect condition, but the asking price was \$225. It had been sitting on a high shelf at the Ray Smith Hardware Store. When the owner finally decided to sell it, I knew of course that buying that pot would have a major impact on our family finances, so I debated with myself for many weeks before finally deciding to buy it. A few days later, I saw Rex Arrowsmith, who said that my purchase of that jar at such a high price was the talk of the town among dealers in Indian art. No one, it seemed, had ever bought a historic Pueblo Indian pot for anything approaching that sum, although Vincent Price, the Hollywood actor, had paid appreciably more than that amount for fabulous ancient Mimbres pottery bowls.

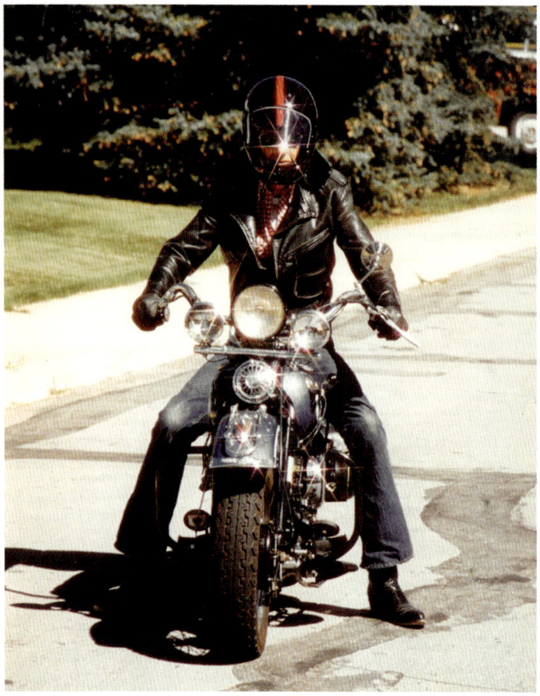

Figure 27. My third motorcycle, a 1940 Harley-Davidson, August 1981. (Photo by Keith Harlow.)

Some years later, around 1980, Dennis Lyon, head of the Russ Lyon Realty Company in Phoenix (which handled only the high end of the market), became infatuated with early historic Indian pottery, especially from the period 1700 to 1850. He frequently consulted with me about the authenticity of examples that he wanted to own. (Because of my books, wealthy collectors who became interested in early historic pottery often asked me to comment on vessels that they might buy.) Dennis became very excited about my Ray Smith jar and offered me a large

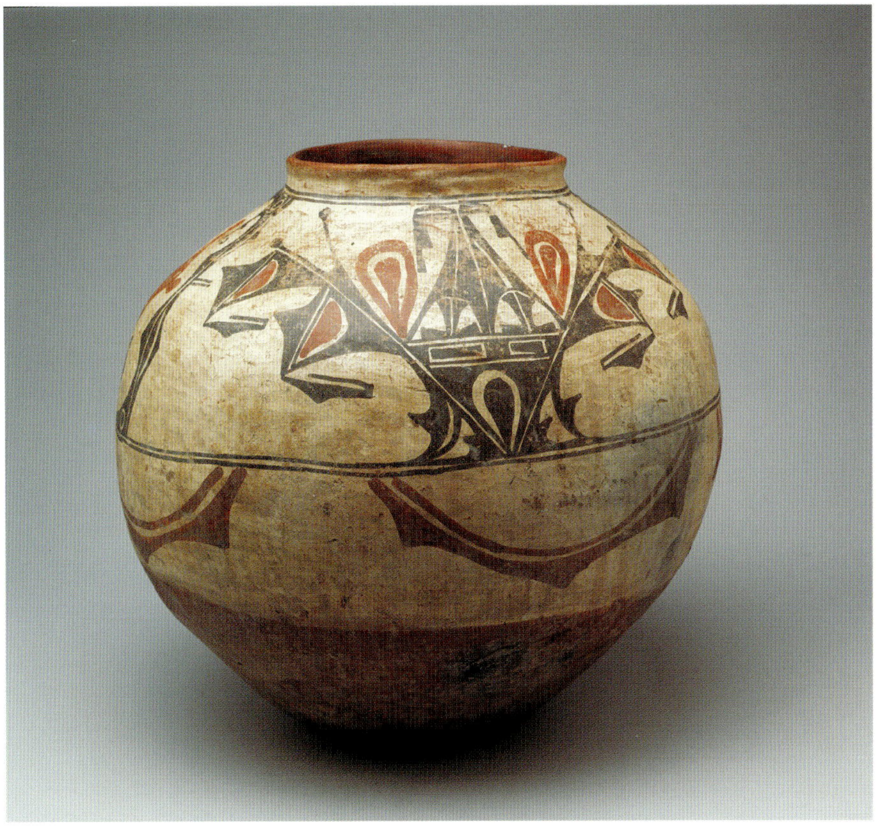

Figure 28. San Pablo Polychrome storage jar, Zia Pueblo, about 1780–1790, 51 x 43 cm. (Photo by Craig Smith, from *The Collecting Passions of Dennis and Janis Lyon*. Billy Jane Baguley Library and Archives, Heard Museum, Dennis and Janis Lyon collection.)

amount of money for it. I said that the only way I'd consider parting with it would be in trade for early historic pots that were of particular interest to me but of lesser appeal to his tastes, and for an old Harley-Davidson motorcycle. His immediate reply was, "You find such a motorcycle for sale, and I'll buy it and include it in the trade." I got copies of *Hemmings Motor News* and eventually discovered a bike that seemed potentially appealing. Dennis said to check it out, so I talked by phone to the seller in Winston-Salem, North Carolina. He promised to send me photographs, which arrived a few days later. I showed them to some of the guys who worked with me in our group at the Lab, who said, "Oh, Frank, don't do it. This is one of the oldest come-on scams in the country. You send him the money and he sends you a basketful of old motorcycle fragments, and there's nothing you can do about it." But the guy sounded so sincere and honest on the phone that I decided to go for it, thus obtaining my 1940 Harley-Davidson motorcycle, which was so similar to my first Harley that it was spooky. The photos showed the same blue color, essentially the same configuration, the same leather packs beside the rear wheel, and everything else that I found appealing, so we went ahead with the deal and the bike was shipped by a private moving company.

"Frank, come home quickly," said Pat on a call to my office one day. "There's a huge moving truck in front of the house and the guy is starting to unload it." I hurried home, bubbling with excitement, and sure enough the driver was working his way into the bowels of the truck to where he said there was, indeed, a motorcycle. He had hooked a ramp to walk up and down, carrying cartons and other stuff to set onto the street. The bike had not yet become visible behind the mass of stuff that had to be moved out of the way. I was appalled to watch his carelessness! He would drop cartons onto the asphalt rather than setting them down gently. One of them had even broken open to reveal an antique spinning wheel. Finally, he reached a large blue packing quilt, which he drew aside to reveal *the absolutely most beautiful motorcycle in the world!* It was vastly more stunning in real life than it had appeared in the photographs. I was thrilled. He started wheeling it toward the ramp. "Let me help you," I offered. "No, this is *my* job," he replied with some impatience. But soon I could see that he was going to miss the ramp by several inches! "Wait," I screamed, "you're going to miss the ramp," and in a split second I was up there with him. He just shrugged as I took hold of the handlebars and pushed the bike backward to achieve a better alignment. I slowly backed down the ramp, guiding the bike to the pavement. He hurriedly reloaded the truck, I signed a receipt of shipment, and he maneuvered the huge truck up the narrow street and was gone.

To register a bike from another state, I had to call the Police Department to verify the serial number. I suspect that they contacted North Carolina authorities to see if the bike had been stolen, but I didn't hear anything back to suggest a problem in that regard. I pushed the bike into our carport, and the next problem was how to get it started. I had no idea what to do and therefore called Ed Soenke at his motorcycle repair shop on DP Road. He said that his partner was an expert on old Harleys. The partner came the next day, and it certainly looked to me that he knew what he was doing. After a little tinkering, he sat on the bike and kicked the starter pedal. Nothing happened, and he tinkered some more. With the third try, the machine roared to life, with the classic sound of the Harley twin cylinders reverberating through the carport.

I never rode that grand old bike farther than just around Los Alamos. It clearly showed its age, but I didn't care; I had no plans for using it on out-of-town excursions. The main thing was that it was beautiful. I've used it as a model in numerous paintings (perhaps approaching a dozen or so), and I enjoyed seeing it on display in the back of the carport, chained to a secure post. "Have you hugged your motorcycle today?" is a bumper sticker that expresses my feelings for that wonderful old bike.

Lots of guys asked me if they could buy the old Harley. Often they came to the front door—delivery people, meter readers, garbage collectors, and others who otherwise wouldn't go along our street but were told by their friends about the bike. If I was not home, Pat would show them the machine and answer questions such as "How old is it?" "Does it still run?" and "Is it for sale?" I estimate that perhaps as many as fifty people made half-serious offers. Some guys who were bike enthusiasts told me that they saw one like it (at some undisclosed place) for sale with a price of $35,000!

My brother, Bruce, was also excited by the bike. Whenever he and Betty came to visit, he wanted to work with the bike, mainly to clean and polish it. (Bruce is a collector of old cars and knows lots about antique vehicles of many different makes and models.) He asked if there was any way he could have the bike for his collection, and I sometimes felt guilty putting him off.

So what has become of the old bike? Duane Anderson, former director of the New Mexico Museum of Indian Arts and Culture (MIAC) in Santa Fe, is a friend and was coauthor with me and Dwight on an Indian pottery book. In 2001 his museum was to have a display of artifacts related to the famous east–west highway Route 66 through Albuquerque. He asked to borrow the old Harley, which he had seen during visits to our house. I agreed, although for a while I had attacks of nervous anxiety over whether the museum would transport the bike safely and keep it from harm while on display. Duane assured me that they would handle it with complete security. The week before the big move to MIAC, Carol and Juris, with our grandchildren Lisa and Adam, came to visit from Sydney, Australia, and they were delighted to join me in a thorough cleaning of the machine for display. At MIAC I saw for myself that the move had been made with no trouble or damage at all. Three or four guys helped Duane load the bike into a large van, for which I had specified the necessary dimensions, and secured it with much bungee cord, so I was indeed reassured of safe transport. I have to say, however, that it was a very emotional moment for me to see the bike depart, and I would have felt it even more so if I had known it would never return.

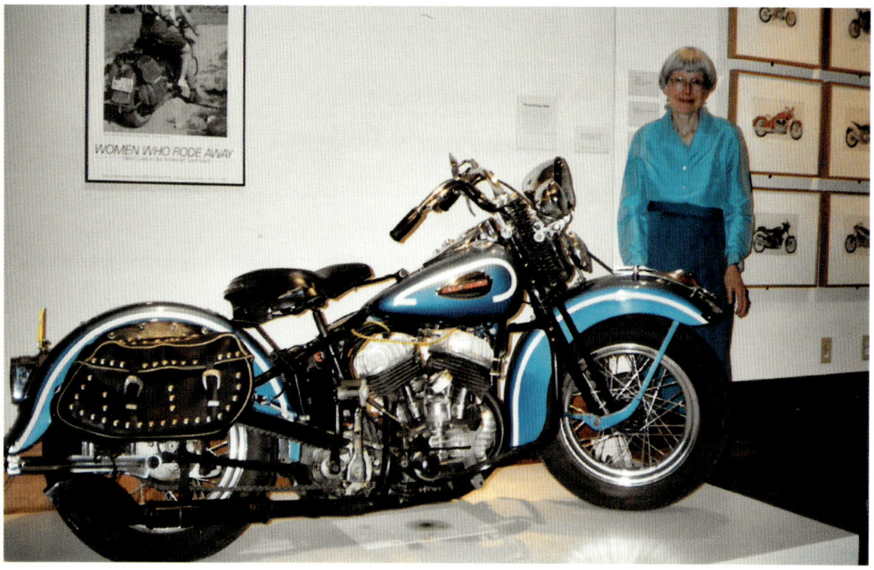

Figure 29. Patty with my Harley-Davidson when it was shown in the Governor's Gallery of the New Mexico State Capitol in 2007. (Photo by Francis Harlow.)

It looked *fabulous* on display in the MIAC lobby, just inside the main entrance. Duane said that it was one of the main attractions in the show and that there had been lots of comments and expressions of awe. All the museum guards were vastly impressed, as was the staff from other branches of the Museum of New Mexico: the Palace of the Governors, the Museum of International Folk Art, and especially the Museum of Fine Arts (now the New Mexico Museum of Art) on the corner of the historic Santa Fe Plaza. I asked Duane if he thought the Museum of New Mexico would like to have it permanently. Without a moment's hesitation, Duane said, "Yes, they would be delighted to take it for permanent care, forever" (whatever "forever" would turn out to mean). After a little thought, I concluded that the museum was exactly where I wanted the old bike to be, so we transferred the title to the Museum of New Mexico, asking in return only that they keep and protect it "forever." The regents of the museum enthusiastically concurred, and the director signed the papers of acceptance. The museum was so pleased that it hired a professional expert to work over every nook and cranny of the bike, cleaning, polishing, and restoring the chrome parts to virtually good-as-new luster. The bike is now considered to be "a classic example of mid-twentieth-century multimedia sculpture." I have none of the papers—my notes on how to start the bike,

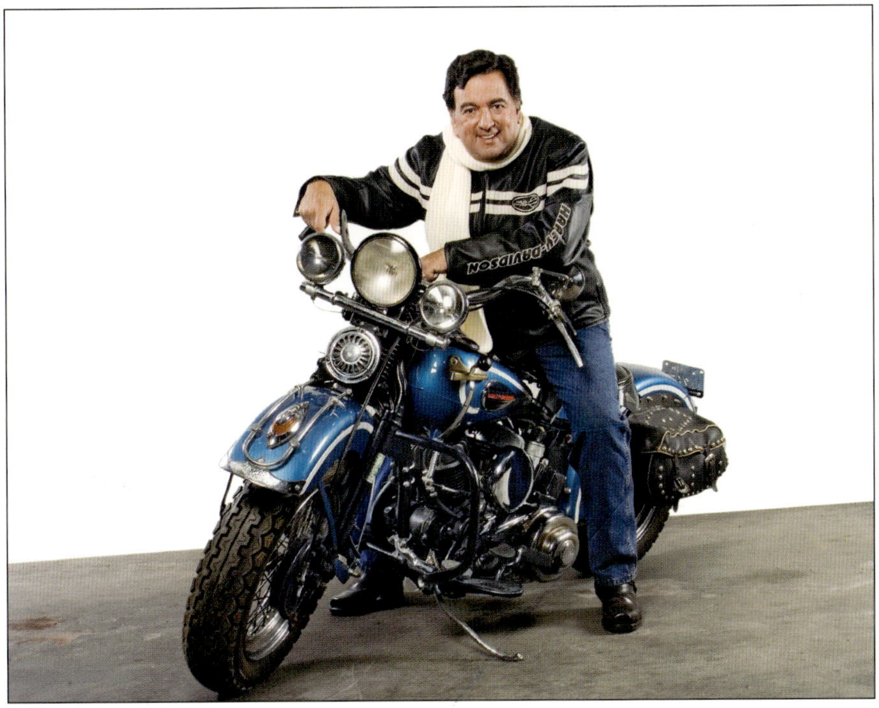

Figure 30. New Mexico governor Bill Richardson on my Harley-Davidson. (Originally published in *El Palacio* 112, no. 1 [spring 2007]: 52. Photo by Blair Clark. Courtesy *El Palacio*.)

the service manual, and so on, all went to the museum. All I have left are photos, paintings, and fabulous memories.

The bike was also shown in 2007 in the Governor's Gallery of the State Capitol in Santa Fe, where it was photographed with Governor Bill Richardson sitting on it. Thereafter, it was on display at the New Mexico Museum of Art until 2014.

8

The Pueblo Indians of New Mexico

By about 1960, my work with fossils was coming to an end. It wasn't that there were no more problems to be solved in brachiopod physiology and taxonomy for the earliest layers of the Pennsylvanian-period sediments. Rather, the difficulty for me lay in the necessity of using sophisticated machinery for producing thin sections of specimens, in addition to being trained to use them and interpret the results. Instead, my interest gradually turned to several nearby Pueblo Indian villages and their people, which eventually led to an immensely enjoyable and productive sideline of my career: the study of their pottery.

The Pueblo Indian pottery of greatest interest to me is vessels made for the purpose of utilitarian or ceremonial activities. The crux of this idea is that the ceramic pieces are made to be *used*, not just displayed, by the recipient (Indian or not). The users might be the potter's family, people in the village or in another village, or even people in a non-Indian town (for example, Santa Fe).

The Pueblo Indians of New Mexico have lived for centuries in small villages called pueblos, of which there were hundreds in ancient days (some are now in ruin), scattered through many parts of the area. Although there were various language groups among those people, their cultural similarities were quite remarkable. Nineteen pueblos are still active in New Mexico, and twelve lie within a forty-mile radius of Los Alamos: Cochiti, Jemez, Nambé, Pojoaque, San Felipe, San Ildefonso, San Juan (today known as Ohkay Owingeh), Santa Clara, Santo Domingo (now Kewa), Tesuque, Santa Ana, and Zia.

A visit to an Indian pueblo can be a wonderful experience. Many of these small villages preserve features that existed before the coming of the Europeans,

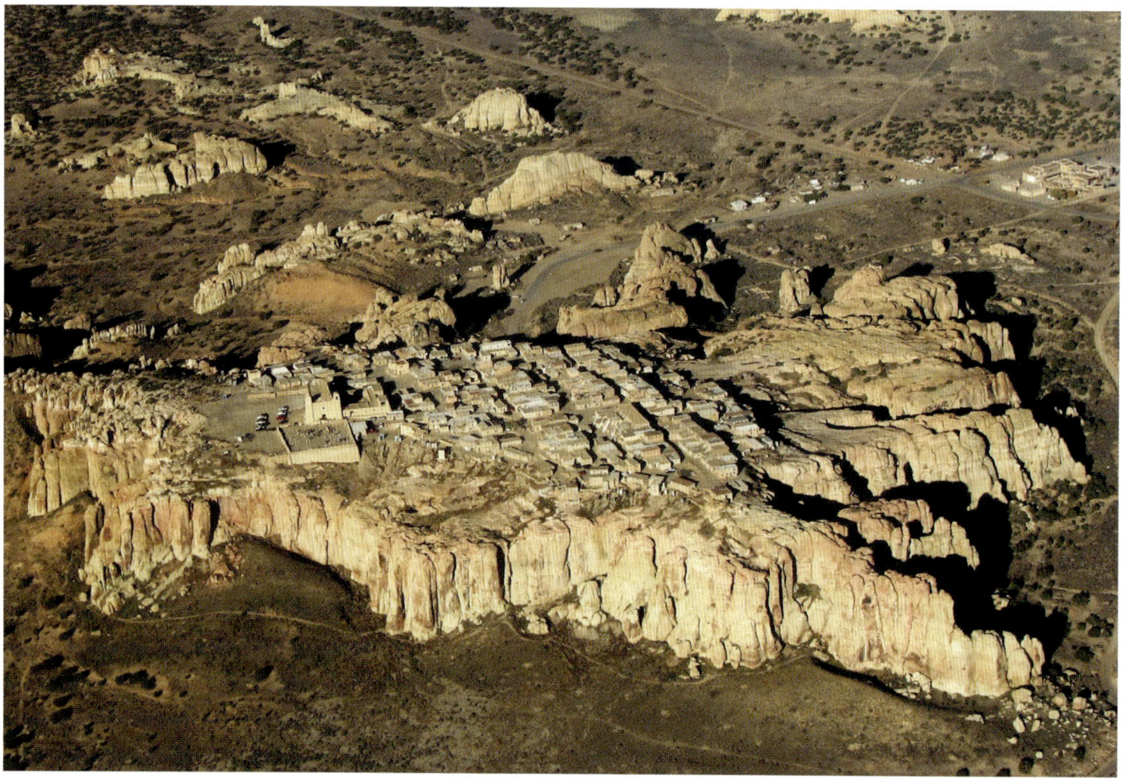

Figure 31. Aerial view of Acoma Pueblo. (Photo by Marshall Henrie, Wikimedia Commons.)

but even during the time we have lived in Los Alamos, we have seen many changes. Instead of the traditional compact arrangement of closely connected, adobe house blocks, the pueblos are moving toward more widely dispersed sets of individual, commercially built homes scattered outside the original village. Some of the more conservative pueblos are resisting this trend, but others now look more like small non-Indian towns in the area. Although the traditional pueblo structure is more interesting to the visitor, the new houses are often more comfortable and therefore are likely to be adopted at all the pueblos before another five years have passed.

In the winter, pueblos are usually quiet and the air is sweet with piñon or juniper smoke. In the summer, lots of kids play in the central plazas and older folks tend to the day's chores. In either season, the weekday population is significantly decreased because many people have jobs in Española, Santa Fe, Bernalillo, Albuquerque, Los Alamos, and other towns in the area.

I have enjoyed many important friendships with Pueblo people. Most of my visits have taken place in their homes, and only a few have occurred at our house.

Following are recollections of some of my experiences with Indian people at nearby pueblos.

SOME OF THE GREAT POTTERS I HAVE KNOWN

Maria Martinez

The pueblo nearest Los Alamos is San Ildefonso. First occupied in the 1300s, the village is situated north of the highway linking Los Alamos and Pojoaque. There is a large open plaza with a circular kiva in the center. Enormous cottonwood trees flank some of the adobe houses facing the plaza, where ceremonial dances take place.

The pueblo—and its potters—became world famous in the 1920s for their stunning, lustrous black pottery. The most prominent among the potters was Maria Martinez. She and her husband, Julian, are credited with reviving an ancient black pottery style made by their ancestors, in addition to developing a method for decorating it with matte black designs.

Maria's fame has been highlighted in many books and articles devoted to her work, written by Alice Mariott, Richard Spivey, Susan Peterson, and others. I can't

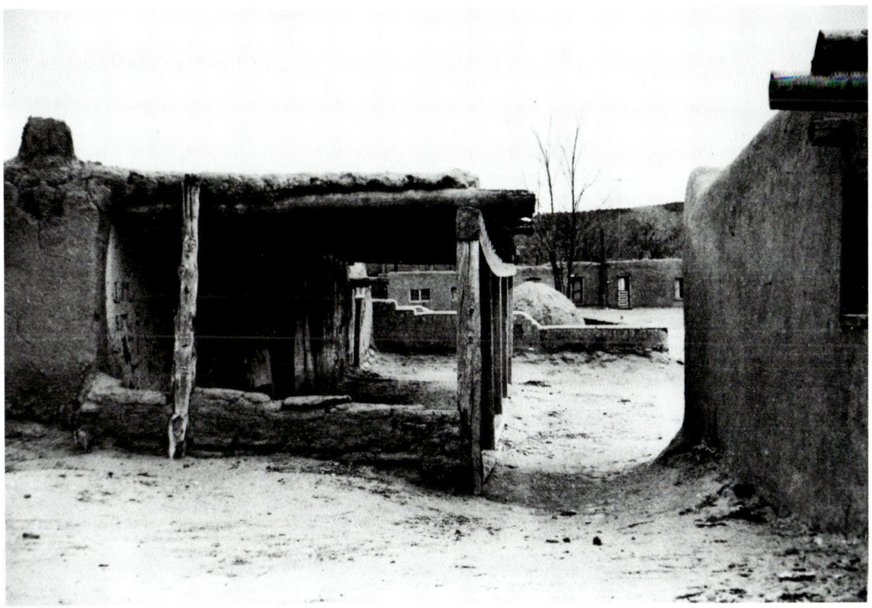

Figure 32. Old houses at San Ildefonso Pueblo, 1950s. These homes have since been razed. (Photo by Francis Harlow.)

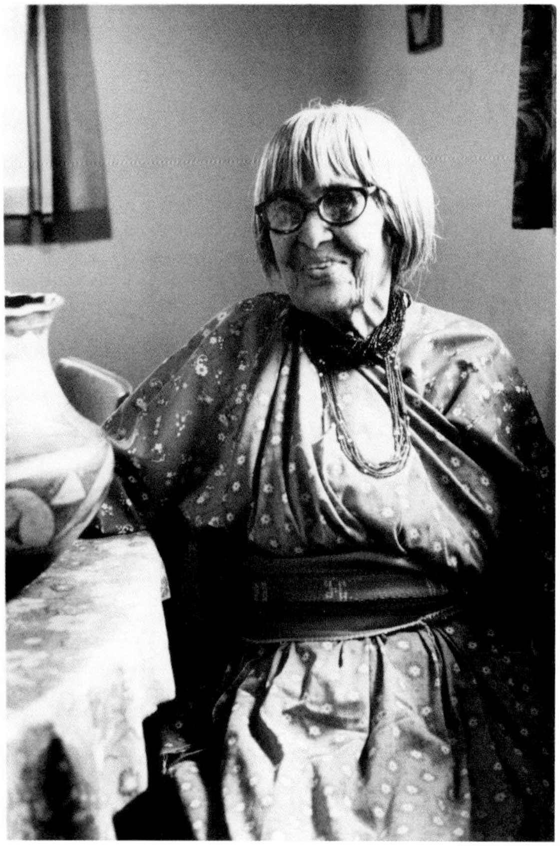

Figure 33. My favorite photograph of Maria Martinez (1887–1980), taken by me at San Ildefonso Pueblo in 1975. (Photo by Francis Harlow.)

compete with their extensive texts and illustrations, but I am able to write about my personal associations with her. I was privileged to visit her twenty-seven times.

My strongest impression of Maria was of her lovely character. We first met in 1961 when our whole family (Pat and I and our four kids) went to the Indian crafts store on the west side of the plaza. In those days, there were still many traditional adobe homes around the plaza. Some of the house blocks were busily occupied, while others were abandoned and starting to return to the earth. Later, to tidy up the village, the abandoned houses were removed, and the plaza, which had been split down the middle by a long house block, was restored to its original single open area. We met Maria's son Tony and his wife, Anita, in the store. At that time, Tony mostly was known by his Indian name, Popovi Da, or Po for short. We may have telephoned ahead of time to express our interest in meeting Po's mother, or we may have arrived without a prior appointment. In any case, our expression of interest in meeting Maria resulted in Po's leaving us with Anita while he went to get his mother. When she came into the room to meet us, her expression was gracious and friendly, but she seemed rather formal in her demeanor. She responded in her Tewa language to our expressions of pleasure at meeting her, which Po translated.

I later found where Maria was living—in a little detached adobe house on the east side of the plaza, and one day I decided to knock on the door to see if she was there. She was, and that was the beginning of a wonderful friendship. The first thing I learned was that she spoke English very well but that when Po or some other member of the family was present, it was customary for her to speak with a visitor in her Tewa language and then be translated by someone else. When she and I were together by ourselves, our conversations were very lively and friendly, and I came to realize what a wonderful lady she was. On the one hand, she knew her proper place as an elder Indian, with completely traditional demeanor, but on the other hand, her conversations were open and filled with personal vignettes that she was willing—even eager—to share with me. She loved meeting visitors and enjoyed opportunities to travel and meet famous people. "I don't want to be like many of the old Indian ladies, who don't act friendly or talk with visitors," she once confided to me. She delighted in telling me a lot of personal things about her life. After a while she would look a bit demure and say to me, "Now don't you tell anyone until we're all dead." A few of these secrets are hinted at in my notes of these visits, and it's now OK for other people to read what I wrote. Other secrets I simply did not write down, and I shall retain them only in my memory without ever divulging them to anyone. (There was nothing shocking in the things she told me.)

I witnessed for myself Alice Marriott's observation (in her book *María: The Potter of San Ildefonso*) that Maria loved to please people; they were especially delighted whenever Maria said that a pot they had brought was, indeed, made by her. The trouble is that there is clear evidence that she was not the maker of some of them. It took a number of visits with Maria to convince her that I was eager for her accurate opinion rather than what she thought I wanted to hear. After we reached that understanding, Maria was very helpful in explaining how she *really* decided whether or not she made a pot. The two principal criteria had to do with the form of the vessel and the designs used in the decoration. In assessing the origin of a pot, she felt down inside "to see how it curves," and she looked at the exterior contours to see the perfection of balance and form that characterize her vessels, especially jars. Regarding the designs, Maria was very open in her statement that she *never* painted decorations, relying instead on her husband, Julian, and other relatives and friends. She characterized the design features painted by each of these people quite consistently and said that the design was especially important in assessing whether she was the maker of a pot. Her assessment depended on her ability to recognize who the painter was.

One pot that I took for her to identify especially delighted her. "That was made by Martina and Florentino Montoya," she said, and she added with genuine conviction, "They were the best of all the San Ildefonso potters!"

She also stated unequivocally that she had made a jar that I showed her in 1973 and that her husband had decorated it. (She is holding it in her lap in fig. 34.) Made about 1910, it is an early example of Tunyo Polychrome, made shortly after the introduction of Cochiti slip. The grainy, streaked appearance of the Cochiti slip is especially evident. A relatively early date for Tunyo Polychrome is indicated by the red rim top.

After a few years, Maria was persuaded to leave her little home and move in with her son Adam and his wife, Santana, both of whom collaborated in her later pottery. When I visited her in her new home, Adam and Santana knew me well enough to let Maria talk directly with me in English. On one visit, I brought a jar (made about 1910) for her inspection. Maria was eager to show me how she could still balance it on her head. She lifted it to her head and moved about the room with her arms to her sides. (She said with complete conviction that it was one she had made and Julian had decorated.) I showed Maria that jar and a few others that she had identified as her work on several occasions some years apart, and she never contradicted her earlier assessment.

Some additional observations about Maria and her pottery, excerpted from notes I made after several visits, follow.

NOV. 25, 1961 Whole family made trip to San Ildefonso with our three old jars from there. At the store we met Popovi Da and his wife, who were very cordial and admired the jars much. . . . Then he went to get his mother to bring to the store, and we met her in the little kitchenette behind the store. She is quite bright and alert and moves quickly despite her age. She talked mostly in Tewa with her son. . . . One polychrome jar was made by Maria and decorated by Ana (Maximiliana) in about 1910, at which time she probably sold it for 10¢. Maria said that she would sign it. (I had asked Popovi Da if she would.) He got a sharp scratching tool, but the surface was too hard. He got a pen and she tried the bottom and then the side, but the surface was too smooth. Then he got a "flow-master" marker and this worked fine on the bottom. Finally, the third jar was made by Maximiliana at an unknown date (circa 1910). We thanked Maria and I quietly asked her son if we should pay her. He said no. He gave her a melon as she left, and I asked him again what we could do. He suggested sending her some nice material for a scarf.

DEC. 29, 1962 Visit with Maria Martinez at San Ildefonso. She says that several features distinguish the old B/W San Ildefonso jars from those at Cochiti. San Ildefonso uses a stone-polished slip (white), while at Cochiti this was not done; the slip was rubbed for polishing. Also, San Ildefonso solid-black design areas are thin and watery-black, while those from Cochiti are dark-black black.

JULY 6, 1963 Maria Martinez, in interview at her home on 6 July '63, told me that in the latter part of the 1800s, the pottery-making families had surnames Montoya, Vigil, Peña, and Sanchez, at San Ildefonso.

FEBRUARY 1966 Mrs. Martinez at her little home. She was charming. She identified 5 or 6 . . . San Ildefonso pots for me. Different forms are characteristic of the various potters; one potter made a big mid-body bulge, another a globular form. Maria's form appears to have usually had a full underbody and relatively tall shape. She says that her old (pre-1915) polychromes are extremely rarely encountered, in almost no collections she knows about. . . . Maria's mother never made pots, but her grandmother did. Maria easily recognizes style and design differences, paint texture, slip polishing method, etc. I am convinced that Maria is a very kind, lovely, genuinely friendly (when she gets to know a person well) person who lives a relatively typical and genuine Indian life. She is modest, frank, dedicated to her position in the pueblo. I come from the interviews filled with renewed respect and admiration for her.

A few days later we saw a half-hour TV program (educational TV station) showing her and Popovi Da. Po made the pottery in the demonstration. The announcer said that Maria makes no more pottery. Maria said only one sentence, that being in Tewa to Po, who answered briefly in Tewa.

I visited Maria again, with a little stone-stroked Black/Red globular jar, which she said was made at San Ildefonso. I asked if it could be from Tesuque, and she said no B/R was made at Tesuque. (I think that in this she is mistaken; black-on-red was rarely made at Tesuque.) She said the jar was much older than from any date she could recognize. I asked Maria about the TV show. She said the only thing that she had said during the show was to tell Po to use a little more water to keep the clay from drying out. He then told her not to talk at all during the show. I asked her about the statement concerning no more pottery making, and she said that she had not heard it said. This visit was on a Saturday afternoon and four 7" jars were drying in the warm sun in front of the house. She said it was such an unexpectedly nice day that she should make some pots, even though it was winter. As soon as the air got cold, she would take them in, even though not dry yet. Maria showed me the pot mold forms she uses. They are fired clay of the form ~6" in diameter. When making a pot, she has to turn the mold 'round and 'round. To keep the bottom from wearing out, she puts the mold into the bottom part of a broken Picuris jar, which then grinds on the turning, but doesn't wear out because it is harder, she claims.

JUNE 26, 1971 [Maria] seems quite tired & frail after her eye operation. (Also, the day is <u>hot</u>.) Today she claims, for the first time, that she made a very small number of stone-polished polychrome vessels, in addition to the Cochiti-slip jars that she usually made. She wished to sign my stone-polished jar as her own, even though I insisted she not do so unless she felt sure she had made it; at the same time, she rejected a beautifully formed Cochiti slip jar as not having been made by her, because it is too heavy and because she does not recognize who painted the designs on it.

Although her one-eyed sight is weak, she recognized the polished vs. Cochiti slip and admired the designs on the former. Her hands seem frail and her hearing is weak. But her humor is fine and she seems to be as alert and intelligent as ever.

JUNE 27, 1971 I am reassured to the viewpoint that she would not sign a pot as her own make unless there was no reasonable doubt. . . . Maria says that one thing that helps her recognize her own pots is to see and recognize designs painted by people whom she would get to do painting for her when Julian was away. Alfredo Montoya (who did not live to be very old) was one of these whom Maria often got. Lightness of weight is another feature that makes her recognize her own work. Maximiliana also sometimes painted pots for Maria.

It seems that the people Maria got to do her painting were people who put on neat designs with some degree of imagination, often with lightness of line work and grace, usually somewhat dynamic rather than stolid and heavy and static.

OCT. 1, 1971 She . . . identified pots made by Martina and Florentino Montoya, which she much admired.

Apparently, the style of Martina & Florentino includes

- Thin walls & hard firing
- Black rim top
- Partial or complete ceremonial breaks
- Cochiti influence in designs
- Beautiful and exuberant designs
- Negative fine lines in black (or red edged with black) designs, e.g.

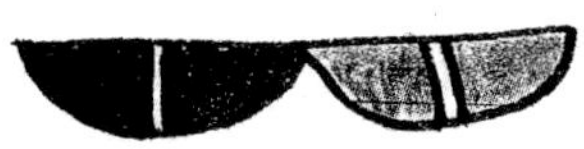

- Relatively heavy jar base
- Manufacture for actual service (at least sometimes)

Maria seems much stronger than a few months ago. Her eye bandages are off and she is wearing very thick glasses, so she does not see well and uses a support stick for walking. Her humor was excellent tonight and she talked a lot to me in English about all sorts of things, including her two doctor's degrees and various non-Indian potters she has recently met. . . .

Maria says sometimes Martina made and fired plain white pots, which were then painted by a Spanish man with flowers and angels, etc. She has never seen one in a museum, however.

MAY 11, 1973 Maria seems to be getting around better. She has thick glasses that give her good vision. She uses a wooden cane when walking and not the aluminum-frame walker any more. She seems as alert and full of humor as ever. I took the large pitcher that she and Julian made for the ranch school at Los Alamos [see figs. 34 and 35]. She and Adam and Santana at once agreed on Maria & Julian having made the vessel. . . .

She and Santana looked at the black-on-black small-jar sherd from Quintana's, 1.3 mi. east of the pueblo. They agreed it was not a Maria-Julian piece because the avanyu faces right (Julian's always face left) and the tail is fatter than Julian would paint.

Adam again reiterates that my "tennis-racket-tail" bird jar was painted by Julian [figs. 34, 35, and 68]. I asked him if it could have been painted by Alfredo Montoya, and he said no, it was surely by Julian.

FEB. 15, 1974 Visited Santana and Adam Martinez at their home in San Ildefonso. They had just finished firing some pottery and it was set out on the dining room table. I think that Santana's work was not up to its usual high standards. The matte black designs were less carefully painted, and the jet black surfaces were not as well polished as I have seen before, being somewhat stroke marked. I asked about Maria and they said Maria is well, sees well, and gets around well. They showed me that some of the smallest pots they had fired were, in fact, some that Maria had just recently made. Santana, as usual, had of course polished them. They were quite plain, no decoration, and the polish was very nice. Santana had

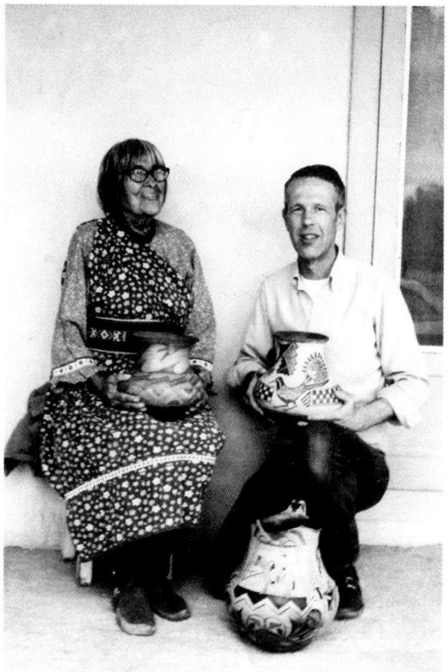

Figure 34. Maria Martinez and I on May 11, 1973, with two jars from our collection and an enormous pitcher that she made, now in the collection of the Los Alamos Historical Museum. (Photo by Adam Martinez.)

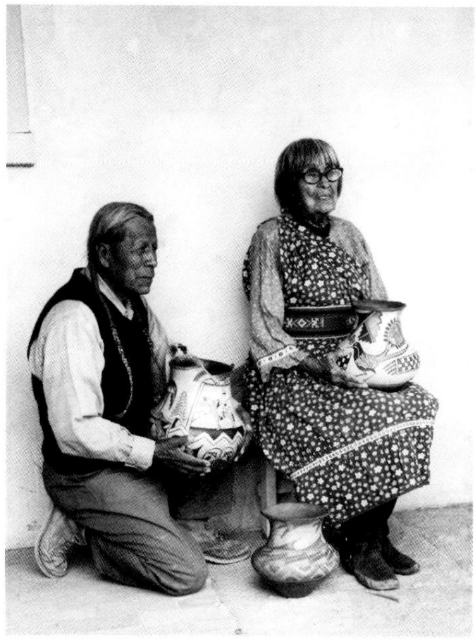

Figure 35. Adam Martinez with his mother, Maria Martinez, May 11, 1973. (Photo by Francis Harlow.)

made a bowl for her own use, rather shallow with flat bottom, polished in and out, which she said would hold water very nicely.

NOV. 4 AND DEC. 5, 1974 Two visits with Maria Martinez at San Ildefonso. . . . She uses her walker around the house, to avoid falling, and led me around to see some pots and awards she'd received. Says she plans to make pots (little ones) next spring. Grasped my hand with strong firm grip. . . . [December 5] Again Maria seems quite well. Santana told me Maria gets $3 for signing the book about her. I gave her $10 for signing the pot, which she thought was fine. I took pictures of her with & without the pot, for which they wanted no further money.

FEB. 10, 1975 (Monday afternoon) Visit to see Maria Martinez at the home of Santana and Adam, who were present. (Also, Maria's sister, Clara, was there.) Maria had been sick with flu the week before but seemed very well today. She walks with a cane only, not the aluminum walker, as before. She seemed very cheerful and talkative. I took a pot belonging to Forrest Fenn, which I felt sure Maria made and Julian decorated. Maria confirmed my ideas without my suggestion of them to her. She signed the pot on the bottom, Marie and Julian, Povika. I paid her $10 for the signing. Then I took the black/white and colored pictures of her sitting by the window with the pot on the table beside her. I paid her $10 for the picture taking session.

APRIL 23, 1975 Visit with Maria at the home of Adam and Santana. Clara was there with us part of the time, but otherwise Maria and I were alone from 1:00 until 1:30. . . . She was in tremendously fine spirits. Clara talks very little, apparently never in English. She polishes a lot of the pottery for Santana and Maria but never makes pots or paints designs. Maria says Clara is very hard of hearing. . . . Maria and I talked about people who decorated her polychrome pots. I showed her a picture of my tennis-racket-tailed bird, and she immediately exclaimed that it's a pot she made. She says it was painted by Crescencio, her brother-in-law, Maximiliana's husband, rather than Julian.

Maria says, quite consistently, that Alfredo Montoya's designs almost invariably have flowers. When Alfredo painted birds, they were always very fancy and had flowers in association with them. Alfredo's Indian name was Huan Tsire (Pine Bird).

Crescencio Martinez, Ana's husband, also painted fancy birds, during his active period of pottery decoration, 1910–1918 (his death, according to San Ildefonso pottery book).

Thus, Crescencio and Alfredo painted fancy birds. In contrast Julian (and Florentino Montoya, who never painted Maria's pottery) always painted much more simple birds and never showed flowers with the birds. Maria says Julian's birds were very much like Florentino's. . . .

Maria says she changed her pot-signing signature from "Marie" to "Maria" because of the book. She did this "after the book came out" (i.e., Marriott's *Maria* book, 1948).

Maria was very talkative and informative. We looked together through Chapman and my San Ildefonso pottery book, and she volunteered a variety of comments on the bird drawings. Noted the following attributions:

- Plate 156p was painted by Alfredo.

- Plate 156e was painted by Alfredo.

- Plates 160a and c are "old style" (i.e., before her early period).

I paid Maria $10 for each pot she signed (she signed them "Maria Povika") and $10 for posing for photos, $40 in all. She also put Maximiliana's name on a pot that she thinks her sister made and painted. The name she put on was "Anna Martinez." I didn't pay her for that signature. She seemed delighted to get the $40.

Vicentita Pino

On a warm and sunny winter day, I visited Vicentita Pino, the famous potter of Zia Pueblo. I asked if she was going to make pottery that day. She said she would love to do so but could not because she had no ——, which was an Indian word that I didn't understand. After further conversation, I realized she was referring to finely powdered, volcanic black lava, which for hundreds of years has been mixed with the clay used to make Zia pots. She went on to say that grinding the lava on a metate was very hard and she didn't feel like doing it that day. I suggested that she make some pots without the ground lava; her response was to the effect that she could not make any pots without the life imparted to the clay by the lava. I think she considered me to be either grossly ignorant of such matters or a heretic. I pretty much knew what her response would be to my suggestion, but I was interested in finding out just how dedicated she was to tradition. My other visits to Zia were directed more toward finding old pottery fragments.

Santana Melcher

On several occasions, the Melcher family of Santo Domingo Pueblo came to visit us in our home. We have also spent many enjoyable hours at their home. The matriarch of the family was Santana Melcher, a charming old woman who spoke almost no English. To her, and her daughter-in-law Crucita, goes the credit for perpetuating the finest traditions of Santo Domingo pottery manufacture. Few examples of the modern wares of that village can compare in quality or beauty to the vessels produced so prolifically by the Melchers.

The head of the family was Ray Melcher, and when they came to visit, Ray and his wife and eldest son and daughter occupied the cab of their pickup truck. In the bed of the truck rode the older mother, Santana, and her youngest grandchild.

The first time I visited the Melcher home in 1962, I was immediately struck by the beauty of an enormous pottery jar in their largest room. It was beautifully proportioned in form and attractively painted with bird designs. The jar was made by Mrs. Melcher in about 1927 and obviously had increased in importance to the family over the years, as evidenced by their refusal to sell it to the various visitors who had offered to buy it.

Accordingly, I was particularly intrigued when one day a long-distance call from the Melcher family indicated that their immediate need for some money was forcing them to sell the old jar. Their question to me was, Could I give them $100 right away if they brought the jar to our house? Of course the answer was yes. Politeness prohibited any discussion of the reason for this need, but even though the amount seemed at that time to be rather steep, I was sure that their need clearly called for the requested assistance. (A few years later, the value of the jar would be at least four times the price then, and its value would continue to rise indefinitely in that fashion.)

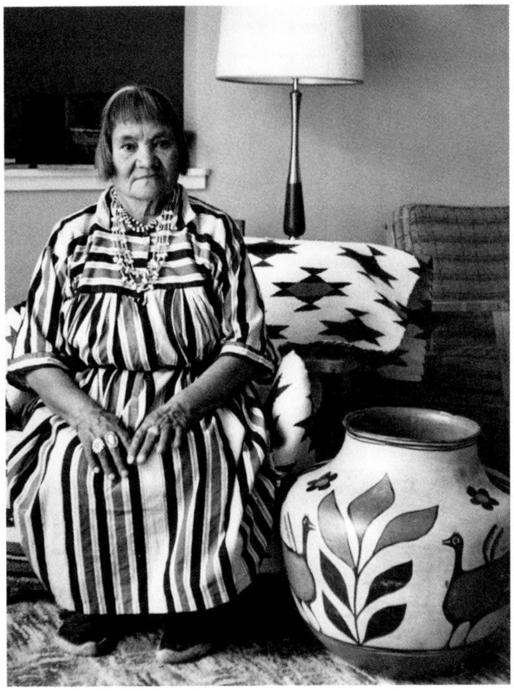

Figure 36. Santana Melcher with a big storage jar that she made around 1927. (Harlow family photos.)

The visit was indeed memorable. As in all visits with Indians, business was never discussed until sufficient polite chatter had relaxed everyone. With the Melchers, this usually meant at least forty-five minutes of pleasantries concerning family, weather, dances, etc. Meanwhile, there in our living room was the Melcher family treasure, to be abandoned to satisfy some emergency requirement of the moment.

As soon as business became the order of conversation, however, it emerged that the intention was for me to keep the jar as collateral for a loan rather than as a permanent sale. That was fine with me, although I knew that parting with the vessel later would be difficult. On the other hand, they knew it would be difficult to raise the redemption money at a later date, so we agreed on an alternative redemption plan: the Melchers would make me another huge jar to replace this one, if they could. This agreement caused me some misgivings, for fear that they would insist on trading a much inferior vessel for the old heirloom. The fear proved not to materialize, however; the whole Melcher family expended enormous effort to produce the finest vessel made in recent years at the pueblo with which to redeem the one they left with me in hock.

I'm glad that I photographed Santana Melcher with her old masterpiece on the day the family brought it. We asked her permission for the picture through her children as interpreters, and she seemed quite flattered. She retired to another room to fix her dress and hair and then settled herself into a chair that I covered

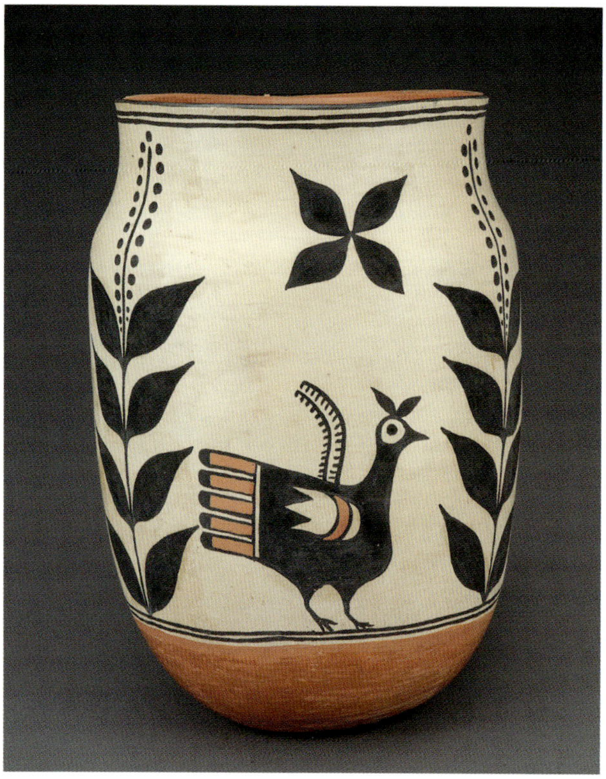

Figure 37. Storage jar made by Crucita and Santana Melcher, Santo Domingo Pueblo, circa 1965, 57.5 x 40.9 cm. (Photo by Blair Clark. Museum of Indian Arts and Culture [hereafter MIAC], 55963/12.)

with a Navajo blanket. I set the fine old jar beside her and took several exposures. I used one of the photographs in my *Matte-Paint Pottery* book.

Several months later, shortly after Easter, we heard again from the Melchers. The big replacement jar was ready. It had been fired on Good Friday (for luck?) and had come out well. Shortly thereafter, our good friends Mark and Tommie Jakobson offered to stop at Santo Domingo and bring the vessel here to Los Alamos. And so they did, in their tiny, crowded Volkswagen, with Mrs. Jakobson carrying the pot like a baby. A few weeks later, I took the old jar back to Santo Domingo.

The replacement jar is indeed a treasure. It was so much work and the firing was filled with such nerve-racking uncertainty that the Melchers claimed they would never attempt such a huge project again. The jar is nearly twenty-three inches tall, and only a very small number of other painted Pueblo pots of that size are known to me. Other people from Santo Domingo afterward told me that half of the pueblo turned out to witness the firing. Indeed, this last of the great Santo Domingo pottery storage jars will long be remembered by the residents of the village, by many visitors to our home, and by those who see it in the Museum of Indian Arts and Culture in Santa Fe, to which it went.

The following year, I saw Ray Melcher at the Santa Fe Indian Market, which takes place each August. He said they were glad to have the old jar back. When it had been gone, there had been much sickness in the family and he had lost his job. As soon as the old pot returned to their home, he got a good new job and the sickness vanished.

Santana, Ray, and Crucita Melcher also brought pottery to our carport to sell to Los Alamos people I had contacted. Their beautifully constructed wares showed traditional Santo Domingo forms and decorations that were very popular.

The prices were low—$10 to $25—so they sold many fine pieces. In general, however, Santo Domingo pottery was much less popular with collectors than wares from such pueblos as Acoma, where fine-line, eye-dazzler designs were painted with incredible precision.

INDIAN DANCES

Indian dances seem to be of two types: those that are truly sacred and those that are presented for the amusement of outsiders. In between these two extremes are the feast day dances—held by each pueblo on the day honoring its patron saint. These are meant to be joyous occasions attended by the pueblo population, by friends and relations from other pueblos, and by non-Indians from surrounding cities. Often the dance is performed in front of an effigy of the patron saint, which is housed in a ramada, a temporary structure covered with branches or boards specifically for the purpose. In this respect, the dances express the serious joy of protection bestowed by the saints, but most of the delight of the day takes place in an atmosphere of joyous holiday. Everyone is fed in their own homes by the hardworking ladies of the village. Tables of locally made Indian crafts are attended by people wanting to sell their wares to any and all visitors. For me, a disappointing aspect of the feast day dances is that the dancers usually wear costumes that are nontraditional in many respects, consisting of white shirts, colorful commercial blankets or sashes, and other similar modern adaptations.

Even more commercial are most of the dances performed away from the pueblo, at fairs or holidays in nearby towns and sometimes even for special faraway events. A notable example was the annual summertime dance sponsored by Santa Clara Pueblo and held at the ruins of Puyé Pueblo, which was abandoned in the late 1500s. A fee was charged to any and all people wanting to attend, and many booths were constructed to sell Indian souvenirs or Native food. The dances were performed in the plaza of the ancient village, which had been cleared of weeds and brush, and the dancers had been recruited from Santa Clara and other pueblos. I attended once and took lots of photographs. Several years after I went to the Puyé dances, the celebrations were interrupted by the kind of summer storm that can gather quickly on a day that starts out calm, clear, and sunny. Out of the thick clouds above Puyé there came crashing down a lightning bolt that killed several people. The Santa Clara Indians considered this to be in retribution for their having profaned both the ancient village and the sacredness of the dances, and the public summer dance at Puyé was never held again.

Actually, some of the tourist-oriented dances can be performed for fun (and profit) in a manner that seems not to offend the spiritual traditions of the pueblo. One memorable occasion occurred at the Wheelwright Museum in Santa Fe at an opening of a wonderful show of Zia Pueblo pottery in 2003. The celebration also commemorated the publication of *The Pottery of Zia Pueblo,* a book written by Dwight Lanmon and me.

The Zia people presented a so-called Crow Dance, conceived and choreographed in such a way as to avoid any sense of mimicking the sacred dances of the pueblo, although the costumes were very much like those of the traditional dances. The dancers (all young men) had their bodies completely smeared with black ashes, to suggest the image of crows (or the ravens that are so abundant in this area). The day was beautiful, and a large crowd of observers surrounded the field near the museum where the dance was held. The drummers and male chorus started the dance beat, and the dancers cavorted about, pretending to be crows scavenging for bits of food. The audience started throwing in money; one or several dancers would depart from the group and, in a squatting run, go over to pick up the dollar bills (or higher denominations) with their teeth and awkwardly squat-run to a central basket, in which the treasure was deposited. From time to time, the crow dancers would form themselves into a line and the drumbeat would change to the rhythm of a traditional Pueblo line dance, with staccato foot motions pounding against the ground. Then the drumming would return to the scavenger's beat and the crows would resume their exhausting squat-runs around the area, sometimes approaching a surprised member of the audience and squawking for food (money). It was delightful and much fun for everyone!

In contrast, the Turtle Dance, held annually at Ohkay Owingeh Pueblo on December 26, is absolutely awesome in its solemn performance of an ancient sacred ceremony in a manner that preserves all the spine-tingling dignity of a centuries-old tradition. We went one cold December day a few years ago when our daughter Carol and our grandchildren Lisa and Adam were visiting from Australia. As best as I could count, there were about two hundred men dancing, all with painted bodies and wearing kilts and other traditional objects of sacred religious significance—especially the carapace of a New Mexico land turtle (about five inches in diameter) with tied-on deer hooves that made a wonderful rattle. This dried shell was fastened behind the right knee of every dancer, who also wore metal bells, so the air pulsated with the rhythm of the dance beat. Of course, no photographs of the dance were allowed, and the visitors (rather sparse on that cold day) were instructed to stand well away from the long, straight double line of dancers. This dance and the Antege

Shade ceremony at San Ildefonso were the most emotional experiences I have ever had at a modern pueblo (this one located on the same site for many centuries—from well before the "discovery" of America in 1492).

An entirely different emotional response occurs whenever I visit the ancient ruins of Tsirege Pueblo, which lies close to Los Alamos, built on one of the mesas of the area. Some of the rooms and ceremonial kivas are still visible. From here, the spectacular view of the mountains twenty miles across the Rio Grande Valley is exactly the same as the sights that moved the ancient Indians to their reverence for nature. Birds and deer still inhabit the area, and in nearby fields, corn, squash, and beans were grown, until a drought in the late 1500s forced the Tsirege Indians to abandon their ancient home and join their Tewa-speaking cousins at San Ildefonso, which lies close to the Rio Grande. Whenever I have gone there, the sights, fragrances of nature, and gentle sound of the breeze have never failed to cast their spell on me. The spirits of ancient inhabitants still seem to hover over the village. Whenever I visit San Ildefonso, I meet the descendants of those ancient Tsirege Indians and something special dances in my mind, even when there are no drums or turtle shells to create the beat.

SANTA FE INDIAN MARKET

Indian Market is now held every August in Santa Fe, where hundreds of Indians display and sell their wares. When we first moved to Los Alamos, the market and the annual Santa Fe Fiesta occurred together in early September on Labor Day. We attended the festivities every year on Saturday morning, when the various arts and crafts were being judged for ribbons and when the children's pet parade wound its way around the Plaza. It was fun to be part of the excitement, although we rarely bought anything. One exception was when we purchased a large polychrome storage jar, beautifully constructed and decorated with birds and rainbows. The jar had been made by Lucinda Torribio of Zia Pueblo, who sold it to us for $100. I met Lucinda only that one time. As I carried the beautiful jar back to the car, there were many admirers along the way. After many years of displaying the piece in our living room, we gave it to our daughter Katie, who now has it in her Albuquerque home. The jar is illustrated in our book on Zia pottery (fig. 14.144).

By the 1960s, Indian Market had increased in size so much that it was no longer possible to have the market, the fiesta, and Labor Day occur at the same time, so the fiesta was moved to mid-September and Indian Market was moved to a weekend in mid-August. (It now draws thousands of people from all across the country.) It is interesting to note that there has also been a tremendous growth of interest in Hispanic arts and crafts, so a separate Spanish Market was also created; it occurs a couple of weeks before Indian Market.

INDIAN ACTIVITIES AND VISITS

We often visited pueblos, sometimes to see ceremonial dances, other times to view and acquire pottery. I usually made notes about what we saw shortly after each visit. The texts of some of those notes follow.

NOV. 12, 1960 Catherine, Carol, and I went to Tesuque—Annual Fiesta. Pueblo was crowded with many cars, and traffic routing was necessary. Dance in central plaza was just starting a new session as we arrived late afternoon. Dancing was in two lines of alternating men & women. Dance was fast and energetic by men who dance around the women. Costumes were elaborate and bright—lots of feathers, sunbursts, etc.—suggesting plains Indians. Pictures were allowed.

FEB. 12, 1961 Pat went to San Idefonso Evergreen Dance. Dance in South Plaza by men & boys—no women, no drummers—men did own singing. Costumes as in Easter Dance (below). Dance was serious and impressive.

EASTER 1961 We all, with John Nystuen, went to the Easter Dance at San Ildefonso. Very impressive, serious, and beautiful. Dance in North Plaza. Four fir trees put in square and dancers danced in straight lines in succession between each pair of fir trees. Men danced and sang; 2 or 3 women kneeling on blankets in middle of line, inside of square, played scraping instruments. A few Indian observers, but only 5 or 10 Anglos besides us. (Gilbert Atencio—23 September 1961—says this was the Antege Shade.) Costumes were quite typical Pueblo. Upper bodies were painted black. No pictures allowed. Well worth seeing again.

SUMMER 1961 We all went briefly to San Ildefonso Corn Dance—arrived just as N. Plaza Dancers retired to Kiva. S. Plaza Dancers later came out to present rather poor dancing—pictures allowed.

JUNE 24, 1961 San Juan Saint's Day Fiesta attended by Catherine and me. Comanche Dance done by younger people—they were wildly decorated, dancing for fun and amusement of onlookers. Plains Indians type dress—bright luminescent colors, sunbursts, feathers, etc. Only a few good dancers—mostly not too interesting. Lots of Fiesta celebrants, holiday mood, food stands.

JULY 1961 Puyé ceremonial—well done, good dances. Costumes not complete—men wore white shirts. Poor contrast to Santa Clara day—see below.

AUG. 12, 1961 Whole family went to Santa Clara for fiesta, arriving about 3:00. There were continuously two dances going on, both very spectacular. Very many people—booths with food, curios, pottery, rugs, jewelry. Happy mood. Shrine (Catholic) erected near rectangular Kiva—always dancers in front of it. Costumes were gorgeous, complete, as compared with at Puyé. Women wore more elaborate decorations. Men had no shirts, had painted bodies and faces, wore elaborate necklaces. Picture taking allowed (w/ prior permission?). Well worth attending again.

SEPT. 30, 1961 We all went to Taos on spur of the moment this beautiful Saturday morning. There we were reminded of the Pueblo feast day, so we went out, getting there at about 3:00 p.m. The clowns (5 of them) were clowning about the pole, and shortly after we arrived, they brought a ladder. One went up and untied the ropes, letting them down to the ground where the other clowns could swing on them. Then he climbed down. Another clown, younger and husky, rubbed dirt on himself and climbed ladder. Another came behind him and 1st climbed on shoulders of 2nd, then climbed the pole to the top, there greeted by applause and car horn honking. He then untied a parcel of bread to be lowered pulley fashion by a rope over a cross-arm on which he sat. Then he lowered several sacks of things and finally a sheep carcass. Then he himself slid down the two ropes. Admission to pueblo: 50¢ per car. Very crowded with cars and people, we hardly could park. Clowns wore cornhusks in hair, belt with loincloth between legs tucked over belt front and back. Some had quite black face paint and all had fairly faint stripes with no strong white or black.

SEPT. 8, 1963 Whole family to Corn Dance at San Ildefonso. Must have been 50 dancers, including perhaps 25 small children. Costumes are still lush. Men have painted bodies, no clothes from waist up. They wear regular dance kilts, embroidered and with the usual white sashes with long fringe, and with fox skins at back. Sandals and skunk skin anklets and armbands with evergreen complete essential costume. Women wore dark mantas over one shoulder, the other bare. There was a little edging embroidery, and many used wild sunflowers, freshly picked, woven into their mantas. All had simple blue-green tabletas on their heads. One drummer, ~6 men in chorus, one standard bearer; standard had a white "flag" with colorful edge embroidery, also numerous feathers, especially at the tip. Outstanding, however, was the appearance of two K'ossa [Tewa clowns], both old men who danced around among the formal dancers with very graceful ballet, especially graceful in hand motion. Between dances, one K'ossa went from house to house, singing and dancing at every approach (often frightening the children on the porch, who scattered). At each house, he collected some food, accumulating a large bundle tied in a cloth, which he finally took to the rectangular Kiva, near the round one being used in the dances. The K'ossas had circular black and white stripes, double corn-husk tassels in hair, and black loin cloths, all seemingly very typical. The large circular Kiva has a ground-level hole just to the left of the stairway (as the latter is approached) through which small children (dancers) squeezed in and out between dances and through which food and drinks were handed.

FEB. 3, 1962 Catherine and Celia and I went for afternoon to Santo Domingo (Carol was sick so stayed home—we had <u>all</u> planned to go). We took many nice baby clothes plus several shirts and my suit, all to trade for pottery. I was impressed with how many homes have and still use the old-style Santo Domingo bowls. Also in use are Zia bowls and jars and Acoma jars. I've not seen Cochiti pots at Domingo. Santana Melcher makes fine old-style pottery, but so, apparently, do many others of the older women. Mostly these potters are the "mother" or "aunt" of the women to whom I talked, and seldom, apparently, do women less than 40 years of age make the old-style pots.

I could see that there was some sort of important ceremony taking place. From one large building in particular many people were going or coming. The men were costumed and painted or partly costumed (partly dressed in usual fashion) and partly painted. No drums were heard. Women carried bowls, baskets, and shawls with food (?) into the building. At ~4:00 p.m., for example, women from all over began to approach the building. One would have a laden shawl over shoulder. Another would have an Acoma jar balanced on her head. Others had bowls or baskets with cloths over them. Then at about 4:45, the "meeting" at the big house broke up and women poured out in all directions with their empty utensils. I noticed at one time a row of empty old-style bowls and "Navajo style" baskets out in front of the big house. I stopped to look at them and a voice cried out, "They're not for sale."

I went to Santana Melcher's house; she was home but shortly thereafter had to leave with a bundle. Mrs. Melcher had two large, nice bowls, rather shallow, with inside decorations (her daughter does the painting). She wanted $20 for the two. One was badly cracked. There was a big storage jar [see fig. 36] at one side of the eating room. Mrs. Melcher had made it 35 years ago—had refused $50.00 for it. Large black and red bird on it, nicely done in strong colors. Also had (I think) minor flower elements in design. Bread loaves (Indian style) were inside; over the top was a thick soft paper of some kind, with an old-style Domingo bowl over that. Jar was perhaps 18 inches high—body was more cylindrical than globular.

Two women offered large Domingo old-style bowls for the clothes. One bowl was especially nice—rim slightly incurved. Reyes Lovato showed me a poorly done, old-style Domingo bowl with no ceremonial breaks in exterior or rim lines.

VISITORS TO OUR HOME

As the size of our collections grew, our home became something of a museum of Indian arts. We mostly collected pottery, but we also had a variety of other materials, including stone, textile, leather, baskets, and wood carvings. And not all of it is from the American Southwest; we also have Peruvian and Near Eastern artifacts. Until we donated most of our Pueblo pottery to the Museum of Indian Arts and Culture in Santa Fe, we displayed it on shelves in a small room that was also my study. We called the room our little "pottery museum," and visitors often came to see it.

One Sunday afternoon in 1969, a friend called and asked to bring over visitors. They were the Tosa family from Jemez Pueblo. Mr. Tosa had a typical Indian visage that may still be seen among conservative members of the villages: long hair tied with a black-and-red sash. Both he and his wife were quite shy and talked little. June Johnson of Los Alamos had encouraged Mrs. Tosa and several other Indian potters to experiment with modern innovative styles. Her vessels were fired and then decorated with black-and-red designs, sprayed with a commercial fixative. The artwork was copied from designs of the early historic period, but little of the old traditions remained in the finished products. She felt that her work was getting to be famous. Indeed, examples were to be found in several Santa Fe shops, and they may still be selling rather well. Mrs. Tosa was disappointed that I did not buy an example for our personal museum.

The week after the Tosa visit, we enjoyed a pair of visiting groups. June Johnson brought the first of these, Grace and Jack Hoover of Santa Clara Pueblo. What a contrast this pair was to the Tosa family. Grace was a Santa Clara Indian, but Jack was an Anglo (a term frequently used in this area to identify non-Indian people of European descent) who had lived in the pueblo since their marriage. They were quite young. Both were very sincere people who talked easily, and they obviously loved the pottery work that supported them. Jack was a big man with strong hands. He did much of the laborious part of the process, preparing the clay, firing the vessels, and carving the patterns. Grace's father was a Pueblo elder who knew something of the traditional designs and laid them out for Jack to execute.

When Grace was a child, she watched her mother make pottery, but like many Pueblo youngsters, she felt that such work was not for her. As a result, the craft is mostly dying out today, remaining only where commercial success with works of art serves as an incentive to continue. Jack, too, never pictured himself as a potter and marveled to see the change in himself that circumstances brought about.

It was fun to watch the delight that Grace and Jack expressed as they admired the various pottery pieces in our home museum. Jack was surprisingly knowledgeable about some of the styles, having committed to memory his observations at various curio stores and exhibits. This seemed like an appropriate time to bring out one of the ancient bowls that I keep to give interested visitors, and indeed they were pleased with the present. They promised to give me a carved black jar in return, and I regretted their feeling of obligation. In this case, however, I have to confess that a beautiful example of that Santa Clara pottery style was a welcome addition.

Another visitor was George Rivera, who at that time was lieutenant governor of Pojoaque Pueblo. George is a very pleasant person. He's an artist, especially a sculptor, who has studied in other parts of the world, including France. George later became Pojoaque Pueblo governor, a position that consumed much of his time and energy.

On several visits, he showed me some extremely interesting pottery vessels that were offered for sale to the pueblo. One of the jars was a black-on-red vessel with a circus of animal designs and an Indian rider on his horse. Another was a large, polished black bowl. But the most intriguing of all were several sacred ceremonial bowls of Tewa origin in the style of the 1700s, which were so unusual as to suggest they might be artificially aged, modern fabrications. I don't think that this initial conclusion was valid, however, because there were so many design elements that I would not expect anyone to know about in modern times. Also, I don't think that many modern potters would have the knowledge of, or access to, the correct materials for the paste and slip of the 1700s.

Among other Indian visitors to our house were Laurencita Herrera and her family from Cochiti Pueblo. Especially noteworthy about that visit was Laurencita's mother's emotional response to seeing old Cochiti Pueblo jars in our collection. She asked through her grandson as interpreter if she could touch some of them, and of course I said yes. Her delicacy and reverence with one in particular were very touching. Her grandson said that they no longer had any ancient pottery treasures at Cochiti and that it was very special for his grandmother to see and hold them. Only after a long time did she reluctantly set the jar back on the floor. I'll never know what special memories were evoked by the visit.

Gilbert Benjamin Atencio, a noteworthy artist from San Ildefonso Pueblo, was another visitor. He concentrates mainly on painting and a little bit of pottery making. He worked for many years as an illustrator in the Theoretical Division of the Los Alamos National Laboratory, and his office was not far from mine, so we had frequent interactions. At one time, Pat and I commissioned him to paint some pictures for us, which we still have. Several show Indian dancers and one has many potters at work on their craft, but the most interesting one shows a baby-naming ceremony, with two women and a baby outside a pueblo house. It is autumn and leaves blow across the scene, one landing on the baby, who is being given the name Ka Fede, which means "blowing leaves" in the Tewa language.

An especially close relationship with a Pueblo Indian woman developed when our children were young and Pat needed someone to come to our house once a week to help with cleaning and ironing. Mary R. Cata from San Juan Pueblo was the person we hired, and she turned out to be wonderful help and also a good friend. We paid her $10 for each half-day that we needed her. When our son, Keith, was born, Mary Cata insisted that Keith have the Indian name Ka Fede.

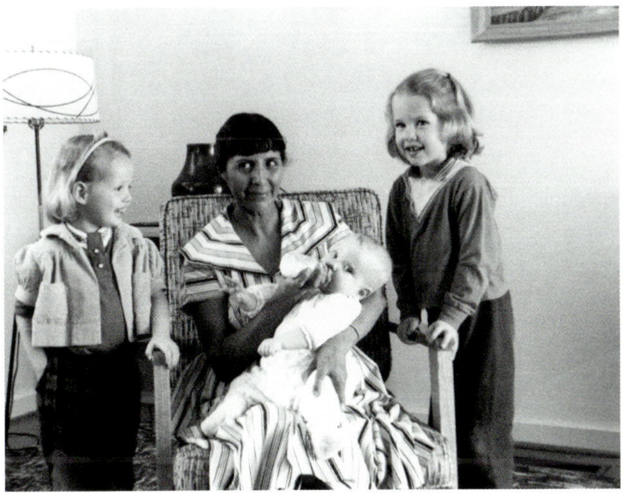

Figure 38. Mary R. Cata with our daughters Carol (*left*) and Catherine (*right*), feeding Celia in our house in Los Alamos, February 1960. (Photo by Patricia Harlow.)

Mary told us that her Indian name was K'unye Tsamwe, which means "blue stone" (that is, turquoise), and I was suddenly inspired to ask her to teach me more of her Tewa language. She readily agreed, and we set aside an hour each week for tutoring sessions. In this way I developed a Tewa language notebook. We explored numerous facets of grammar, and she wrote translations of stories that I made up. Sometimes we would be only partway through a story when it was time for her to leave to catch her ride. She said that during the whole next week, she was eager to hear how the story ended, and I think she enjoyed the sessions as much as I.

Mrs. Cata occasionally made pottery in the style of her village and gave us some pieces that now reside with our collection in the Museum of Indian Arts and Culture in Santa Fe. After her work for us came to an end, we continued to visit her and her family at San Juan several times a year for many years thereafter. We were invited to both the Catholic church and Indian weddings of one of her sons, Herman Cata, to Aurelia. The Indian wedding was especially impressive. There were long speeches in Tewa, together with ceremonial exchanges of necklaces, all followed by a big feast. Herman and Aurelia were divorced a few years later. Herman changed his name to Herman Agoyo and for years was prominent in Indian politics while managing an organization called the Eight Northern Pueblos, an advocacy group working to advance Indian rights and to sponsor a big yearly show of Indian arts and crafts.

Some of my favorite visitors were groups of children. There were dozens of such visits, generally by school classes in which one of our kids was a student, Cub Scout dens, and church groups. The kids ranged from kindergarten to sixth grade, rarely later. I liked the fourth- to sixth-graders best of all. They were always alert and asked good questions. Older children were usually more interested in each other than in the displays, although one junior high group was especially enjoyable. The lower grades used to worry me for fear that clumsy fingers would knock a precious specimen to the floor, but there never was a casualty, even from boisterous first-graders.

Our usual procedure was to have the tour convene in the living room, which has space for up to thirty people. I would give a brief talk and then guide about eight of the youngsters into the much smaller museum room. Pat took over in the living room, showing jewelry, baskets, a drum, and other artifacts. The smaller groups stayed for about ten minutes each in the pottery room, where the level of discussion was geared to the age group. Favorite items always included the three-toned Mexican music bird from Jalisco and a mysterious pot up in the corner with hands reaching out. Corny as it was, I kept it set up because of the comic relief it afforded to an otherwise rather serious dose of "culture."

The mysterious pot was a large Papago Indian jar, in which I put a pair of old leather gloves filled with tissues so that from the outside it looked like someone was trying to climb out. Often it took a while for one of the kids to notice. Then I'd tell them a little story about a windy night when the window started to rattle and I opened it up to see what was happening. Right then and there, a strange spirit flew in and jumped into the jar, I said. Trying to climb out, it grabbed the jar rim and pulled itself up, but it bumped its head on the ceiling and has been quiet ever since.

I had (and still have) a little carved animal of white rock with turquoise eyes. It lives in a little leather sack on top of Indian-ground cornmeal in a little brown ceremonial jar. I would take the fetish out of its sack and get one of the kids to take a pinch of the meal and insert it into the sack. Then the animal would be reinserted into its leather-sack home, with its mouth pointing toward the bottom of the sack so that it could feed on the corn.

I had a native New Mexico turtle shell, about five inches across, into the top of which I had drilled one (or two) holes, through which leather thongs passed, each with an object tied to the end. When the shell was jiggled, the objects hit the shell, making a dry rattling sound. Such rattles are worn behind the right knee of men performing the Turtle Dance at San Juan Pueblo. The question for the kids was, What are the objects tied to the end of each thong? The answer was deer hooves.

On several occasions, years after a kid had come to our house to see the little museum, that same person would speak to me on the street, saying that the visit had been one of the high points of his or her childhood memories. It was sometimes hard for me to remember the specific visit, but it was always pleasing to hear.

9
Pueblo Indian Pottery Studies and Collecting

When I first began collecting and studying Pueblo pottery, my feeling was "the more ancient the better," but with more familiarity and some guidance from Roy Tilghman, a Santa Fe dealer in fine Indian pottery, it became clear that the most interesting and challenging period for me was the "early historic" years, from about 1550 to 1850.

THE ESTABLISHED COLLECTIONS

In Santa Fe, the Laboratory of Anthropology housed the principal collection of Southwest Indian pottery when I first became interested in the subject in the early 1960s. The laboratory was a beehive of activity, with numerous staff members, students, and professional visitors busy at work washing sherds, sorting them, and marking them with codes that identified the location and collector's information. In the basement were long tables with people analyzing the material, piecing broken pots together, and recording their observations and conclusions. Fred Wendorf was the director at that time, with Ed Dittert taking over later. I had important interactions with both of them.

As soon as my intentions were recognized as serious, the staff gave me lots of attention—tutoring, mentoring, and advising—and access to the collections. The focus of my interest was contained in three rooms downstairs. Collections managers were usually at tables in the first room; among them, I remember Betty Toulouse, Barbara Mauldin, Nancy Fox, and Marina Ochoa. The walls were lined with huge metal cabinets filled with pottery fragments, and more cabinets were present in the middle of the floor, filling one-half of the room.

The second room was filled with rows of shelves along the walls, filled with hundreds of prehistoric pots. Most of the vessels were from New Mexico, Arizona, and the southwest corner of Colorado. I was fascinated to look at them, but mostly my activities lay in the next (third) room, which likewise was filled with numerous many-shelved storage units, all unbelievably crowded with pottery. Except for a couple units of gorgeous old Casas Grandes pottery, the collections in this third room consisted of historic-period pottery arranged in groups of vessels from each of the pueblos represented. At the far end of the room, a stairway led back up to the main floor, secured by a corrugated iron gate to prevent passage by anyone without a key. There was also a door that led to the furnace room, which likewise had shelves that played an important role for me when I worked on mending the vandalized Fred Harvey collection (see below).

The basement had other rooms; if I turned left at the bottom of the stairs, I could follow a hallway with a door on the right to the sherd-washing room, containing big sinks and shelves. I also remember low cabinets along the hall with cartons of human remains. Because the lab was built on a hillside, there was a loading dock, reached by a steep road alongside the building. Long tables with busy workers were present, but the most interesting attraction for me was reached by means of a steep stairway down to the sub-basement, which was almost overflowing with large cartons of material from various excavations of Indian ruins conducted in the years before my arrival. I didn't know it at first, but some of those cartons contained a lot of important pottery fragments from Cuyamungue, a village north of Santa Fe that was abandoned at the time of the Spanish reconquest in 1694. Later, Fred Wendorf permitted me to analyze this material.

It was surprising and delightful to get acquainted with the staff people, who were always friendly and helpful and never turned down my requests for information. Besides the names mentioned above, there were Bertha Dutton, Al Ely, Stewart Peckham, David Snow, Kenneth Chapman, and others whose names escape me now.

There's no way for me to remember how many days were spent in the third room, with the historic-period pottery. With my camera and notebooks, I spent countless hours making detailed records of the pots. Sometimes the end of the day would creep up on me almost before I knew it, and Bertha Dutton would ask if I was at a good stopping point, because it was time to close. I'd tell her about a particularly important pot that still needed a lot of study, and she would say, "Well, go ahead and take it home for a week or so." She marked it down, and I would put the vessel carefully on the backseat of my car, bracing it with my black leather motorcycle jacket and/or an old gray woolen blanket. Only later did I realize what an exceptional thing it was to take home in such casual fashion such rare and fine national treasures, which today are virtually untouchable objects in extremely secure vaults.

It was also delightful to take, one at a time, my preschool children to spend the day with me in the third room. They would alternate between playing with one of their toys and holding Dad's notebook and/or camera as I moved pottery pieces on the shelf to reach some that were less accessible. At noon we would sit on the concrete floor or a stool and eat the lunch we had brought. After that, I would spread a quilt on the floor, and the kid would take a nap for an hour or two. Sometimes I was aware of people coming quietly into the room and peeking around one of the huge shelf structures to observe the highly unusual sight of a child napping on the floor.

One especially interesting project was proposed to me in the 1960s, after I had been visiting the lab frequently enough to establish my serious interest in the evolution of early historic Pueblo Indian pottery styles. I think it was Bertha Dutton who showed me several cartons of broken pottery. "There's nothing like putting together broken pots to learn about them," she said to me. There were thirty-four cartons of fragments, more than eighty pots altogether. "How were they broken?" I asked. She replied that back in the 1940s, there was a famous Fred Harvey Museum in Albuquerque, where these pots were a main part of the exhibit. One night, vandals broke in and indulged in an orgy of destruction. What a mess! After the insurance claims had been processed, the Fred Harvey Company gave all the pieces to the University of New Mexico's Department of Anthropology. At that time, Ed Dittert was a graduate student in the department, and you know how graduate students earn a minor stipend for graduate student research work (that is, slave labor). Well, Ed was given the project of gluing all the pots back together again. He dutifully laid out all the pieces according to various attributes such as paste, slip, designs, etc. Then one day, after realizing the gigantic nature of the project, he rebelled. "Getting a PhD is not worth it!" he said to his adviser, who looked at the huge agglomeration of fragments and agreed that it was not a fair task to ask of a graduate student. So it was decided that faculty and students would be allowed to take samples to use for future reference. After a while, someone realized that this was not a proper thing to do at all. Someday the pots *had* to be put back together; they were far too rare and important to be scattered to the wind. So they boxed them all up into cartons and donated them to the Laboratory of Anthropology, where they've been sitting gathering dust.

It was clear where she was heading in this conversation. She wanted me to take the material home and assemble the pots (as a "means of learning more about historic-period Pueblo ceramics"). I naively agreed, loaded them into the car (a Plymouth station wagon), and brought them home in about three trips. Within a week or so, there were eighty-four piles of fragments in various rooms and hallways of our house. Patty was very supportive of the work and willing to put up with the inconvenience as long as I'd work as fast as possible to get them glued back together again. Actually, it wasn't necessary to keep them in piles on the floor; as soon as I convinced myself that the sorting was accurate, each pile could be put into a separate sack and stacked along the wall in what we called our pottery room. It took some months, but I was indeed able to assemble the material into the vessels from which they had come, with only a double handful of leftover tiny pieces of grit that never would be able to fit together. The biggest challenge was to put together bowls and jars with large holes for which the pieces were missing (having been taken by UNM staff and students for "reference" purposes). Nevertheless, most of the vessels are now whole enough to allow serious and meaningful study. But at the time I was taking them back to the lab, a few each trip, there was no plan for integrating the restored vessels into the collection, so most of them were simply placed on the shelves in the furnace room. It wasn't until many years later that the pots were properly cataloged (I was asked to help) and integrated into the collections. Through this whole episode, I did indeed learn lots about Pueblo Indian pottery of the 1800s. (There was nothing earlier in the collection of fragments.)

I also undertook other pottery-mending activities for the Laboratory of Anthropology. In particular, it was very interesting to work with its collection of Mimbres bowls—dating from the 1100s and made in southwestern New Mexico. These vessels represent one of the high points of ancient Pueblo Indian artistry. Some of the bowls are decorated with fish, insects, mammals, and even people, all executed with astonishingly precise line work. The movie actor Vincent Price recognized the beauty and importance of Mimbres pottery and was willing to pay very high prices to dealers for outstanding examples, thereby bringing this ancient artwork to the attention of many people from different parts of the world.

It was a genuine pleasure taking home Mimbres examples, which had been collected in the form of some number of fragments, and to assemble fragments into a nearly whole bowl. (Whereas bowls are relatively common, there are only a few jars of classic Mimbres pottery and none that I can remember being decorated with animal life.)

I was having fun with all my Indian pottery activities at this time. It was also pleasant to receive expressions of interest in my work, such as when I was appointed research associate of the Museum of New Mexico in 1965. Shortly thereafter, I was invited to become a trustee of the Indian Arts Fund collection of especially rare and precious pottery vessels from the early historic period. The appointment did not last long because after due consideration, it was decided to establish a new and different organizational relationship that brought much of that collection into the possession of the School of American Research (SAR), which was able to raise sufficient funding to build a fabulous building to house the collection. I later became a research associate at SAR (now the School for Advanced Research).

In those early years (the 1960s), I was also involved with detailed analysis of two major collections of fragments excavated from famous localities. One of them was obtained at Acoma Pueblo by Ed Dittert as part of his doctoral research. Ed's careful work in a trench near the Acoma church produced an abundance of material from seven different layers, from which the evolution of styles from about 1300 to about 1680 could be determined in an orderly sequence. Ed did not foresee having enough time to make a careful analysis of the material, and he suggested that I undertake the project. It turned out that the results had a degree of consistency far beyond his or my initial expectations. I was able to work out a four-level evolutionary sequence, identified (in analogy to Rio Grande Glaze Ware sequences) by the Greek letters alpha, beta, gamma, and delta, and to describe the continuity of variations from one level to the next. These results were described in a report I prepared for him in May 1965, in which I made the egregious error of listing only my own name as author. His revenge was wreaked at a ceramics conference he assembled, at which the results of my analysis were discussed in great detail but without the identification of my authorship, except for the inconspicuous presence of my name on a summary chart included in the published proceedings. Needless to say, our subsequent relationship was cool, although it always had the appearance of cordiality. I later included the full text of my analysis as a chapter within the book Dwight Lanmon and I published in 2013, *The Pottery of Acoma Pueblo*.

The other major collection of fragments that I examined during the 1960s was excavated at Cuyamungue Pueblo by Fred Wendorf and his crew. I won't go into details about the material because the major conclusions are described in my *Matte-Paint Pottery* book. The whole activity was lots of fun, and the human interactions were completely cordial.

Several other established collections have had significance for my Indian pottery studies. One of these is in the Maxwell Museum at the University of New Mexico in Albuquerque. I visited there only one time but nevertheless got some very useful data and pictures of Puname-area pottery (Zia and Santa Ana Pueblos), especially of the 1600s, as described in our 2005 book, *The Pottery of Santa Ana Pueblo*. And although I've never visited these collections in person, Dwight Lanmon has gone to the Smithsonian Institution in Washington, DC, the American Museum of Natural History in New York City, the Heard Museum in Phoenix, and several others, from which he has brought back numerous photos and notes for description in our books. By *numerous*, I mean many thousands of annotated photographs—more than two thousand from the Smithsonian alone!

POTTERY FRAGMENTS (SHERDS)

Although it is pleasant to study whole pottery vessels, there is much that can be learned from the examination of fragments (called *sherds* in the Southwest and more generally *shards* elsewhere). One advantage of sherds is their revelation of the materials used in constructing a vessel. This information can be especially important in determining the pueblo at which the pot was manufactured, because each village (or small group of closely situated villages) has its own signature composition, whose use may persist for centuries. With a whole vessel, the composition of the body is usually revealed only where the vessel has been eroded from hard use or where it has been chipped.

I've spent many hours scrutinizing sherds from many locations using a hand lens. More sophisticated techniques require that thin sections be cut from the sherd and examined under a microscope. Anna Shepard and Helene Warren have extracted very useful information by this laborious process. Shepard, for example, was able to demonstrate conclusively that large amounts of pottery used at Pecos Pueblo had been imported from the Tewa pueblos near Santa Fe, while Warren examined glaze ware sherds from many villages south of Santa Fe and extracted considerable information about the trading of vessels from one village to another. I've never used this technique, having concentrated more on hand-lens observation combined with observation of easily visible features that enable considerable useful progress in interpretation of what was happening in the ceramic evolution at many of the New Mexico pueblos during the historic period. Because the conclusions from all of those studies have been described at length in my other publications, I focus the discussion in this section on interesting vignettes associated with collecting sherds at a variety of locations I have visited.

The most interesting of my sherd-collecting activities took place at Nambé Pueblo. It was obvious, even the first time I walked around the little village, that there were abundant fragments of historic-period pot sherds scattered in and around the dwellings. It is, however, never a good idea to pick up any of these pieces without first getting permission from the pueblo governor. He and I got acquainted, and he became quite interested in the studies that were so fascinating to me. He was glad to give his permission as long as I picked up pieces only from the surface and promised not to do any digging. He then suggested that Nambé children could help if I wanted. This, of course, was an excellent idea.

The next Saturday, I went back with sacks, a carton, and a pocket filled with change: nickels, dimes, and quarters. It was a beautiful day, and lots of kids were playing in and around the plaza. They needed very little persuasion to join in the treasure hunt and quickly scattered in all directions to see what they could find. As I remember, about a dozen youngsters gave serious attention to the task. Soon they came back to where I was looking for fragments. If the kid brought me a few sherds that were small and nondescript, I paid a nickel. For larger sherds, especially those with diagnostic designs, a dime seemed appropriate and was much appreciated. Some pieces that were a significant fraction of a bowl or jar deserved a quarter, resulting in tremendous excitement for the kid.

Whereas some of the kids gradually lost interest, perhaps because they ran out of places to look, it soon became apparent that two brothers, Carlos and Dennis Vigil, were especially enthusiastic. The Vigil brothers didn't mind looking farther away, and with their sharp eyes they continued to bring me special discoveries: half a bowl of a rare type made in the middle 1700s, a tobacco pipe in two pieces that I was able to glue together, and several large pieces of pottery storage jars, together with many hundreds of smaller sherds from which to make statistical counts of various features, in addition to a fibrolite scraper carved out of speckled white-and-green stone.

One of the most significant of the resulting analyses had to do with the presence of relatively large flakes of mica in the paste. Eventually, I was able to demonstrate that the presence of large mica flakes is a strong indicator of a Nambé Pueblo origin and that the rather poor-quality slip and nature of the designs correlated to a pottery type that I call Nambé Polychrome.

Eventually, even Carlos and Dennis could find no more items of interest, but by then I had plenty for my purposes of analysis, so I quit going to Nambé to gather material. (All the pottery fragments, large and small, were later given to the Laboratory of Anthropology for permanent retention and storage.)

That was in the middle 1960s. Now fast-forward to summer 2004 and a chance encounter with Carlos Vigil, who was then employed with Los Alamos National

Laboratory. We met near the loading ramp of the Administration Building, where another guy introduced us. "Carlos Vigil?" I gasped, "from Nambé Pueblo?"

"Yes indeed," he answered, "and I remember you very well." We talked a little about those days of collecting and how much he enjoyed the idea that his material was making a contribution to the history of his pueblo, but our conversation was brief, ending with the idea that we should get together for a longer visit someday.

Returning to the 1960s, one very interesting thing that Carlos showed me was a much more ancient village on the other side of the Nambé River from the modern pueblo. The older village was occupied around AD 1000. The pottery sherds from that site are very different in material, paint, and design from the Tewa sherds dating after about 1250. They are closely related to pottery from the area around modern Gallup, New Mexico, and I think it has been concluded that there were incursions of settlers from that area to the Rio Grande Valley.

Another site dating to that early period is found on a famous formation just east of the Rio Grande and north of San Ildefonso Pueblo. Its English name is Black Mesa, in Spanish it is called Mesa Huerfano (Orphan Mesa), and in the Tewa

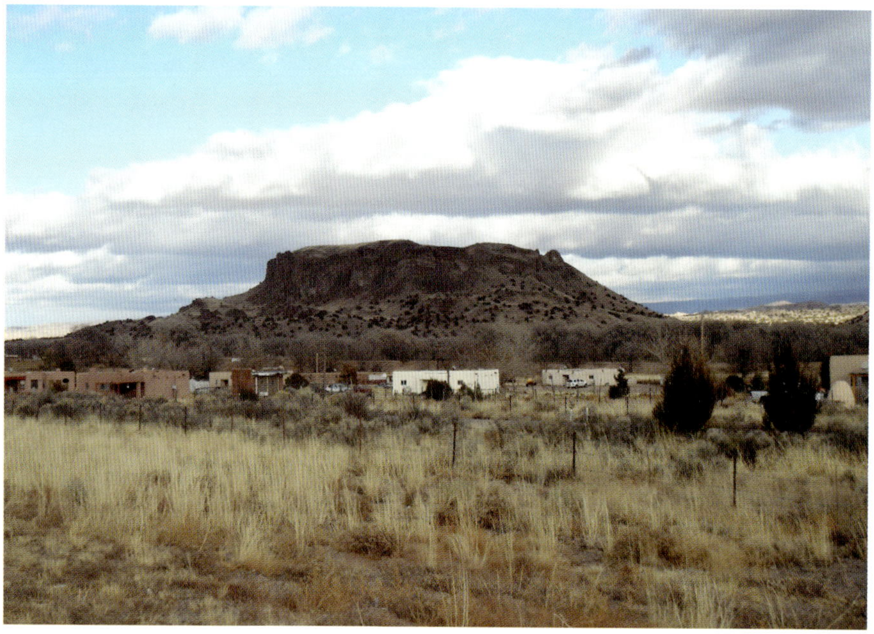

Figure 39. Black Mesa with San Ildefonso Pueblo in the foreground. (Photo by Em-jay-es, Wikimedia Commons.)

language it's Tuño Piñ. Over the most recent thousands of years, this formation has been a tall and isolated landmark, perhaps three hundred feet high and six hundred feet across. It consists of volcanic lava on its upper layer, with ancient river sediments below. Half a million years ago (or perhaps earlier), it was one of the lowest points in the valley. In one of the periodic volcanic eruptions, the ground split open and volcanic lava poured out, settling in the depression like a pond. As the lava cooled and solidified, one or several rivers flowed over its top, leaving river-tumbled gravel that can still be seen on top of the mesa. Gradually, over long periods, the soft sediments around the lava puddle were washed away, leaving the lava at the top of the geological structure as a hard cap with relatively little susceptibility to erosion. With the softer sediments tending to undermine the lava cap, even that hard rock started breaking off, leaving large boulders scattered down the sides.

For some reason, the more or less flat top of the formation attracted Indians from the west, who came to this area around AD 1000 and established a small settlement on top. They had long since left when Tewa Indians settled Powhoge Pueblo (commonly called San Ildefonso), a short distance south of the mesa, around AD 1250. It is very likely that from the beginning of San Ildefonso, the Indians considered the mesa to be a sacred place and performed ceremonial rituals on top, as they continue to do now. In 1694 the mesa top experienced one of the most dramatic periods in its history. Pueblo Indians had driven Spanish settlers hundreds of miles to El Paso in the south in 1680. In 1692 Spanish soldiers under the leadership of commander Don Diego de Vargas reconquered the Pueblos, some of whom apparently welcomed their return. Earlier attempts at reconquest had resulted in a decade of bloody and futile battles led by ambitious Spanish commanders, who were rebuffed at a terrible cost to the pueblos and their inhabitants. In 1692, however, there was no Indian resistance to the reconquest (known as the peaceful *entrada*). De Vargas took his troops back to the area around El Paso, where the expelled Spanish settlers were living, and in 1694 they returned to Pueblo Indian country, expecting a welcoming reception but finding instead renewed animosity. De Vargas, in his eagerness to protect the Spanish settlers and to insist on the Indians' sworn allegiance to the king of Spain and to the Catholic Church, was forced to lead his soldiers into continuing disastrous battles, which resulted in the abandonment of several pueblos and the establishment of refuge sites where the Indians could get away from their hated conquerors. Much has been written about the travails endured by the Indians, and the top of Black Mesa was the site of one interlude of suffering. Tewa Indians from several nearby pueblos occupied a hastily constructed village there for seven months in 1694, with Spanish soldiers forming a sparse siege encirclement. The siege was breached, with Indians stealing down at night to gather food, water, and other supplies. But eventually the Indians capitulated and returned to the valley floor.

Every time I drive by Black Mesa in my comfortable car, I am filled with wonder at what the Indians endured in this tragic period of their lives. I've climbed the easy southern route to the top of the mesa twice, and even today one can see remnants of the seven-month occupation. Indeed, the pottery sherds found up there serve as very useful time markers of styles during that occupation, but there's also something else very precious to find on the top: the peace that pervades the atmosphere, the gentle breeze and warm sun, the view in all directions across the wide valley, the sight of the Rio Grande close by, and all the fragmentary reminders of a million years passed by.

The Pueblo Revolt of 1680 had repercussions beyond Black Mesa. It resulted in the permanent destruction of some of the older pueblos (such as the large village of Cuyamungue) and the creation of new ones (such as Laguna Pueblo). It brought Pueblo people from various villages into closer contact with each other than ever previously had occurred. In the refugee sites near Walatowa (Jemez) Pueblo, displaced people from five pueblo areas, speaking different languages, suddenly lived alongside each other. From the standpoint of Pueblo Indian pottery, many influences between villages resulted in complex mixtures of styles. I found that fascinating and saw my interest to be strongly concentrated not only on revolt-period pottery but also more generally on the early historic period, from about 1550 to 1850. I remember Stewart Peckham, who was a wonderful source of information at the Laboratory of Anthropology, cautioning me against involvement with that period because of its extreme complexity. But his advice in that regard had the effect of enhancing my eagerness to figure out what was going on with early historic Pueblo Indian ceramics.

I worked with many sherd collections associated with that period—many that I formed myself and others that were supplied to me by other collectors. Some of the collections (especially those from White Rock Canyon and from the Jemez refugee sites) presented problems regarding ownership of the material, and I had interesting discussions with representatives of Los Alamos County, the National Park Service, and the New Mexico Attorney General's Office. The dilemma was always the same. Should the material be ignored? confiscated? used for pottery studies but intended for permanent placement in a public museum? Fortunately, the last approach prevailed, and indeed both the studies and placements have been accomplished.

One of the things I learned in dealing with fragments and whole pots at the Laboratory of Anthropology was how to clean them of adhering caliche—a layer of soil in which the particles have been cemented together by lime (calcium carbonate, or $CaCO_3$) from burial—to reveal the decoration. After consulting with my friends at the laboratory and trying their suggested techniques on some pottery fragments, I felt confident that I could make significant improvements to the vessels in the laboratory collection. The procedure consists of several steps:

1. Soak the vessel in clean water long enough to fill the pores with water.
2. Immerse the vessel in a bath of dilute hydrochloric acid, keeping an eye on the gentle fizzing of the caliche as it is softened by reaction with the acid.
3. Remove the vessel from the acid bath, and put it into a bath of soda water to neutralize the acid.
4. Rub the surface very gently with a soft cloth to remove the softened caliche.
5. Repeat the above steps, removing a little of the caliche at a time, until the desired cleanliness of the surface has been achieved.

COLLECTORS AND DEALERS

One of the most interesting aspects of my Pueblo Indian pottery studies has been the fascinating people I've met, both Indians and settlers (by which I mean Anglos or "palefaces," Hispanics, and other non-Indians). Santa Fe has been the focus of Indian pottery sales to the world since about 1880. Yes, one can also find dealers in Albuquerque, Taos, Phoenix, Tucson, and other cities. It is also possible to buy pottery directly from the Indians, both in their pueblo homes and on the Plaza in Santa Fe all year-round under the portal of the Palace of Governors, and nowadays through Indian Market, which fills the Plaza and spills down Lincoln and Washington Avenues in August.

When we came to Los Alamos in 1953, the annual Indian Market, which had been established in 1922, was much smaller than its present size, being mostly confined to the area under the Palace portal. But in the middle 1960s there was a burst of recognition across the whole country—and even in other parts of the world—for American Indians and their crafts. In movies, Indians had been portrayed as enemies and cowboys as heroes, but that changed around 1965, a few years after I commenced my Indian pottery studies, so I watched the revolution of attitudes toward Indians and their crafts with interest.

Until my first books (real books, not earlier booklets) were published in the 1970s, historic Pueblo Indian pottery vessels were not much appreciated. As Roy Tilghman explained to me, those pots were worn and dirty, not like the new and fresh vessels made to be beautiful for the collectors' market. Pottery made by Maria Martinez and her family was eagerly purchased, even at their high prices, which could be as much as $100. (Today those same pots sell for at least a hundred times more.) Joseph Lonewolf of Santa Clara Pueblo made tiny pots with exquisitely detailed carving and sold all that he made for prices in that same range, and there were many more potters with great skill whose wares were much in demand.

If a pot showed the results of extensive usage, then it had to be truly ancient (that is, prehistoric) to interest collectors. Santa Fe dealer Forrest Fenn claims that I played a significant part in opening people's eyes to the wonderful world of early historic Pueblo Indian pottery, but that was later, after the transition of attitude had been well established.

The Original Curio Store

One of the most intriguing shops selling pottery of the 1900s was the Original Curio Store, which was said to have been established in the 1600s (but more likely in the late 1800s). The proprietor for many years was Mr. Candelario, whose activities have been described in several books. When we arrived in New Mexico, the place was being run by Walt and Alma Wright, who were friends of mine for many years. In addition to their mineral specimens—their principal focus in the little shop they owned on Cerrillos Road in Santa Fe—the Wrights became dealers in Indian crafts. The store on West San Francisco Street, about three blocks from the Plaza, was a fascinating place to visit. The walls had large murals, painted many years earlier (today covered up), and shelves with pottery from the early 1900s that was not for sale. It was as much a museum as a store. Toward the back, floorboards could be lifted up to reveal an unfinished basement of fairly large size. There one could see old dusty storage trunks that looked as though they had not been opened for many years. "Go ahead and look," Alma said to me one day. "If you find anything interesting, let me know." So I started exploring. One of the trunks had numerous Tesuque "rain god" figures made of pottery. At that time, they were considered to be crude tourist-ware pieces with no traditional roots. (Duane Anderson's book *When Rain Gods Reigned* discusses the history of this particular pottery form at length.) One discovery I made was of a little narrow-mouth pottery bottle with circumferential broad-line designs, undoubtedly made by Tewa Indians in the 1400s or 1500s. I showed it to Alma, who said, "If you want it, you can have it for fifty cents," which was fine with me. I kept it for many years and eventually gave it to one of our grandchildren visiting from Australia.

One terribly upsetting incident with the Wrights occurred one winter day when they lent me several beautiful pottery jars made at San Ildefonso Pueblo in the first decade of the 1900s. I braced the pots in several cartons with lots of tissue paper. Arriving home, I discovered that the sidewalk in front of our house was treacherously icy, and despite my attempts to walk very carefully, I slipped and fell on the end of my spine, which was quite sore for several weeks. Although a bruise will eventually heal, the disastrous consequence of falling was the breaking of a fine black-on-red jar, one of the Wrights' display treasures, which was a wound that will never heal. Needless to say, I was enormously flustered! I glued the pieces back together, but the jar was never going to be in the pristine form it took when they generously trusted me to treat this treasure with extreme care. To mitigate the situation somewhat, I took from my collection a polychrome jar of comparable size, made by the famous Maria Martinez, and drove that plus the broken jar back down to the shop. Walt and Alma were very gracious about the incident and agreed to accept the Maria jar as compensation for the damage. They even suggested that if they ever sold the Maria jar, they would give me half of the sale price. Over the subsequent years, I lost track of what happened to either of the two jars. Later, after Walt and Alma sold the shop and all of its contents to Bob Ward, they said that the Maria jar had gone to Bob, probably for around $500; they were true to their word and gave me half. (At the present time I think the Maria jar would easily sell for $35,000.)

The only other Pueblo Indian pot I have broken is the first one we ever bought, an ancient pitcher of Reserve Black-on-white purchased for about $25 at a little mineral and fossil shop on the highway (Route 66) east of Albuquerque, toward Tijeras Canyon. (At that time the urban part of Albuquerque began to thin out to pasture fields, with occasional houses and a few businesses at the sides of the road, a rather short distance beyond the university and the New Mexico State Fairgrounds. Today the houses and businesses are solidly packed together all the way to the canyon entrance. The highway was then called Central Avenue.) I don't recall the details of how the pitcher got broken. It is now part of the Harlow collection in the Museum of Indian Arts and Culture in Santa Fe.

Bob Ward soon sold all the pottery treasures of the Original Curio Store. I bought one of them, a very interesting polychrome ceremonial bowl from Tesuque

Pueblo. I got to know Bob quite well. He was so friendly that he invited Joseph Lonewolf and me to have a two-man show at the shop, Joseph selling his small pottery treasures and I selling my paintings. A few years later, Bob sold the shop, and the new owners converted it to an incredibly close-packed store filled with trinkets for the tourist market. Bob bought or rented a second-story place on San Francisco Street south of the Plaza. The necessity of climbing the long steep steps cut down appreciably the number of walk-in visitors. Mostly his merchandise was of little interest to me, but I nevertheless stopped by occasionally to say hello. One of those visits, however, was especially noteworthy. On the top shelf against one of the walls was a large bowl with polychrome decorations and a label proclaiming the bowl to be a very rare Indian pot dating to at least two thousand years ago; the price was $450. The identification was way off; polychrome vessels with split-feather designs were not made in the Southwest that long ago. Indeed, the bowl was a superb example of Ako Polychrome (a pottery type I named in one of my publications, from Acoma or Laguna Pueblo), dating around 1710. The price was a lot to pay in those days, but I nevertheless bought it. It has appeared in many of my paintings and now is housed in the Harlow collection at MIAC, where its identity and rarity are understood (see fig. 51).

Mr. and Mrs. Julius Gans

Also on San Francisco Street, near the southeast corner of the Plaza, was a store run by Mr. and Mrs. Julius Gans. As at the Original Curio Store, high shelves along the walls displayed lots of Indian pottery, in this case from the 1800s. There were fine classic water jars and large storage jars especially from Cochiti, perhaps thirty of them in all. An interesting feature of the store was the opening in the floor, through which one could see Indians making fine silver jewelry in the basement. I got to know Mrs. Gans quite well and started hinting to her that I would like to buy some of her pottery. For years, it had been for display only, not sale, but she never said either yes or no about selling some of it to me, until one day she said that the store would not be there much longer and that I could buy a few pots. One deterrent to her selling those fine old vessels was the haunting memory of how she had acquired them. "Many years ago," she told me, "we'd take a wagon out to one of the pueblos and buy these pots for fifty cents to a dollar each. Now I'd have to charge $25 to $100 for them," which made her feel guilty for having exploited the Indians. I ended up buying two or three of them and sending Mrs. Gans $10 a month in payment. In later years it became clear to me that I should have gotten a bank loan to buy them all; by 1990 the price for those beautiful vessels had risen by a factor of at least a hundred, although I would have had no intention of selling them.

Rex Arrowsmith and Forrest Fenn

Rex Arrowsmith's Indian crafts store was a quarter of a mile away from the Plaza, where East De Vargas Street meets Old Pecos Trail. Rex and I became good friends soon after meeting. He was a quiet and pleasant kind of a guy, and from him I acquired some nice pottery examples, again by sending him $10 per month. After a few years, someone who changed things considerably for Rex came into his life and also had a strong effect on my own activities. That person was Forrest Fenn, a retired air force fighter pilot with the rank of major and a large retirement salary. Rex and Forrest were about as different as two people could be. Rex was quiet and conservative; Forrest was brash and a risk taker. Perhaps they thought their contrasting personalities would complement each other, and they established a partnership. They built a combined foundry and art gallery on Paseo de Peralta, about half a mile southeast of the Plaza, but their partnership was later dissolved.

Among Forrest's experiences had been conducting archaeological excavations in southern Arizona, and when I first met him, he had some choice examples of Salado Indian material that he had uncovered. Pueblo archaeology and early historic pot collecting were passions he could indulge in as a result of his successful business activities. He bought some rare, expensive, early historic Pueblo Indian pottery and requested my help in identifying and authenticating the vessels, which I did on many occasions. He also craved owning some important Indian ruins and was eventually able to purchase a large part of San Lazaro Pueblo, which was first occupied around 1300 and was abandoned in the late 1600s. There he initiated a plan to excavate major parts of the village, much to the displeasure of professional archaeologists in the Southwest, who were far from happy with his excavating techniques. But they could do nothing to stop him because the law gives a person permission to excavate on his or her own land.

Forrest and I engaged in a variety of philosophical discussions, ranging from topics of science to the lives of ancient people to his interactions with rich and famous modern-day people and many other topics. He always had interesting observations to share. Among other things, he persistently encouraged me to do things that could make me rich, especially in the careful marketing of our Indian pottery collection and in charging people for authenticating and appraising Indian pottery specimens. "It's who you know that counts," he often told me. "You have to mingle with them, go to their parties, host some parties of your own," he would say with conviction as he gave me examples of his own networking techniques. "But on the other hand," he continued, "just remember that you'll never make it big financially by giving things away. Any gifts you present to someone must be a carefully calculated investment."

Forrest played a major role in two of my publications. He encouraged me to write *Modern Pueblo Indian Pottery,* furnishing secretarial help in preparing the manuscript and arranging for its publication by Northland Press. He also asked me to write a descriptive text on the pottery of San Lazaro Pueblo, which was included as a major section in his book on the excavations of that village. Dwight Lanmon joined me in that project. When I saw the finished book, my excitement for being a part of it was unbounded. It's an absolutely fabulous book. Forrest wrote a wonderfully readable text and illustrated it with excellent photographs and drawings. I've heard well-deserved praise for the book from many sources—and no criticisms—despite the earlier outrage of professionals regarding his excavating techniques. A book could (and should) be written about Forrest Fenn's life; I know it would be fascinating to read.

Larry Frank

Larry Frank, who lived a few miles north of Taos in an old Spanish Penitente morada, is another pottery dealer–collector with whom I had many interactions. Larry purchased the entire C. G. Wallace collection of Indian pots, dating mainly from the 1800s and early 1900s. Through careful and clever merchandizing techniques, he was able to turn this material into a fortune. When I first saw the collection, it was stored in a specially constructed building near his home. There may have been several hundred extremely fine and important vessels. He and I did some trading; in retrospect, I can think of some exchanges in which he got the better deal and some in which I came out ahead.

Larry and I decided to write a book together on historic Pueblo Indian pottery, using examples from both his and my collections, and other places as appropriate. *Historic Pottery of the Pueblo Indians, 1600–1880* was published by the New York Graphic Society in 1974 and has been reprinted since.

Dennis and Janis Lyon

Dennis and Janis Lyon of Phoenix, Arizona, have been especially interesting and delightful to know. Dennis was the head of a large real estate company that specialized in the high end of the market. He and Janis have been interested in

Pueblo Indian pottery for many years. At first their collecting concentrated on famous modern potters—Joseph Lonewolf of Santa Clara Pueblo was, as I recall, one of their favorites. Gradually, their collecting interest shifted to include superb examples of both prehistoric and early historic pottery. It was a time when early historic pottery was still widely available but at prices that were escalating rapidly into five figures for the most important pieces. It was through their interest in ensuring authenticity and establishing dates and sources for their examples that they learned about my studies in this field. Over the years, they visited our Los Alamos home around a dozen times, bringing one or several treasures for me to study. Jack Beasley, from Farmington, New Mexico, was an especially prolific source of beautiful pottery, collected for them at various refuge sites in the vicinity of Gobernador Canyon in northwestern New Mexico.

The Lyons and I also did some trading during those years. (See chapter 7 for a notable incident involving an old Harley Davidson motorcycle and an early historic jar from Zia Pueblo.) Their friendship and generosity also resulted in their supporting the publication of four of our books.

Bob Gallegos

Bob Gallegos from Albuquerque has been a dealer in historic Pueblo Indian pottery and other Native American artifacts for many years, and beginning in the late 1970s, we visited each other's homes. Most of those visits occurred when Bob brought examples to our home, being interested in identifying type and pueblo of origin for many of the treasures he had acquired. He has become very knowledgeable about pottery from 1700 to 1900 but nevertheless continues to show me vessels for confirmation of his thoughts.

In the late 1980s, he decided to sell many of the pots that he had collected through the years. He and the director of Morningstar Gallery on Canyon Road in Santa Fe decided that the best way to market the collection was to publish a book with illustrations and a descriptive text for each vessel, and they commissioned me for the project. To heighten excitement for the sale, the gallery arranged for an invitation-only opening for serious collectors from all across the country. I was at the opening, mainly to autograph the book and to engage in conversations with the attendees.

At the opening, the gallery was crowded with people, and the sales procedure was announced. Slips of paper were furnished to each guest, and there was a receptacle in front of each pot. Anyone wishing to purchase a vessel would insert a note into the receptacle, thereby indicating a commitment to make the purchase. It was not an auction—the price for each piece was marked on a label alongside each vessel. At 9 p.m. the fun began. One slip of paper was withdrawn from the receptacle for each pot, and the lucky purchaser's name was announced. Some of the pots were not of sufficient interest to attract a buyer; for others there were multiple names, and in one case, someone who wanted the pot very much—but whose name was not drawn—put on a significant show of disappointment. The jar that sold for the highest price was an Ashiwi Polychrome vessel from Zuni Pueblo, dating from the early 1700s. The price was $48,000. The interesting thing to me about that particular pot is that I once owned it and had traded it for a vessel of greater relevance to our collection. The total price for Bob's collection was nearly $1.5 million.

Jim Riley

Jim Riley, who had an Indian artifacts shop on West Plaza Avenue, about a block from the Plaza, once showed me a large storage jar that had been made at the old Santo Domingo Pueblo before it was destroyed by Rio Grande flooding in 1886. I dated the jar to about 1830. It had recently been dug out of the ruins of the old village (the present pueblo is on nearby, higher ground), and a piece of the rim had been broken out, but it was easily glued back into place. Jim wanted $50 for the jar and could not find a buyer. I bought it from him, and today the value of his vessel would likely be $30,000. It now resides in the permanent collection of the MIAC (see fig. 58).

Many other collectors and dealers could have been discussed in this chapter. They include Richard Howard, Jack Silverman, Fred Boschan, Bob and Kitty Whiteside, Art Rogers, and probably twenty or so more.

REPRODUCTIONS

One distressing consequence of the tremendous increase in prices for historic Pueblo Indian pottery is the increasing presence of reproductions that have been sold to unsuspecting purchasers as the real stuff. This knowing misrepresentation is legally classed as fraud, and several cases have been prosecuted. (Reproductions sold without deception are perfectly legal, and I've seen many handsome examples, along with others that are atrocious.)

Several years ago, Santa Fe was flooded with purportedly ancient Indian pottery, which turned out to be fake. Many dealers got stung, and I was asked to go to their stores to inspect the vessels they had for sale. Some of the fakes were so obvious that I could tell they were bad from across the room. The giveaways were the style of vessels, most being figurines, constructed and decorated in ways that were extremely different from any that were familiar to me. In one notable circumstance, I expressed doubt about a jar that had been constructed and decorated with great skill. It required considerable close inspection for me to produce a convincing demonstration as to why I thought it was a fake. The owner was not convinced; he had paid a lot of money for the jar and could sell it for a lot more if the vessel could be authenticated. (In a situation like this, I'm careful not to use the word *fraud* or *fake*, which implies illegal deception. I merely state that I can't give a certificate of authenticity.) To make a long story short, the vessel was indeed proven to be of recent manufacture, and the seller was located, indicted, and tried. He admitted guilt and was sentenced. The New Mexico attorney general was involved in the process.

In a follow-up incident, the attorney general was impressed with the fact that I had been the first person to indicate problems with the jar. It was summer, and the annual Indian antiques market was about to be held at the Sweeney Center in Santa Fe. The attorney general asked me to attend the opening and walk through all the display booths to see if more fakes could be spotted. The State of New Mexico paid my $50 entrance fee for the opening, and then the hard work began. The attorney general followed me around the room, and I struggled to be as accurate as possible in the identification of suspicious pots, but the room was large and there were MANY dealers, so the two-hour inspection was excruciatingly tiring. In the end, I could not see anything that was obviously bad, and the attorney general may have been disappointed.

On quite a few occasions, fraudulent pots have been brought to me for authentication. It is always sad to see an owner's unhappiness at bad news about his or her purchase.

POTTERY TALKS

Pueblo Indian pottery is a lot more interesting to most people than fossil brachiopods. They want to hear about Indian ceramics for any of various reasons, and they have occasionally asked me to give talks, either at our home, where the collection was available to show, or at some other locality, where I relied mostly on slides to illustrate styles from all ages (AD 600 to present) and from abandoned or still occupied southwestern pueblos. So, you might ask, how many talks have I given? I suppose, on average, about four a year over a forty-year period is a reasonable estimate.

I prefer an hour for a presentation. After that, the attention of the audience seems to dwindle slowly, and I also tire. I can remember a few that lasted three hours; these were usually at SAR or MIAC, and they were often intended to educate museum docents or were enrichment sessions for tours to the Southwest arranged by some professional (or ad hoc) group. One time at SAR many years ago, I was scheduled for large parts of both the morning and afternoon, which was exhausting.

Invited talks are of several different types. Some are for the after-dinner amusement of attendees at a technical conference. Some are for special programs sponsored by SAR, MIAC, Crow Canyon Archaeological Center, and similar organizations interested in anthropology and/or archaeology. In all these circumstances, there is usually an honorarium for me in the amount of $100 to as much as $300. Usually, these talks are lots of fun, and I throw myself into the presentation with genuine enthusiasm. (In fact, sometimes comments after the talk suggest that the audience enjoyed the "performance" as much as the subject material.)

One notable exception occurred when I was asked to give an after-dinner presentation to attendees at a large Los Alamos National Laboratory conference. The banquet was held at a famous restaurant in the valley, about twenty miles from Los Alamos. (At banquet presentations, I never eat there, preferring instead to have a rather light supper at home.) The layout of space was not well suited for a talk. The eating area was divided into connecting rooms, so everyone could more or less see everyone else, but it wasn't ideal for placing a clearly visible screen, except by the door to the kitchen. To show slides, it was necessary to have the projector raised several feet above the dining tables, which was accomplished by putting two cardboard cartons on a table as a rather precarious support. The audience crowded into viewing positions, and individuals were packed closely together. Finally, everything was set up, and I asked the manager to quiet the kitchen noises, which I think he tried valiantly to accomplish, but with no success. I had no choice but to give my "talk" by yelling to the audience as loudly as I could. It was terrible. The strain on my vocal chords and on my nerves was almost intolerable. To make matters even worse, the slide projector kept slipping from its perch on the cartons and needed to be straightened and adjusted again and again. That was the worst lecturing circumstance I ever have endured. Fortunately, most talks are situated in much better surroundings, and the noise level is well controlled.

On another occasion, at MIAC, a large number of visitors were present for the opening of a rather special display. The auditorium there is very nice but quite small, so it was arranged that I would give my talk twice. Both times the space was completely filled, with the fifty or so people crammed in. Indeed, for the second presentation there was such a long line of people that I was persuaded to announce that I would be giving the talk a third time. Big mistake! The first talk went quite well. I was pleased and the audience was strongly enthusiastic, both during the talk and in conversations between first and second performances. In fact, the people had so many comments and questions that getting across the lobby to the men's washroom seemed impossible without being rude. So I was rude and brushed the people off rather brusquely, because it was clear that I wouldn't last through the second presentation without a few minutes of relief. The second talk went fairly well but not as well as the first one. I found myself continually questioning whether I had already presented an idea in *this* talk or in the *first* talk, in which case, I could state it again. (I seldom allow two talks on the same subject in the same day, exactly because of such confusion as to when a particular idea was expressed.) Well, you can imagine the job I did during the *third* time presenting the same material. I'll spare you the details, but I assure you that it was gruesome!

PUBLICATIONS

One incident that has had a great bearing on my recent book writing occurred some years ago, probably about 1997 or 1998. At an exhibition opening at the Wheelwright Museum in Santa Fe, Duane Anderson, then director of the Indian Arts Research Center at SAR, asked me to write a book on the pottery of Santa Ana Pueblo. His part of the project would be to contact all relevant institutions in the world to locate examples that could be photographed for inclusion in the book and to work with the current population of the pueblo to gather as much material as possible about the pottery-making activities of the 1900s. The suggestion made lots of sense to me. For one thing, I already had first drafts describing the Puname and related ceramics that led to splitting apart the work at Zia and Santa Ana, around 1760, when differences in materials allowed for unique differentiation between the styles of those two villages. For another, I had pretty much stagnated in my pottery studies and needed a strong boost of enthusiasm, which Duane's persuasive suggestion furnished.

In 1999 Dwight Lanmon moved to Santa Fe and began volunteering at the Indian Arts Research Center. When Duane Anderson told him of our work on a comprehensive book about Santa Ana Pueblo pottery, he suggested that we also do a companion volume on the pottery of Zia Pueblo—which we did. Following that, Dwight and I published two more books, one on the pottery of Zuni Pueblo and the second on Acoma Pueblo pottery, in addition to seven articles on various aspects of Pueblo pottery. A list of all of the papers and books I have published on Pueblo Indian pottery and paleontology is included in the bibliography.

In 2012 I received a Lifetime Achievement Award from the Antique Tribal Art Dealers Association (ATADA) in recognition of my research and publications on Pueblo pottery. News of that award was published in the winter 2012 issue of *ATADA News* and is available on the ATADA website.

I have also published 152 scientific papers. They are listed in the footnotes of my article "Fluid Dynamics in Group T-3, Los Alamos National Laboratory," which was published in 2003 in the *Journal of Computational Physics*.

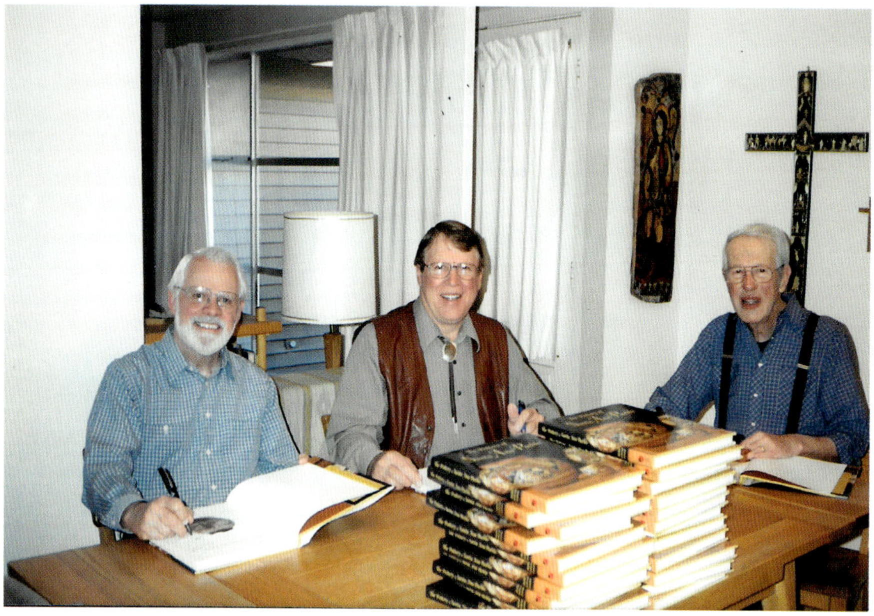

Figure 40. Coauthors signing copies of *The Pottery of Santa Ana Pueblo*, January 31, 2005. To the left is Dwight Lanmon; I'm to the right; in the middle is Duane Anderson, who brought Dwight and me together in 2000 for the writing of four comprehensive books on the history of Pueblo Indian pottery. (Photo by Patricia Harlow.)

10
Our Pueblo Indian Pottery Collection

In May 2000 a disastrous wildfire, the Cerro Grande Fire, swept through the forests west of Los Alamos. As it approached the edge of town, the population was ordered to evacuate. We went to the home of our daughter Celia and her husband on the south side of nearby Española. The five days that passed before we could return were a time of anguish, and we watched TV for news updates and smelled the smoke that was blowing directly toward us. At night, we could see the flames wherever the obscuring smoke parted. Especially frightening was the news that ferocious flames driven by high winds from the southwest had burned to the ground many houses in Los Alamos. As it turned out, four hundred families lost their homes and all their possessions, but it could have been much worse. Thanks to the heroic efforts of the firefighters, the advancing flames were halted before they consumed all of Los Alamos.

On the morning of evacuation day, the fire seemed destined to miss the town. The Laboratory had been closed, so I was at home. It was even announced that the County Planning and Zoning Commission was going on with its plans for a meeting that night. Our neighborhood was much concerned that the nearby YMCA might be rezoned to commercial, so Pat and I had circulated petitions against this action and gotten lots of support. We wanted as many objectors as possible at the meeting to show the solidarity of our objections. At about 11 a.m., I was going around the neighborhood ringing doorbells to make sure attendance would be large. As I walked up Nugget Street toward our home, I became aware of an enormously frightening sight. A tremendous plume of smoke on the other side of town showed me—even before I listened to the radio—that there would be no meeting that night. The plume was so large that it reminded me of what I had seen at Bikini Atoll many years earlier. Just as I anticipated, the radio and TV were telling residents to leave town as soon as possible. We rounded up a few essential items in the Explorer, and Pat, Lindy (our dog), and I headed out to join the throngs of cars traveling east. The whole town was evacuated in the remarkably short time frame of four hours. That evening, the destruction of homes began; it lasted through the night.

For months thereafter, the firefighters who saved the town were recognized as grand heroes, and celebrations were held in their honor. For the roughly one thousand people who lost their homes, however, the recovery was distressingly slow, even though the US government accepted full responsibility for starting the fire (as a "controlled burn") and was generous in settling claims for the loss of property and possessions.

What does the Cerro Grande Fire have to do with my Indian pottery activities? The answer lies in our longtime plans to donate our collection to the Museum of New Mexico, which has been so very good to me through all the many years of my studies and also has the facilities to carefully maintain these treasures "forever." Indeed, many of them are national treasures, being very rare surviving examples from an extremely poignant span of Pueblo Indian history. After the fire, we realized that the time had come for us to make the transfer of our collection to the secure vaults at the MIAC in Santa Fe, recently built close to the Laboratory of Anthropology, where I had spent many hundreds (perhaps even thousands) of hours working with materials and interacting with the staff. Pueblo pottery in our collection ranged in date from the AD 1000s to 1880s. Some

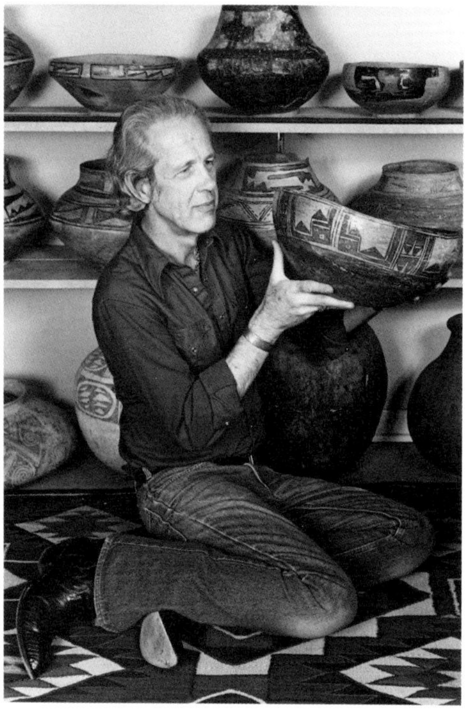

Figure 41. In our pottery room, May 1983. (Harlow family photos.)

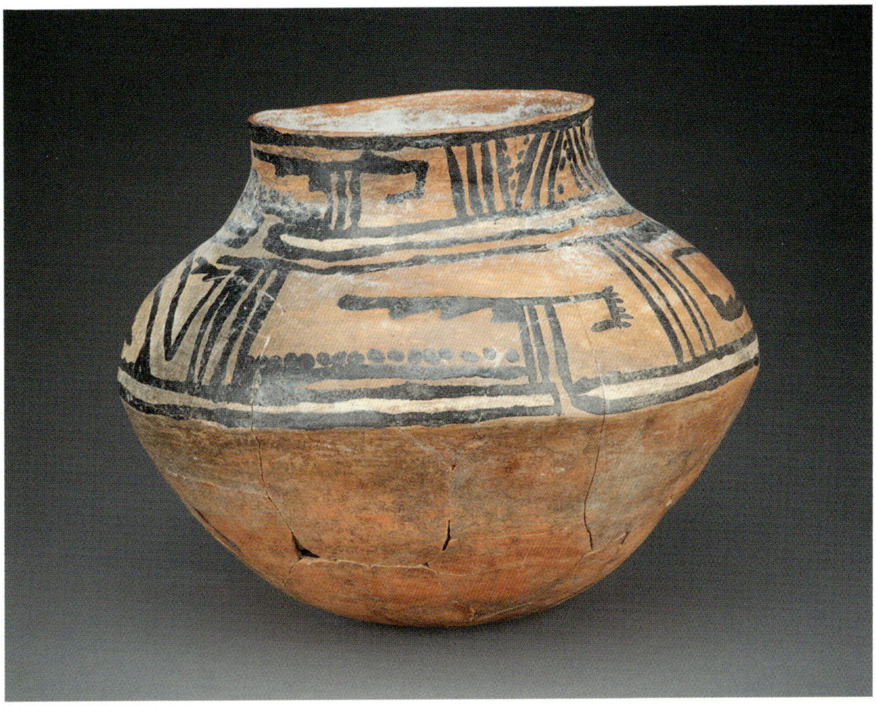

Figure 42. Pajarito Glaze-on-red jar (glaze period D/E), circa 1480, 24.0 x 31.4 cm. (Photo by Blair Clark. MIAC 55768/12.)

specimens of pottery dating before about 1300 had been previously donated to the Laboratory of Anthropology, while later pottery, including many very rare examples of historic pottery made after the arrival of Europeans in the late 1500s (identified as pottery from the historic period), was transferred to MIAC in 2001.

The Harlow collection is especially noteworthy for the number of nearly complete examples of pre-revolt pottery, in addition to many important examples made after the revolt. Following are photographs of about 15 percent of the pottery vessels in the donations, organized roughly chronologically.

Pottery vessel shapes, of both bowls and jars, furnish important clues to the age of the vessels. The jar in figure 42, from the Pajarito Plateau, exhibits a form that was very characteristic for the Pueblos prior to the 1500s: a globular body, a convex base, and a rather weak neck emerging from the top of the body. The overall form almost always shows a greater diameter than height, and often the middle-body diameter is even greater than on this jar.

Bowls and jars from the Pajarito Plateau are of two main types, differentiated from each other by the color of the slip on the exterior surface. A light tan color is the more common of the two on the so-called Biscuit Wares and their descendants over the period from about 1200 to the present time. The strongly contrasting, red-colored slip was much less common, and its use ended around 1500.

Decorations on the light tan jars and bowls were painted with the boiled-down juice of available vegetation, especially the Rocky Mountain bee plant. Red-slipped vessels were decorated with a vegetal liquid, to which was added a finely crushed mineral containing lead oxide. The mineral liquefied at around 880°C and reacted chemically with the clay body to form a more or less lustrous finish called a glaze when it cooled and solidified. Glaze paint was never applied over entire vessels to make them waterproof. Water was the main material stored in these jars, and the evaporation of seepage through the walls cooled the water within.

A rare feature of this jar is the addition of white slip in two black-edged bands around the body. Each band has an interruption, sometimes called a ceremonial break. This feature has a history of nearly a millennium of use on pottery from almost all Pueblo Indian villages until the early years of the 1900s.

On this very rare jar are several depictions of a figure called the Pajarito Bird, which has a long, stair-step tail, a bent-over head, and a triplet of legs. Behind the birds on the upper half of the jar is a row of black spots, perhaps representing eggs or some other substance emitted by the birds as they walk.

The handsome bowl shown in figure 43 has a remarkable history. It was made at Zia Pueblo about 1600, and its unusual form for that village suggests a ceremonial usage for the following century.

After the Pueblo Indian revolt against the Spanish in 1680, there were fourteen years before the Spanish returned from their exile and settled down in their previous homes. Their subsequent treatment of the Indians was mostly unfriendly, so it became the Indians' turn to become refugees, and to escape, they moved to various other places. Many migrated from villages along and near the Rio Grande to more distant regions, where they established new villages, seeking refuge from Spanish oppression. One group moved west to the present-day location of Laguna Pueblo, while others moved as far as Gobernador Canyon, two hundred miles distant in northwest New Mexico. Some even moved more than three hundred miles to northeastern Arizona to live among the Hopi. Among these refugees were people from Zia Pueblo. Along the way, they carried—among other things—this sacred bowl.

Partway to their destination at Gobernador Canyon, this bowl got broken, leaving a hole in the bottom about two centimeters wide. There was no point in carrying it farther, so it was ceremoniously left on the ground, surrounded by a circle of large rocks.

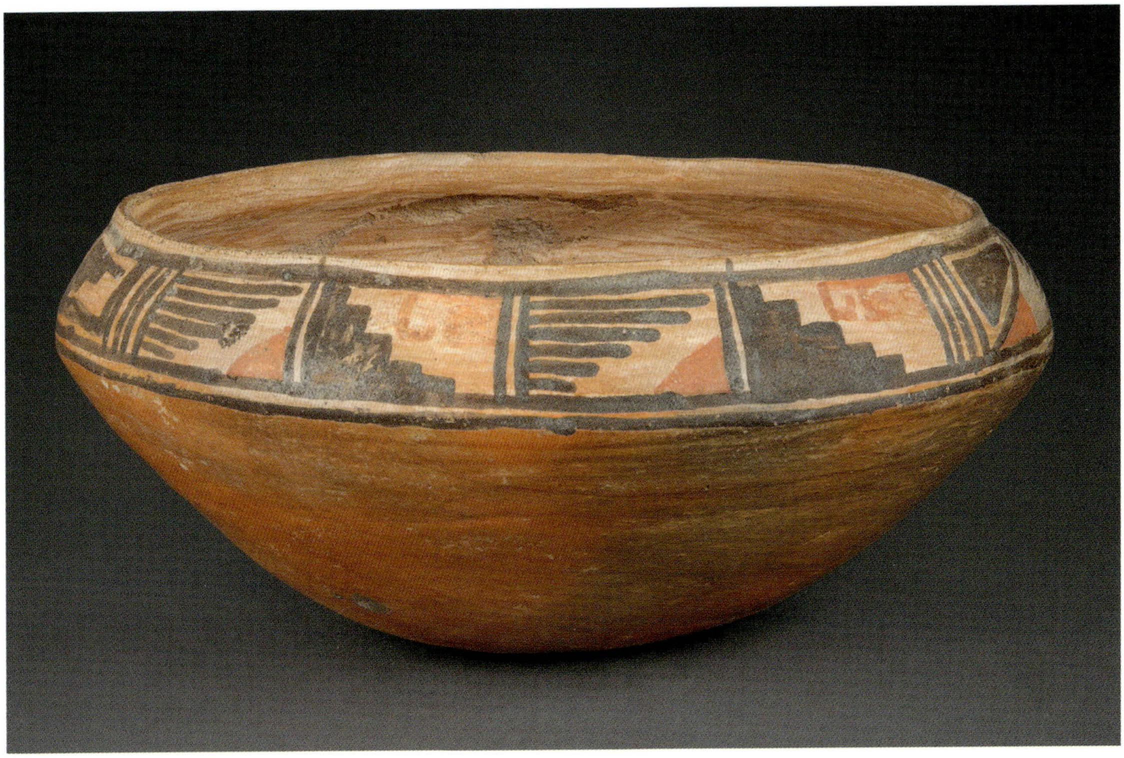

Figure 43. Zia glaze ware bowl, circa 1600, 10.9 x 25.3 cm. (Photo by Blair Clark. MIAC 55776/12.)

Nearly four hundred years after it was made, several deer hunters from Los Alamos found this bowl perched on top of a pillar of sand whose sides had been eroded by numerous rainstorms. (The effect was like the much larger Black Mesa, shown in fig. 39, chapter 9.) The bowl was then carried back to Los Alamos, where it was traded to me for a group of small pots that the hunters planned to give as gifts to their family or friends.

The magnificent jar in figure 44 shows beautifully the evolution of Pueblo pottery jars from the form shown in figure 42. The base is now concave for carrying on a person's head or setting on a flat surface, where it was much less likely to be tipped over. This jar is also from the Pajarito Plateau, and it shows the light tan slip described for figure 42.

This jar was found in pieces by local hikers on the wall of a canyon above the Rio Grande. When they brought it to me for inspection, I told them that it was a very rare treasure, and they soon went back to find more pieces, which nearly completed the jar. After making a trade with the finders, I enjoyed its presence in

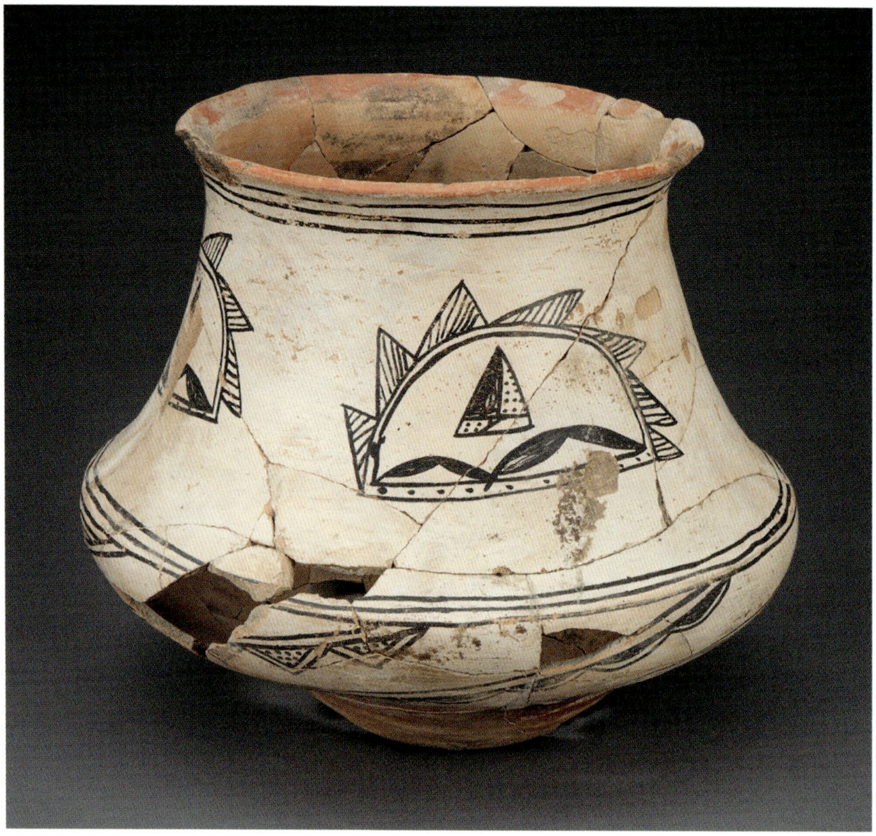

Figure 44. Lineage I jar, circa 1680, 26.5 x 32.3 cm. (Photo by Blair Clark. MIAC 55757/12.)

our collection very much, and I also appreciate the care that it is now being shown by MIAC staff.

The glaze ware jar in figure 45 comes from the southern side of the Pajarito Plateau and is almost identical in form to the jar in figure 44. This form, with flared rim, tapered upper body, flaring mid-body bulge, and concave base, slowly migrated to many of the pueblos that lie near the Rio Grande, but potters at pueblos to the west—namely, Acoma and Zuni—did not adopt the concave base until about 1700.

This jar was fired in an upside-down orientation, as shown by the messy running of the glaze toward the mouth, rendering indecipherable whatever the intended design was. The pattern consists of thick, dark brown glaze and thin fingers of glaze that ran from it. This suggests that there were two mineral components in the glaze material. While both are lead-oxide-based glazes, one component was much more fluid than the other during firing, creating the running effect. These nearly transparent, runny fingers are found almost exclusively on glaze ware jars and bowls made between about 1650 and 1700, so they serve as strong evidence for the purpose of dating.

The lovely jar from Zia Pueblo shown in figure 46 has the Tewa jar form (as seen in figure 48a). Here, however, the decoration contains elements that are very rare—or missing altogether—on jars from the Rio Grande pueblos. Especially significant is the shaft-feather figure, which was used only on Zia pottery.

The other figure of particular significance is the large triangle attached to the upper black-edged red band around the jar. The lower apex at the bottom of the triangle has a much smaller triangle attached and a triplet of downward-pointing dashes. Figures like that also appear on jars from Acoma and Zuni Pueblos. So-called key figures are seen in the band located at the largest diameter.

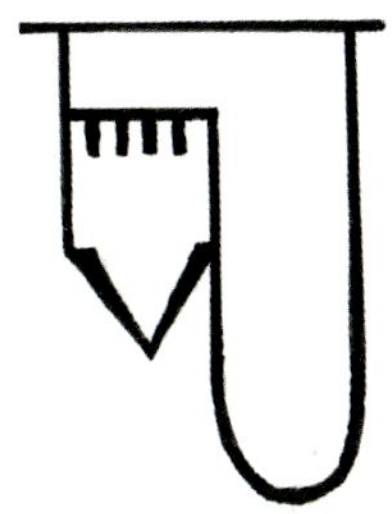

Shaft-feather figure

The type name of this glaze ware vessel is San Diego Polychrome, in recognition of pottery made just before and during the refugee period (1680–1700) in villages on the tops of mesas alongside San Diego Canyon, through which the Jemez River flows.

I enjoyed making a painting of this jar, which is now owned by Dwight and Lorri Lanmon.

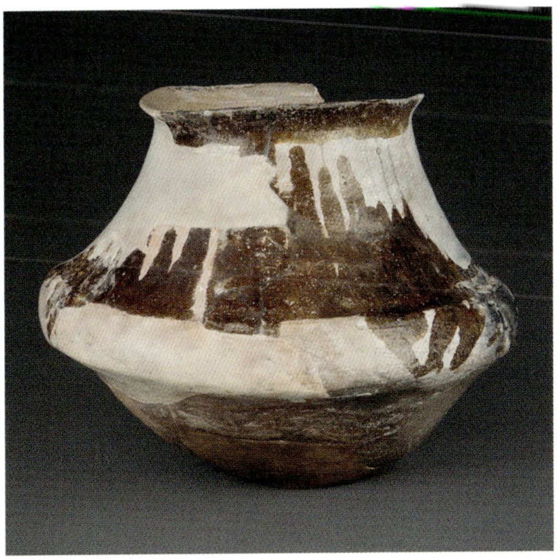

Figure 45. Glaze period F (San Felipe) jar, circa 1680, 27.8 x 34.6 cm. (Photo by Blair Clark. MIAC 55820/12.)

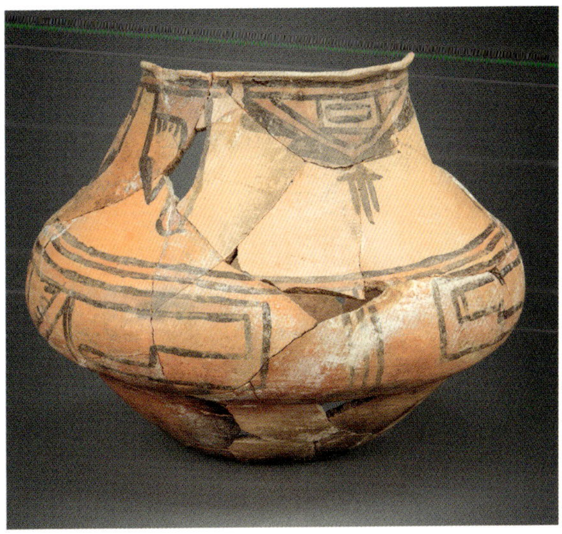

Figure 46. San Diego Polychrome jar, circa 1660, 24.7 x 31.8 cm. (Photo by Blair Clark. MIAC 55792/12.)

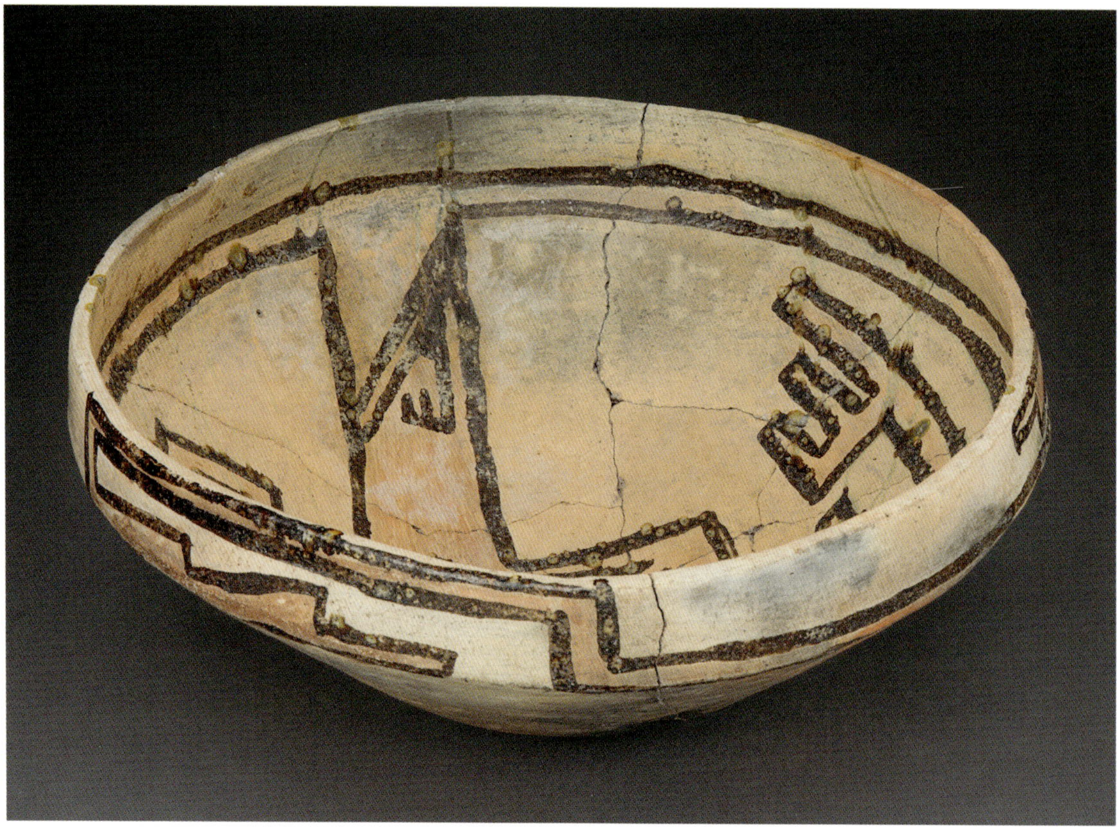

Figure 47. Kotyiti Polychrome glaze ware bowl, circa 1660–1680, 11.8 x 30.5 cm. (Photo by Blair Clark. MIAC 57128/12.)

The bowl shown in figure 47 is one of my favorite glaze ware vessels. I like the form, with the sharp angular fold on the exterior separating the underbody from the vertically rising sides. Notice how prominently the interior black-edged red band displays its single break. The interior isolated figure reminds me of the Pajarito Bird (see figure 42), but the bowl was made quite a bit south of the Pajarito Plateau. The exterior design displays key figures like those seen on the mid-body band of the jar in figure 46. Altogether, this bowl is a gorgeous example of Pueblo pottery vessels made during the early historic years, about 1660 to 1680. It carries the type name of Kotyiti Polychrome.

The remarkable vessel in figure 48a is another handsome Tewa jar form. As you can see, I made a painting of it and also a painting that shows the virtually unique occurrence of designs made by scratching the upper red-slipped area with ceremonial figures, including a corn plant, clouds, and other elements. Although

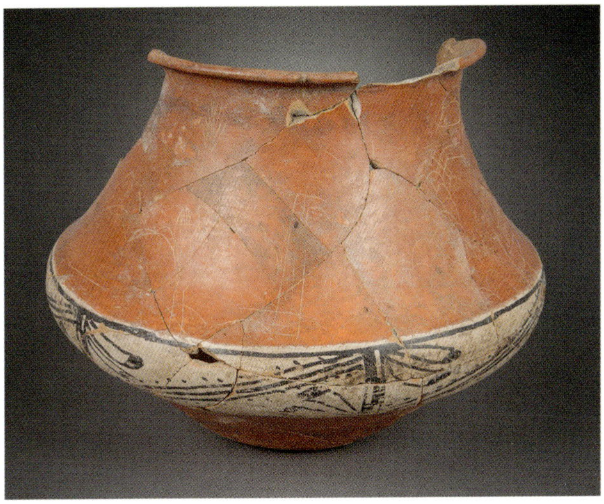

a

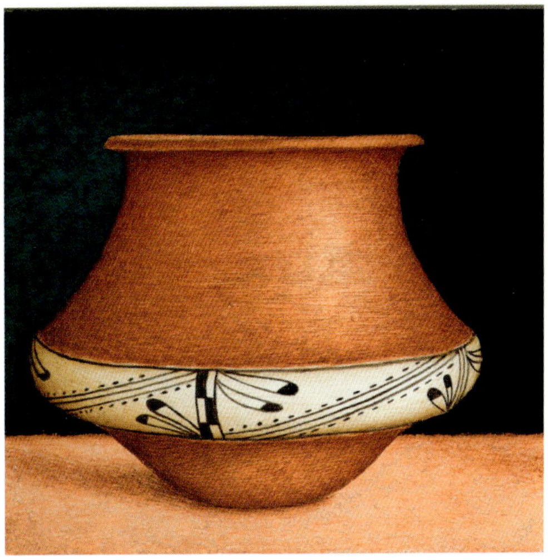

b

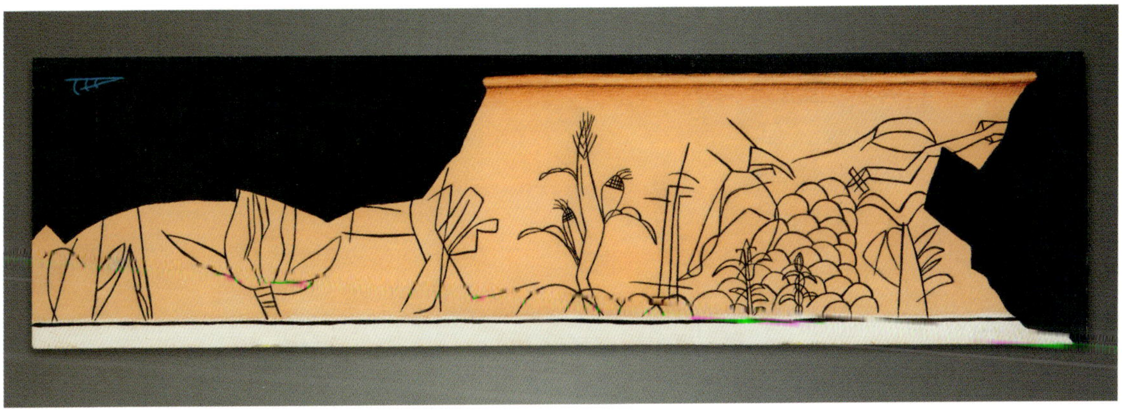

c

Figures 48a–48c. Lineage II jar, circa 1690–1700, 26.7 x 39.3 cm, and my reconstruction of its original appearance (12 x 16 in., December 1979); detail showing the scratched decoration on the upper body (6 x 22 in., January 1988). (Photos by Blair Clark. 48a. MIAC 55758/12; 48b. MIAC 56009/13 [FH-1165]; 48c. MIAC 56006/13 [FH-1341].)

parts of the jar are missing, this example of Pueblo Indian pottery is an important national treasure.

The jar in figure 49 is an early example of the transition from glaze-paint pottery to a purely matte-paint decorated vessel. The cause of this transition was that Spanish people returning after the 1680 Pueblo Revolt refused access to the lead mines from which potters had been extracting their pigments.

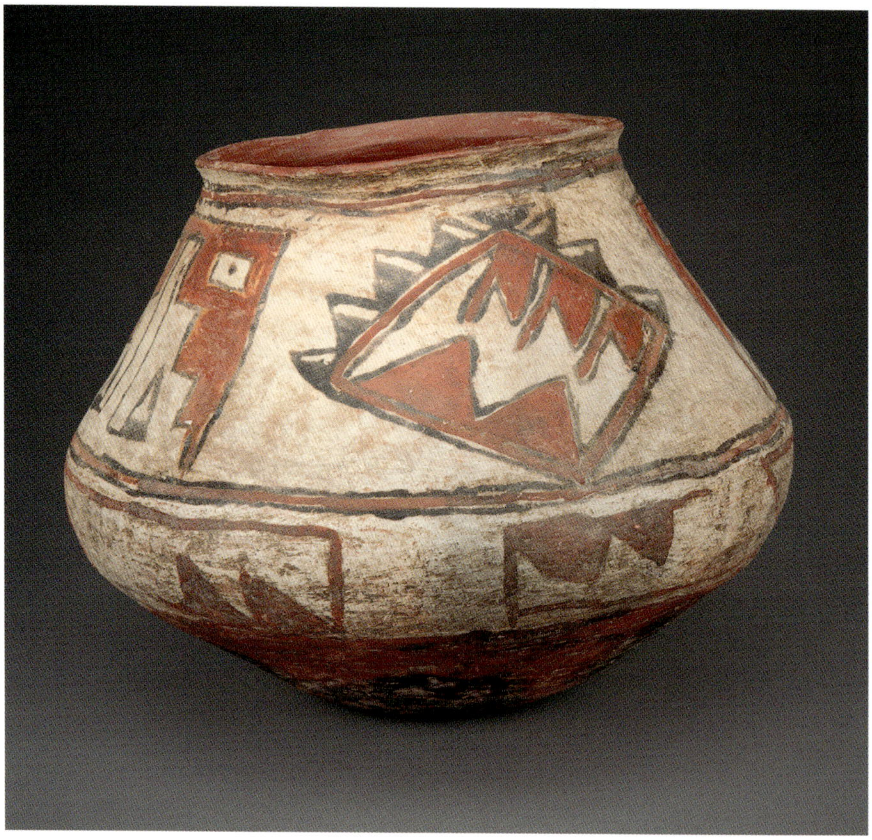

Figure 49. Puname Polychrome jar, Zia Pueblo, circa 1710, 24.0 x 31.2 cm. (Photo by Blair Clark. MIAC 55765/12.)

On this jar, the red decoration was produced using slip, while the black is a mixture of a vegetal material (probably from boiled-down foliage of the Rocky Mountain bee plant) and an iron- or manganese-rich crushed rock. In the earliest days of Puname Polychrome, Zia Pueblo potters continued to use black-edged red bands in their decorations. Also present on this jar are large key figures with square eyes.

Our collection contained three jars of this type of pottery, which show a consistent digression from the Tewa form seen earlier on Zia jars. What was happening at all the pueblos was a slow but sure transition from the beautiful Tewa form toward a more spherical configuration, which was essentially complete by about 1770. Still present, however, were the concave base and short neck. What was the incentive for this transition? Perhaps it was easier to make the spherical shape than to build the earlier sculptural form.

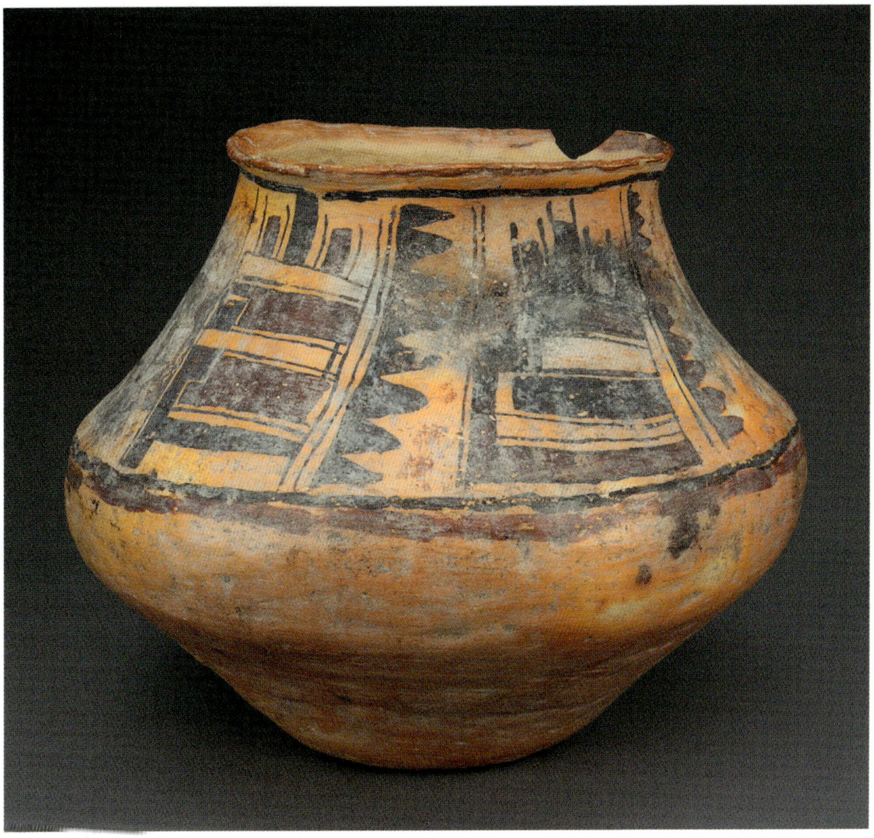

Figure 50. Payupki Polychrome jar, Hopi Pueblo, First Mesa, circa 1700, 24.1 x 29.8 cm. (Photo by Blair Clark. MIAC 55764/12.)

At the time of the refugee period, some Indians living near the Rio Grande fled more than three hundred miles to the Hopi First Mesa in what is today northeastern Arizona. There they established a new village called Hano, where the Tewa language is still spoken.

The jar in figure 50 is a handsome example of the integration of Hopi and Tewa traditions. The jar form is Tewa from the Rio Grande pueblos, and some design features are from Zia, Acoma, and Zuni, although much of the design style of this jar is principally Hopi. One interesting feature is the unedged red band below the design area, a style used at many of the eastern pueblos until as late as about 1930. This jar, however, has a break in this lower band that is never seen on pottery made in the eastern pueblos. Note also that the color of the unslipped surface is an orange-yellow hue, which is characteristic of Hopi pottery.

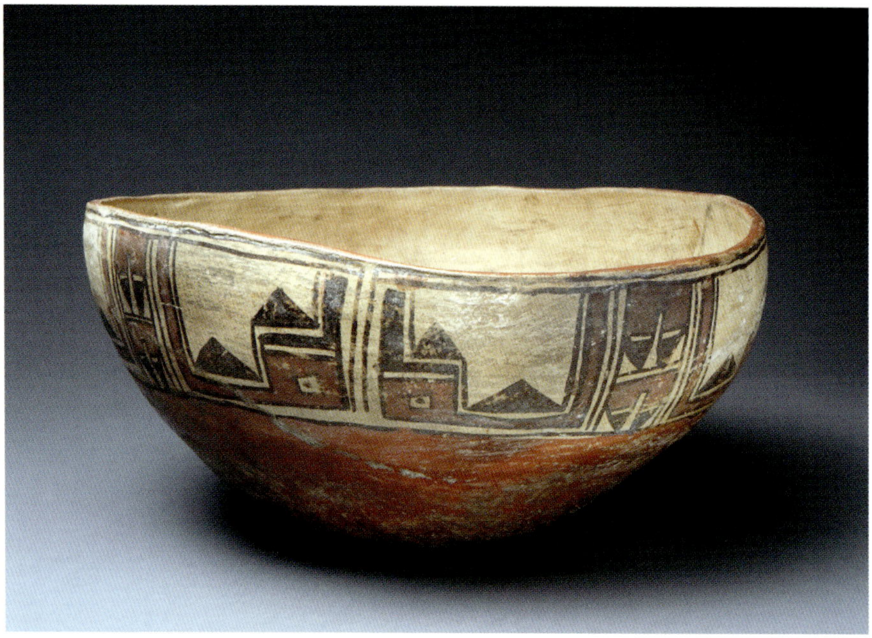

Figure 51. Ako Polychrome bowl, Acoma Pueblo, circa 1720–1740, 19 x 40 x 37 cm. (Photo by Blair Clark. MIAC 55740/12.)

I have not figured out a way to date the various later Hopi vessel forms and designs on Hopi ceramics. Experts on Hopi design styles have also found this to be difficult up to the time of work by the famous potter Nampeyo, whose personal style of decoration is now widely recognized.

The wonderful bowl in figure 51 sat on a high shelf in a Santa Fe gallery, where it was described as being made more than a millennium ago. I knew at once that the bowl was not that old but was made instead in about 1730. The price was reasonable for a vessel of that rarity, so I bought it, knowing that it was a major example of Pueblo Indian pottery from Acoma and needed to be cared for in a museum, where it would be available for study by many future generations. Its beauty led me to include it in several of my paintings.

Its decorations include several features of great symbolism for Indian religious activities, including both sharp-tipped feather pairs and red/black key figures with square eyes. The upper pair of boundary lines has classic line breaks. Their original meaning in the 1300s is unknown with certainty and is now described by Indians in various ways, including the following:

- The breaks are pathways for the vessel's spirit to escape in the event of impending disaster.
- The breaks are pathways by which the potter inserts her spirit as the vessel is being constructed. Some carry this idea even further, believing that if a potter completes a circle, she will become infertile.

The strange-looking jar in figure 52 is almost laughable for its contorted shape. But it has a very significant and tragic background. As a result of the Pueblo Revolt in 1680, many Pueblo Indians fled from their homes to escape war with the Spanish conquerors.

The group that fled to Gobernador Canyon developed a new pottery type called Gobernador Polychrome, based to some extent on their homeland styles.

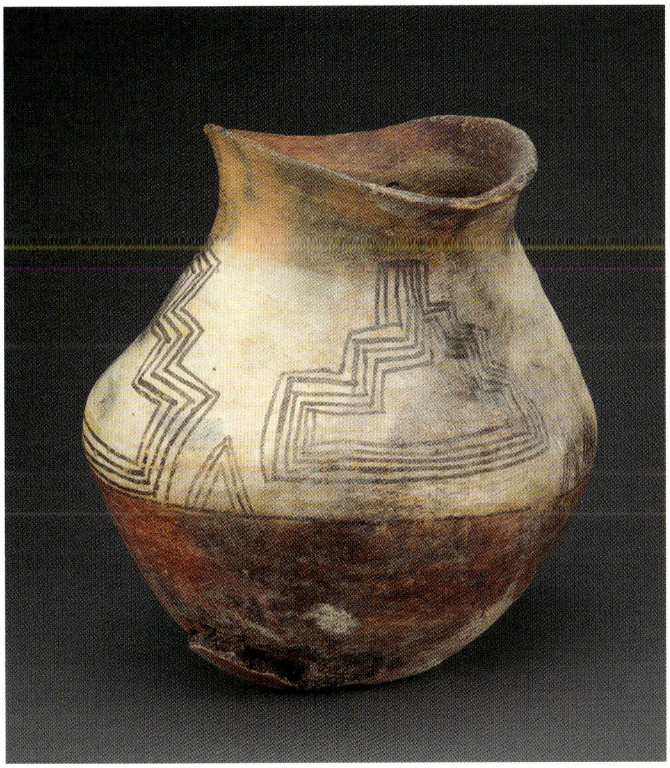

Figure 52. Gobernador Polychrome jar, circa 1700–1720, 28.1 x 27.0 cm. (Photo by Blair Clark. MIAC 55771/12.)

The clay for this new type of Pueblo pottery could be fired to an unusual degree of strength and was thus quite useful. A characteristic effect of this new (to them) material was a tendency to distort in firing. However, I don't think that distortion was the sole cause of this unusual shape. It seems likely to have been an intentional effect of the potter's desire to create a different form, with the widely flaring rim making pouring less messy.

The design on this jar consists of a pyramidal structure with five lines in a stair-step pattern. The idea seems vaguely related to some design styles of Jemez Black-on-white, a pottery type made earlier at Jemez Pueblo (also known as Walatowa).

The fascinating jar of Kiapkwa Polychrome shown in figure 53a was made at Zuni Pueblo in about 1780, a time when pottery jars made at almost all pueblos had returned to a more or less spherical shape. The older concave base, however, remains in most cases, and a short neck with a rather simple design is present. The body of the jar has a very complex pattern, with fine cross-hatching between somewhat heavier, parallel lines. This design style occurs in many different forms during the early years (1770–1790) of Kiapkwa Polychrome made at Zuni Pueblo

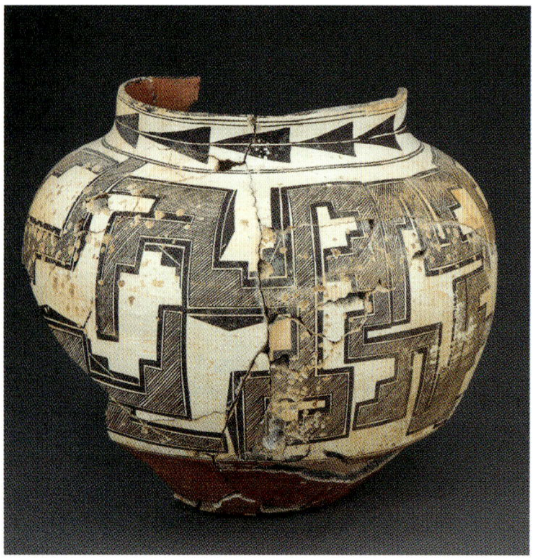

a

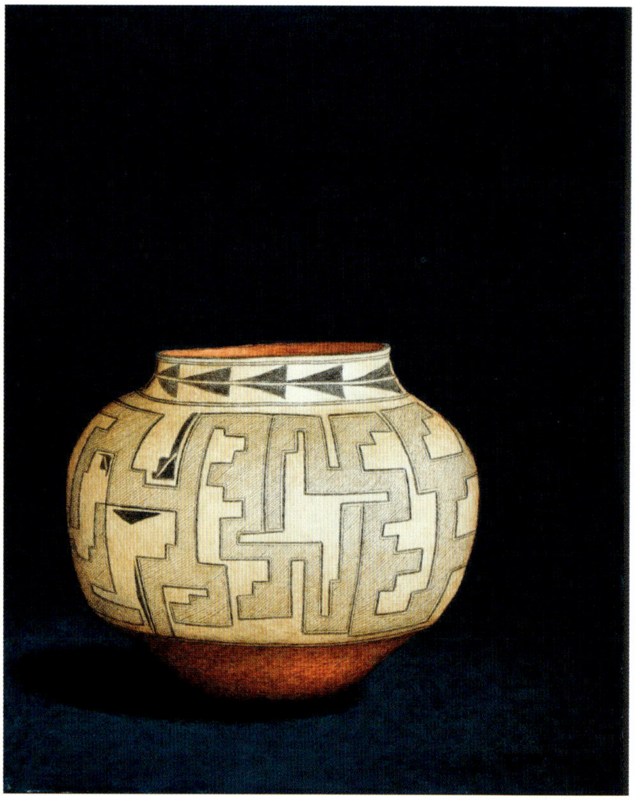

b

Figures 53a–53b. Kiapkwa Polychrome (Zuni Pueblo) jar, circa 1770–1790, 31.1 x 24.5 cm, and my reconstruction of its original appearance (16 x 20 in., January 2005). (Photos by Blair Clark. 53a. MIAC 56211/12; 53b. 57161/13 [FH-1553].)

and must have been of great significance to the artists who painted it. I speculate that the patterns represent some kind of living spirit. Such patterns usually occur twice on each jar, with care being taken to make them identical. A later version of this decoration is present on some jars of Zuni Polychrome in a form called the Rainbird, in which parallel lines with internal hachure terminate with a solid black structure containing an eye and leading to a sharp-tipped beak. (I did not own a Zuni jar with that design.)

As an interesting sidelight, the jar in this figure is one that both Dwight Lanmon and I consider a favorite in this collection. As can be seen, I've painted a picture of this jar (fig. 53b), on which the tedious crosshatch design was a major accomplishment for me.

The beautiful jar in figure 54 is in nearly perfect condition, which is quite unusual for a vessel of this vintage. Again we see the nearly spherical form that

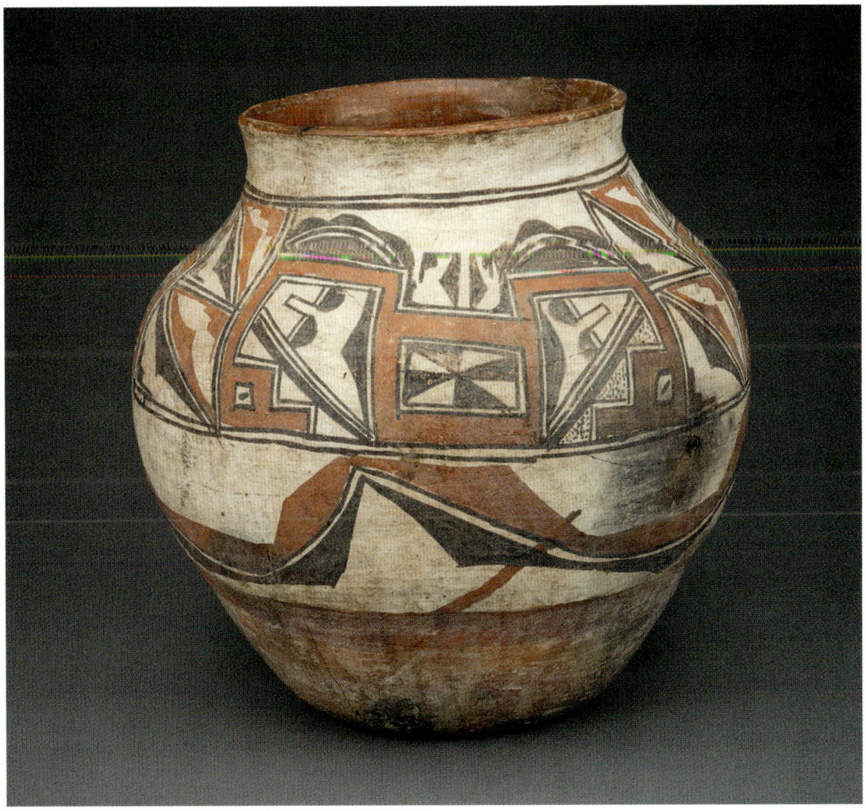

Figure 54. San Pablo Polychrome (Zia Pueblo) jar, circa 1780, 27.2 x 27.9 cm. (Photo by Blair Clark. MIAC 55763/12.)

swept the Pueblo pottery world after about 1760. An especially prominent feature of this jar is seen in the lower design band, which consists of a series of arcs painted in black and red. This in itself is enough to designate an origin at Zia Pueblo. Below the arcs is a red band, which is virtually ubiquitous for pottery made at pueblos close to the Rio Grande.

A prominent feature for the main design band is an angular structure that we call a cadre pattern. It is entirely constructed with red pigment edged in black. From the rectangular middle, the red band sprouts up from each of the two upper corners and bends over to form a key figure with a square eye. The design band is split from top to bottom with a very narrow, black-edged gap that breaks the framing lines on both the top and bottom of the wide band. In characteristic form for San Pablo Polychrome, the main design band consists of four panels, two that are wide and two that are narrow.

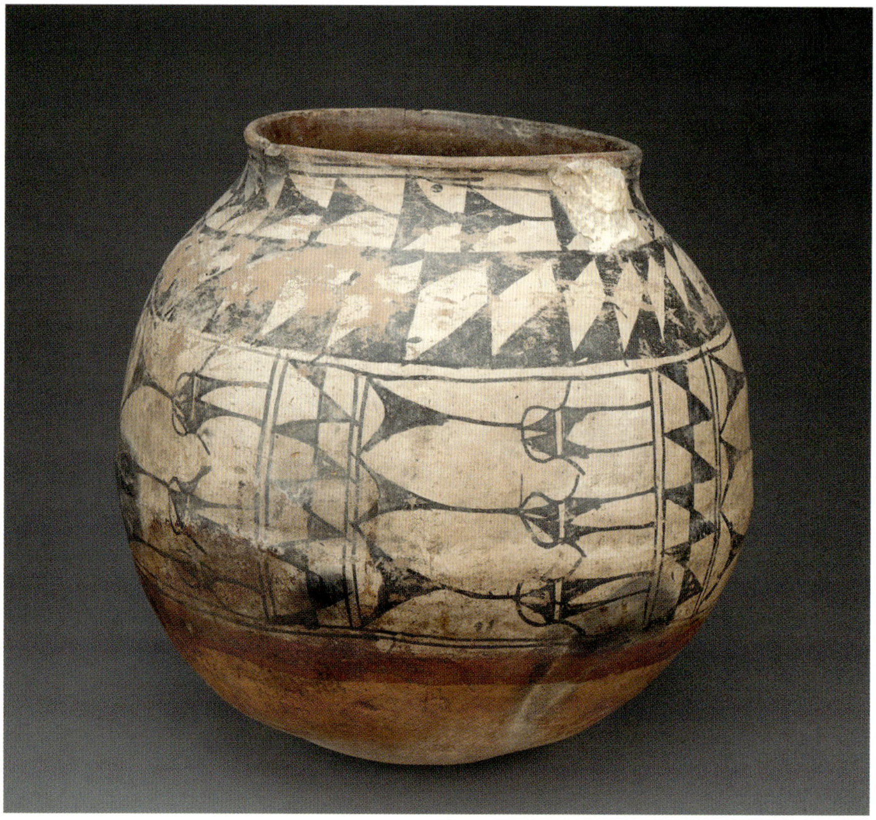

Figure 55. Nambe Polychrome storage jar, circa 1780–1800, 38.2 x 39.4 cm. (Photo by Blair Clark. MIAC 55817/12.)

The flaring neck carries no design, a feature that persists at Zia until about 1820, when that area commences to be decorated, resulting in a pottery type called Zia Polychrome.

The lower design band of arcs found on Zia jars does not occur on jars from the nearby pueblo of Santa Ana. We think that this difference furnishes a clue to distinguishing between vessels made at the two villages. Other, somewhat subtler features existed for at least a century before potters from Santa Ana changed the nature of the temper that was mixed into the clay to decrease the chances of damage before and during firing. (See below the discussion of the Santa Ana jar shown in figure 56.)

Nambé Pueblo owns Nambé Falls and the nearby fossil beds described in chapter 6. The pottery made there before the opening of the Santa Fe Trail to eastern states in 1821 was quite similar to that of San Ildefonso and Tesuque Pueblos. Traders brought many metal and ceramic pots, pans, and dishes, which made the production of pottery vessels less important to the Pueblo people. One result was that potters at Nambé and other nearby pueblos decreased their production of pottery, and those at Nambé completely ceased the making of decorated vessels.

The storage jar shown in figure 55, however, was made before 1800, and it shows some features that allow it to be distinguished from vessels made elsewhere. One subtle feature is that the clay contains grains of mica that are larger and more abundant than those at San Ildefonso and Tesuque. More easily visible, however, are the differences in slip and design. The slip is usually of poorer quality, being softer and thus more easily damaged during use. Another feature is that the vertical boundaries between design panels often occur in two adjacent pairs, between which was placed a relatively simple design, as shown on this jar. These features are sometimes missing. Thus, Nambé Polychrome remains a pottery type that some pottery specialists refuse to acknowledge.

The horizontal figures in the wide mid-body designs are like plants attached to the vertical panel lines, and then they extend to the right, where they expand into a pair of sharp-tipped flowers with narrow curved lines at each side. Sometimes I think they might be descendants of the feather clusters seen on the pots of various pueblos in the early to middle years of the 1700s.

In any case, I really like this old middle-sized storage jar, and I felt a twinge of nostalgia on the day it left for its new home in the basement of MIAC, where the rest of our collection is now.

The ancient pueblo of Santa Ana (also known as Tamaya) lies close to the Jemez River, west of the Rio Grande. The location is rather barren and the

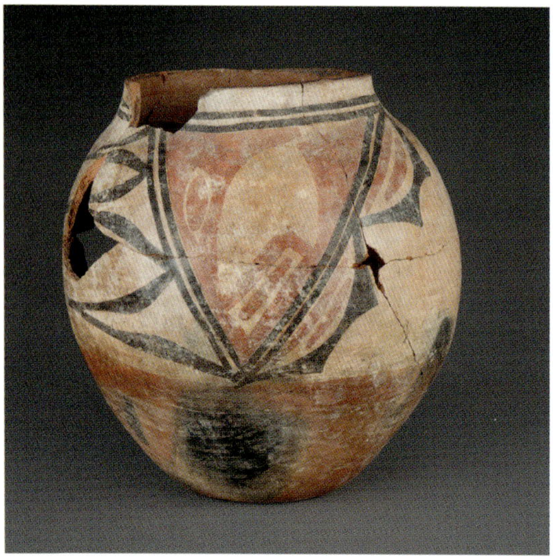

Figure 56. Ranchitos Polychrome jar (Santa Ana), circa 1800, 28.3 x 28.7 cm. (Photo by Blair Clark. MIAC 55770/12.)

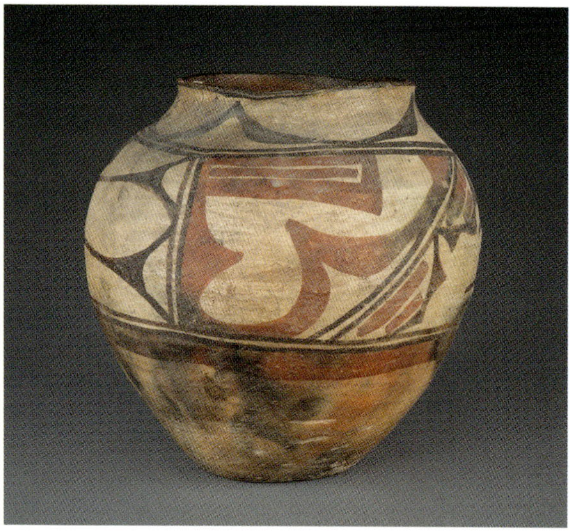

Figure 57. Early Santa Ana Polychrome jar, circa 1825, 29.0 x 30.4 cm. (Photo by Blair Clark. MIAC 55848/12.)

farming land is poor, so the residents of Santa Ana sought to obtain land along the east side of the Rio Grande in the 1700s. They acquired five parcels and established the village of Ranchitos, which became the principal village of the pueblo. The people return to the ancient village for ceremonial purposes.

The two jars shown in figures 56 and 57 are striking because of the similarity of their designs. It is a rare coincidence when two early vessels are so alike but are recognized as being of two different pottery types. In this case, the jar without neckband designs (fig. 56) belongs to the Santa Ana Pueblo type called Ranchitos Polychrome, while the jar with the neckband designs (fig. 57) is an early example of Santa Ana Polychrome. Coincidences like this make pottery research especially fun.

What we see in these two jars is the transition from a pottery type made from about 1770 to 1820 on which the neckband designs are always missing, to a pottery type with neckband designs, made from about 1820 to the late 1800s and even occasionally during the 1900s. In both cases, the designs are evolving to patterns of decoration very different from what is seen at all the other pueblos. The Santa Ana style is much bolder in its use of black and red and the omission of fine-scale configurations, which reappear only in the later years of the 1800s.

The big storage jar in figure 58 was made at Santo Domingo Pueblo in the old village near its present location. In 1886 much of that village was destroyed

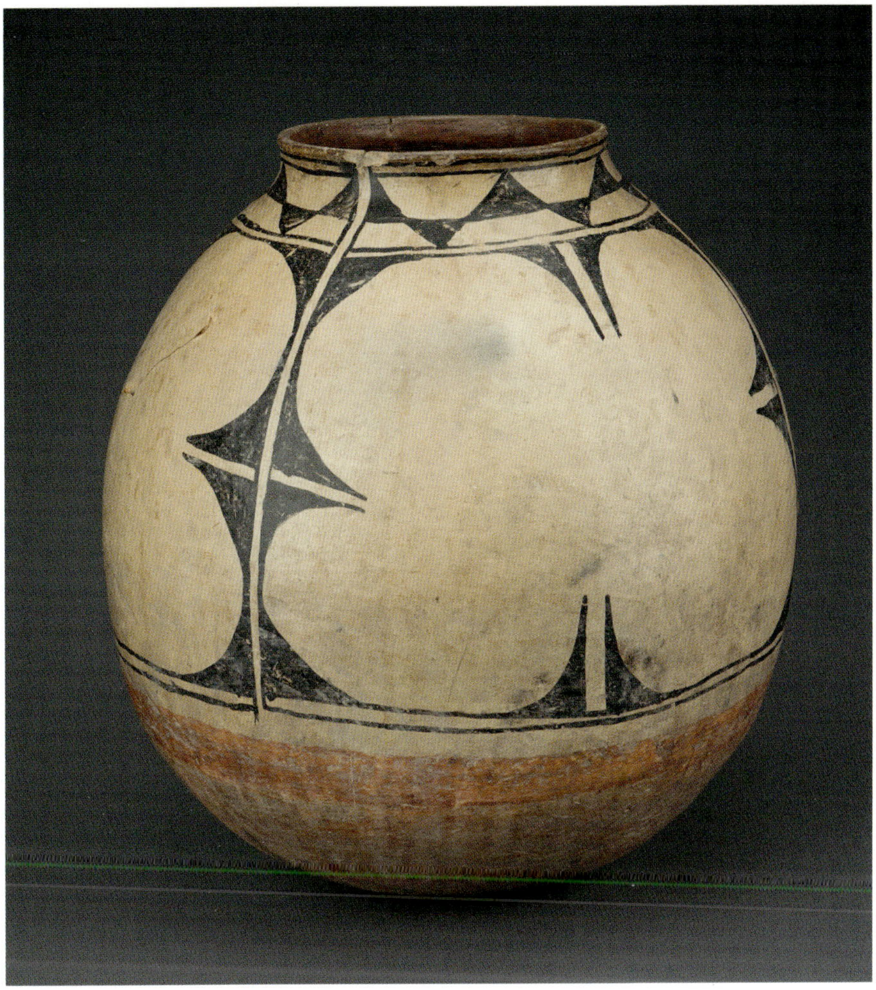

Figure 58. Kiua Polychrome (Santo Domingo) storage jar, circa 1800–1850, 49.4 x 47.3 cm. (Photo by Blair Clark. MIAC 55802/12.)

by flood, and this jar is said to have been later dug from the silt by the family of Nesario Tenorio.

This beautiful example has very simple designs on the body and a zigzag pattern around the neck that is characteristic of pottery made at Santo Domingo during the first half of the 1800s. The only red on the jar lies below the design area. This feature is used at many of the pueblos near the Rio Grande. At Santo Domingo and Cochiti, the red band is relatively wide and almost light red-tan in color, while at San Ildefonso it is narrower and more strongly red.

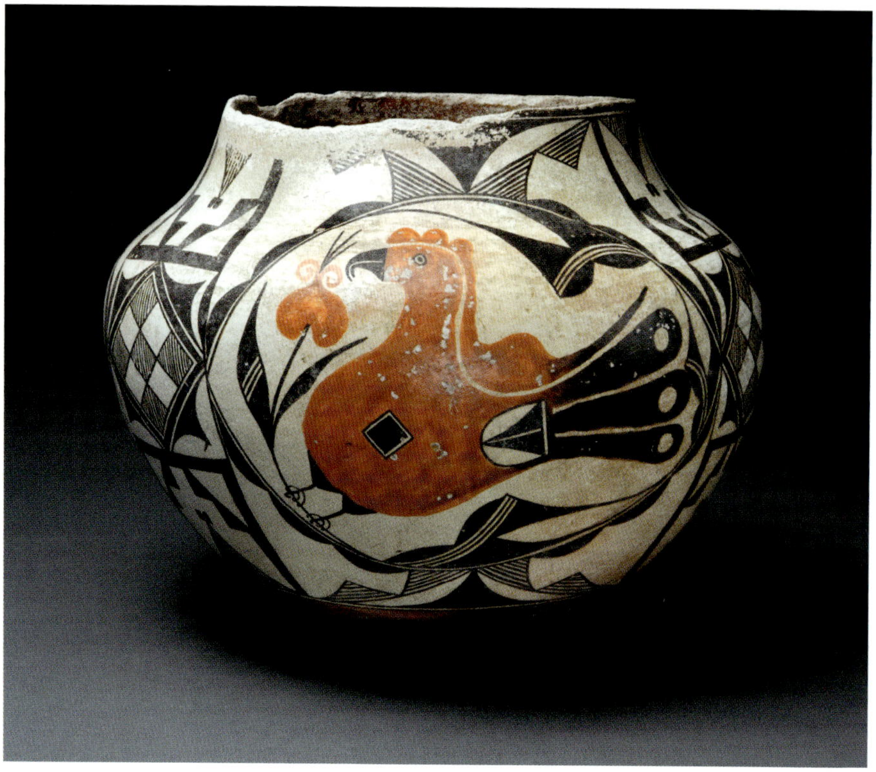

Figure 59. Acoma Polychrome jar, circa 1920, 17 x 30 cm. (Photo by Blair Clark. MIAC 55612/12.)

I got this jar at Jim Riley's store in Santa Fe for a relatively low price because of a broken piece, which I was able to glue back into place when I got home. I'm very fond of this handsome example of a type called Kiua Polychrome, bearing an earlier spelling of the Indian name of the pueblo, which is now spelled Kewa.

Acoma pottery has a great reputation, as seen in the gorgeous jar in figure 59 with bird decoration. I like this particular jar so much that I used it in the painting for the cover of our book *The Pottery of Acoma Pueblo* (Museum of New Mexico Press, 2013).

The bird has a down-curved beak, which suggests that it is a parrot, possibly a macaw. It is perched on a branch with a flower, a typical position that contrasts with the birds on Zia jars, whose feet are usually firmly attached to the ground. The tail feathers on this Acoma bird are black, which is seldom seen on Acoma birds.

It is not clear to me what kind of flower is intended here. The checkerboard with hachured squares occurs often on Acoma pottery of the 1800s and early

1900s. More recent Acoma pottery is often characterized by eye-dazzling patterns, but I've never owned such a piece.

The black-on-red jar in figure 60 is intriguing for a form that's similar to the classic Tewa jars of the 1600s (such as in figs. 44 and 45). It has a concave underbody, a mid-body bulge sporting its own band of decoration, a tall upper body, and a sharply flaring rim. It is the work of the San Ildefonso potter Domingita Pino (1860–1948), whose distinctive style has been well established. Her specialty was vessels with red-and-black decoration on stone-polished slip.

What a beautiful jar this has been for our collection, and I'm happy to know that it will be well protected for numerous future generations of people to see.

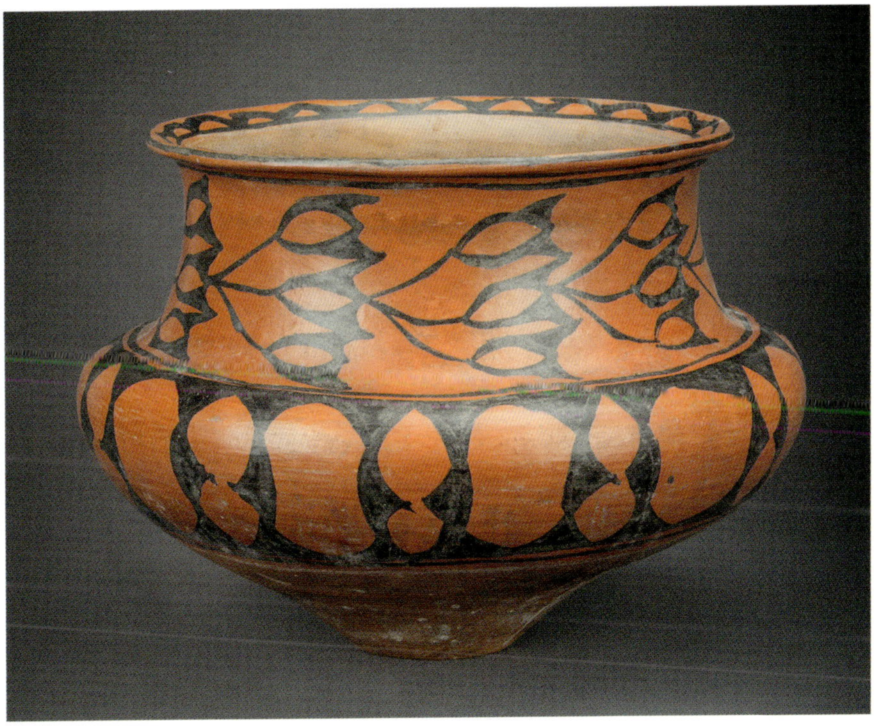

Figure 60. San Ildefonso Black-on-red jar, made by Domingita Pino, circa 1880–1900, 23.0 x 32.2 cm. (Photo by Blair Clark. MIAC 56209/12.)

11
Paintings and Art

It is lots of fun observing the forms, designs, and colors of beautiful things and capturing their images through the processes of drawing and painting. With practice, achieving satisfying results can be a joy.

Prior to 1967 I did very little painting, although there exists in my scrapbook a little abstract oil painting and a couple of drawings. My main exposure to art had been a few grade-school art classes of mediocre quality and also meeting Waldo Chase. He was a cabin-in-the-woods hermit who lived near Hood Canal in Washington, and he supported himself making woodblock prints that are quite nice. We have one at home, which is inscribed to my Aunt Bessie, and there are one or two of them mounted in my scrapbook.

In the 1960s I started drawing the designs I observed on Pueblo Indian pottery, and with patience and several hundred experiments, I was able to produce accurate depictions of vessels. Then I began wanting even more—namely, to depict the colors that occur in many of the patterns. I drew a set of Pueblo Indian pots for inclusion in my little book *Historic Pueblo Indian Pottery*, published in 1967, and about that same time, I prepared numerous drawings for my following book, *Matte-Paint Pottery of the Tewa, Keres, and Zuni Pueblos*, which, after considerable delay, was published in 1973. Eventually, I thought that some of the pictures were pretty nice, and I got the courage to show them to friends and even to exhibit them in places where they would be seen by strangers.

Why draw and paint? For money? For fame? For me? The question is closely related to the reasons for riding a motorcycle. In essence, it all boils down to a few incentives that may be described in fairly simple terms. In reality, though, the matter is considerably more complex, in ways that I can sense but don't have the ability to convey in writing. The simple reasons are, first, to demonstrate that I have the skill to produce a reasonably decent drawing and, second, to give myself a vehicle for expressing thoughts, feelings, and ideas that churn in my mind. Here, I concluded, was a hobby that involved my fingers and arms in slow-muscle activity, which worked out quite well in contrast to the fast-muscle activities that I realized I could not master (such as playing the cello or engaging in fast-action sports).

I then started branching out to subjects other than pottery and found some that worked quite well. Especially exciting was capturing the likeness and facial expression of people and succeeding in representing the textures of the clothing they wore. For those paintings, I had to understand the surroundings of the people and the situations being depicted. In my eyes, some of these paintings turned out to be better than anything I was seeing in some art galleries in Santa Fe—not a modest thing to say, I know, but I do still get pleasure looking at what I think are the best paintings I have done, especially as I age past the stage of my life when my hands were steady. I am sometimes amazed at the skills I once had but that I no longer possess.

In an article in *Esquire* magazine from around 1967, Winston Churchill described a little black dog nipping at his heels, a euphemism for depression. To outrun the dog, he turned to politics, writing, and painting pictures. He also advised that anyone who wishes to paint pictures should start before the age of forty; otherwise, it is too late to focus the necessary energy on this pursuit. My age at that time was 39.7 years, so I decided it was urgent to get some pigments, brushes, and surfaces to paint on. I've used acrylics and gesso from the start, and I hope they continue making this material for as long as I keep painting. I've used a variety of brushes, especially plastic-bristle flats from one-quarter to three-quarters of an inch wide, in addition to a lot of little sharp-pointed, hairlike brushes. Others are useful for various special needs, and I have a drawer with numerous brushes, both new and well used. (I almost never throw a brush away, no matter how stubby it becomes.) For the surface, I virtually always use one-eighth-inch untempered Masonite, which is available in sheets measuring four by eight feet and can be purchased in Santa Fe. I get them to cut the boards, because the largest size I can handle is two by four feet. I always paint with the board lying flat on an old wooden desk. Illumination sufficient for my needs is supplied by a 150- or 200-watt bulb in a lamp attached to the wall on my left (fig. 61).

I once described the excitement I get when a painting I am working on seems to be progressing well: "My mind goes into a sort of euphoria when I'm painting

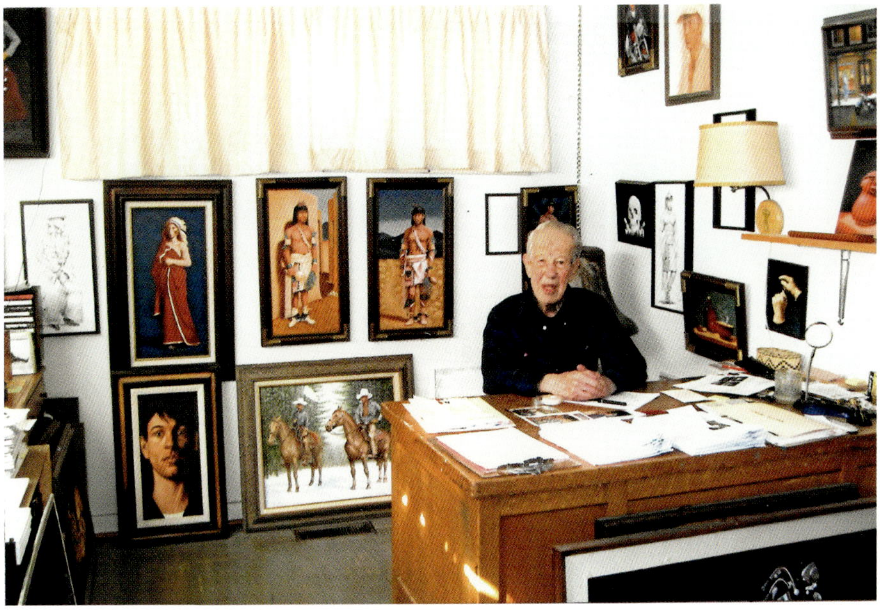

Figure 61. My painting room in November 2014. Some of the paintings you see here are reproduced in chapter 12 of this book. (Photo by Patricia Harlow.)

. . . the brush seems almost alive. It is a very exciting thing to do: to paint, to see it happening in front of your own eyes" (quoted in Jeanne Hassenzahl's 1975 booklet *Harlow*).

The themes of my paintings are pretty much realistic representations of things that interest me, sometimes with a surreal touch (for example, a floating glove; see fig. 80) or a distortion of perspective (which can actually enhance the impression of a realistic setting), but I never paint abstractions. I've thought about doing so and even tried a few times, but the results are meaningless messes, so about the only abstractions in my paintings are in the composition and sometimes the color of an object, but not its form or decoration. Portraits of people are as accurate as I can depict or else are an idealization that suits the mood of the painting.

I've never learned to draw the basic forms of objects easily. Sometimes I can fill in a form with my own imagination, as when I've drawn the basic structure of a person's head and wanted to fill in my own invention of detailed features. One thing that I've learned from this is the crucial significance of the structural details, especially the mouth, for which even seemingly minor alterations can change the mood of expression.

It would be easy for me to invent the form and designs of a Pueblo Indian pottery vessel, and virtually anyone would think that the picture represented a real pot. I did this occasionally many years ago, but in recent decades I've tried to be as accurate as possible in the representation of both form and design. Only the color of the surface is sometimes altered a bit from the actual color of the specific pot being depicted, and sometimes I transform the realism of a fragmentary piece to show how it looked before it was broken.

Depictions of Pueblo Indian pottery vessels constitute by far the majority of my paintings. A very rough estimate is around eight hundred total paintings out of a lifetime total of perhaps thirteen hundred pictures, but not that many still exist, because sometimes I decide that a painting is not worth keeping for a variety of reasons—most often, awkwardness of composition. In some cases, the difficulty was corrected by covering part of the surface with gesso and repainting that area; in others, such a remedial process seems not likely to work, and I cover the whole surface with gesso in preparation for a completely different painting over the first one.

I rarely paint landscapes, except as very simplified or idealized backgrounds of the dominant subject matter, which most often includes cowboys, horses, motorcycles and the bikers who ride them, and Pueblo Indian people. A few of the people are representational portraits of specific individuals; the rest are all me. (Even if they don't look like me, they look the way I feel or want to feel.)

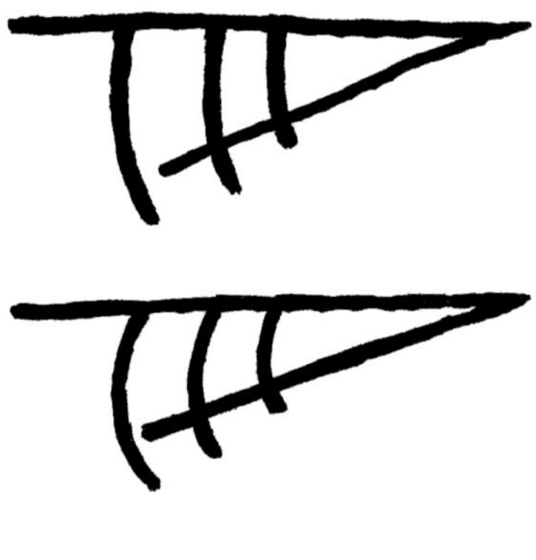

Two versions of my signature on paintings: the earlier (*top*), and the later, more graceful version (*bottom*).

In a painting that has many such figures (of cowboys and/or bikers), I can simultaneously be all of them (except where certain individuals are recognizably portraits of other specific people). I've tried painting only two self-portraits that were intended to actually look like me, but I destroyed both long ago.

One exception to the idea that any or all of the bikers and/or cowboys are *me* is seen in paintings I've done to illustrate the guys in one of my favorite books, *All the Pretty Horses* by Cormac McCarthy (see fig. 73). In those depictions, the guys are my inventions of how John Grady Cole and Lacey Rawlins should look. Those pictures are identified on the back with the characters' names.

I sign my paintings on the front with an abstraction of a black leather right-hand glove pointing to the left. (See the illustrations in chapter 12.) This signature is usually about as inconspicuous as I can make it; sometimes the viewer needs to hunt for it. On the back of each painting I write a title for the picture (sometimes), my full signature, a catalog number, and the month and year.

Sometimes there are additional comments on the back, identifying the subject matter of the painting. The catalog number is recorded serially in a catalog of my paintings. In the early days, the catalog numbers were based on the date of completion, but in September 1975, I started labeling them with a four-digit number, starting with FH-1000 and up to the current FH-1600.

Regarding technique, I never had any art lessons after grade school. Never having learned to draw the overall shapes and proportions of objects, I resort to the use of a pantograph to enlarge pictures or sketches in my extensive files. These pictures are combined on the gesso-covered board into the desired overall composition. Then the process of painting proceeds without any further mechanical assistance.

Learning to paint requires a fire-in-the-belly dedication to spending much time experimenting with brushes and pigments, subjects and forms, the handling of light, the associations among colors, perspective, and other matters. Especially important to me is development of an ability to see the continuously evolving elements of a painting in reference to the subject being depicted. Achieving this has been a primary motivation, and I continually readdress the issue to refine my capability over and over again while I paint. Anyone can look at a Pueblo Indian pot or a human face, for example, but to depict the image realistically requires conveying what is happening with the brushes and paints. I'm convinced that learning to see is the greatest and most difficult thing that a would-be artist must address.

In that regard, one of the most exciting moments for me occurs in painting a human face. After working for a while with all the technical elements, there comes a time when the face suddenly becomes real and human, representing either the intended expression of a specific model or the desired nature of an invented face. Many times my human faces turn out OK, but only rarely does the achievement of a perfect depiction occur with such power as to kick me across the room. Altogether I have had perhaps a dozen such occurrences, and they stand out in my mind as among the most thrilling moments of my life (fig. 72). On June 15, 1971, I wrote a few words that are relevant to this experience: "To execute a portrait requires concentration on the elements of dark and light, as well on as the feelings that are to be expressed by images on paper. The barest flick of line or turn of shadow affects the whole in subtle ways that the mind can scarcely state in words."

Incidentally, I learned long ago that it is foolish to complete a painting that is recognizably awkward in its intermediate stages. Sometimes I've pushed on with the painting to some semblance of completion, but rarely does the final result have enough virtue to overcome the facets of awkwardness. One exception is my first portrait of Maria Martinez, the famous potter of San Ildefonso Pueblo (fig. 68). The group of pots on the right side is a bit awkward, but I think the portrait itself is so nice that I've preserved it. I gave the painting to my son, Keith, in 2008.

One question that I've not discussed very much is, What will happen to the pictures? In the early days, it was fun to sell some of the paintings, and I have had one-man exhibits at the Jamison Galleries in Santa Fe, the Mendosa Gallery in Taos, and the Cliff Dwellers Gallery in Los Alamos. Altogether, I estimate that about 250 of my paintings have been sold.

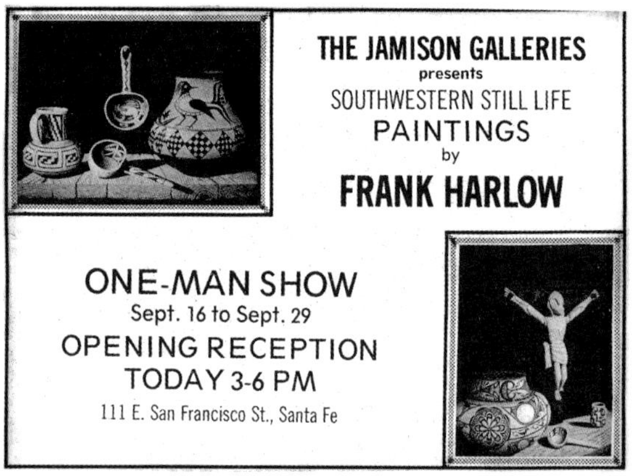

Figure 62. Announcement for the exhibition and sale of my paintings at the Jamison Galleries in Santa Fe, 1973. (Courtesy Zeb Conley.)

As I approached my fiftieth birthday, I was strongly tempted to see if I could move to Santa Fe and make a good living as a professional artist. "Yes," said Forrest Fenn, who owned and ran an impressive gallery on Paseo de Peralta in Santa Fe. He described with enthusiasm and clarity what I would have to do to make a successful career: "We can make it happen. I'll give you a one-man show to get you started. You will have to prepare quite a few large paintings of Indian pottery in the style you do so well. Maybe someday it will be your paintings of motorcycles and Indians that will make you famous, but not now. We'll have to make sure that lots of art magazine articles are written about your work and that a richly illustrated book written about your life and paintings is also produced. You'll have to attend many art show openings of other artists, which works wonders in getting you known, and also lots of social events: parties, celebrations, and the like." He also urged me to capitalize on my knowledge of Pueblo Indian pottery by becoming a professional appraiser, thereby meeting important (rich) people from around the country who were at that time starting to recognize the rarity, value, and importance of early Pueblo pottery and starting to build collections by paying large amounts of money for the most significant available examples. (Forrest said my publications were responsible for stimulating the growth in this market.)

He also told me how he was at the time guiding a young artist along such a path—an artist whose work I had seen and admired. (I don't remember his name.) "His big one-man show here will open in a couple of months from now.

He's currently working hard to complete the number of paintings necessary for a full-scale show. I can give you a brochure with the date." Pat and I went to see his paintings a few days after the opening and quickly realized the dismal truth of what had happened. His paintings were far from the quality we had seen before; they showed the effects of pressure to produce the required number, and as I remember, only one of them sold. It was a disaster from which I think the young artist never recovered. His name disappeared in the Santa Fe art community, and I suspect that he moved out of town or turned to some other line of work.

Forrest assured me that he would give me lots of assistance in all these matters and that with lots of hard work, I could succeed. I got so carried away with the excitement of this adventure that for a while it became settled in my mind that this was what should happen. Pat was dubious and uneasy about it all, but she felt bound to support whatever I decided. We even went so far as to submit $500 as earnest money for a $50,000 house on Armenta Street in Santa Fe, and I wrote a letter of intention to retire from the Laboratory. But soon it became clear to me that it would be foolish (insane even?) to follow that course of action, and we were able to reverse the process, even to the extent that the real estate agent was willing to tear up our earnest money check. (As an aside, the value of the Armenta Street house would now be about half a million dollars or maybe even more.)

I became completely turned off about my dream of becoming a famous moneymaking artist, and I'll always be grateful to Forrest for showing me the reality that I was completely unaware of. Indeed, soon after that, I realized the value of continuing my own profession in science at the Lab, and it was wonderful to have painting as a relaxation and as a means for exploring my daydreams and fantasies instead of as a means of funding our existence.

After I decided to stop selling paintings, the question became what to do with them. Many have been given away to friends and to other people who have exhibited a sincere

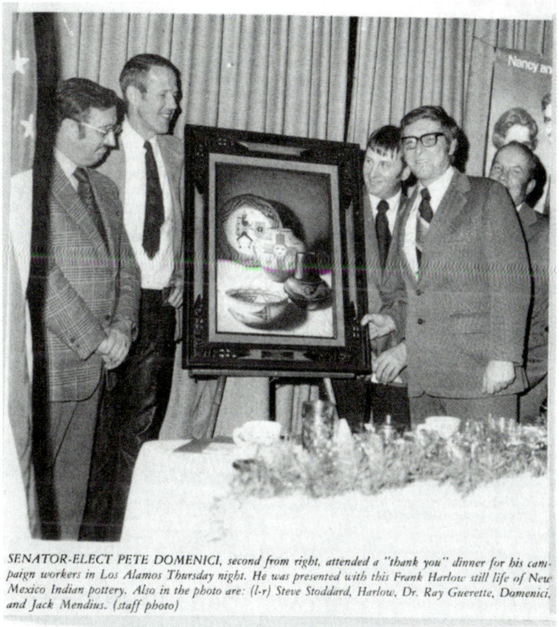
SENATOR-ELECT PETE DOMENICI, *second from right, attended a "thank you" dinner for his campaign workers in Los Alamos Thursday night. He was presented with this Frank Harlow still life of New Mexico Indian pottery. Also in the photo are: (l-r) Steve Stoddard, Harlow, Dr. Ray Guerette, Domenici, and Jack Mendius. (staff photo)*

Figure 63. Senator-elect Pete Domenici receiving a Harlow painting at a thank you dinner for his campaign workers in Los Alamos in 1972. *Left to right:* Steve Stoddard, Frank Harlow, Dr. Ray Guerette, Senator Domenici, and Jack Mendius. (Photo by *Los Alamos Monitor* staff. Courtesy the publisher, David B. Puddu.)

interest in owning one. Wedding presents serve as a useful means for the distribution of paintings. One of the highpoints in my painting "career" occurred when the director of the Los Alamos National Laboratory used one of my drawings as the official holiday greeting card for the Lab.

Senator Pete Domenici of New Mexico kept two of my paintings in his office in Washington, DC. In 2003 there were twenty-three in my office at the Laboratory; ten are in the Francis H. Harlow Conference Room of the Theoretical Building; fifteen are in the Group T-3 hallways; and six are in more distant parts of the Laboratory. (Thus there are fifty-four of them in the Laboratory.) There are (an estimated) ten in Russia, three in France, two in Australia, one in India, two in Japan, and more in foreign countries that I don't remember or that were sold by galleries to other parts of the world without my being told where they went. Many of them are in private ownership in various parts of the United States, with the greatest concentration in north-central New Mexico. MIAC in Santa Fe has around thirty of my paintings.

These figures account for only a fraction of the paintings I have done, so where are the rest? In many cases, they have been destroyed for various reasons—mainly because I concluded that they were not good enough to be preserved. The paintings still in my possession include some of the best I have ever created. What will happen to them when I die? I've been investigating various possibilities. I would have liked very much to have them permanently kept by the Fine Arts Museum (New Mexico Museum of Art), part of the Museum of New Mexico. My good friend Anita McNeece, former registrar of collections at MIAC, discussed the possibility with the Museum of New Mexico collections committee and was told that any paintings of pots we donated to MIAC would appropriately be accepted for permanent storage, but she reported that my other paintings were too much like magazine illustrations, rather than what the Fine Arts Museum was seeking—paintings on the cutting edge of modern trends. As a consequence, I donated twenty-two of my best paintings to the Arts in Public Places program of the Los Alamos County government, in addition to a group of photographic images of some of my favorite works. Several of those paintings are shown in chapter 12. There is, of course, the possibility that one or several of our children would like to have them, to keep or to give away or sell.

I paint less frequently and more slowly these days. My hands are not as steady, and my skills are slowly slipping away. Nevertheless, I still try to paint for a few hours every week, knowing perfectly well that none of the results will be as good as some of my best from previous decades, but I have some half-finished ones that I plan to putter with.

Age has been an accomplice in slowing down many facets of my life. I no longer work on physics research; the pottery books we have published will be my only ones in that field of activity; and this memoir will soon be completed. But I've been working on some philosophical essays.

What comes next? Patty says, "Hey, don't worry, Frank. You always find a new direction for intense focus of activity when each old one is completed, and I'm sure that you'll be finding another one soon." She has been the real treasure and focal point of my life for more than sixty years!

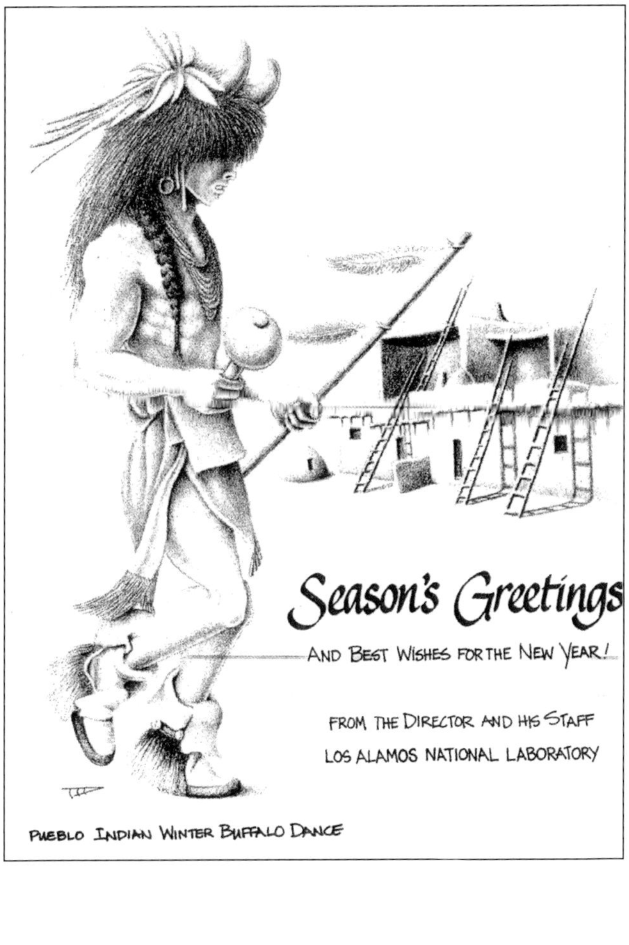

Figure 64. Official year-end greeting card from the director of Los Alamos National Laboratory featuring one of my drawings. (Courtesy Los Alamos National Laboratory.)

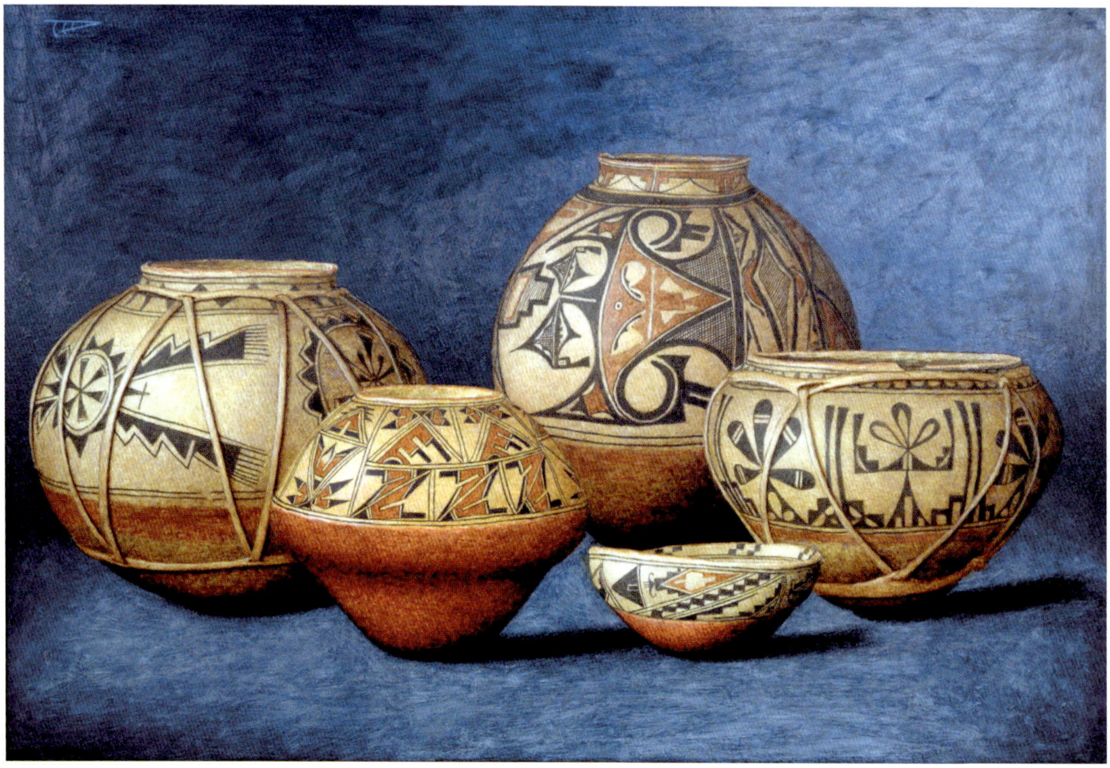

Figure 65. *Historic Pueblo Indian Pottery*, May 2004, 24 x 36 in. (Photo by Mike O'Keefe. LACC, FH-1545.)

12
Album of Some of My Favorite Paintings

It has been interesting to go through hundreds of photographs showing paintings that I have produced over the last forty-six years and to choose a group of my favorites for this book. Many of my paintings are now owned by the Los Alamos County government's Art in Public Places program. Others I still own and are displayed in our home.

The largest of these paintings is twenty-four by forty-eight inches. Others are as small as nine by twelve inches. Almost all of them were painted on untempered Masonite, while a few were painted on very stiff cardboard. The paint itself is usually smooth, but it may be textured for background or other purposes.

Here are some of my favorite paintings.

The five vessels in the painting in figure 65 are magnificent examples from the historic period of Pueblo history. They are vessels that I never actually owned, so I painted them in order to study them carefully and to capture them for my imaginary museum collection. The three large vessels are (left to right) from Cochiti Pueblo (circa 1790, from a private collection), Zia Pueblo (circa 1820–1830, from the Indian Arts Research Center [IARC] at SAR), and Tesuque Pueblo (circa 1810, from MIAC). The two smaller vessels are from Acoma (jar, circa 1700–1750, from IARC) and Zuni (bowl, circa 1750, from MIAC).

In painting this picture, it was necessary to make a pleasant composition of the jars, to choose background colors for the table and wall to contrast with the colors of the jars, and to decide on the direction of lighting and the resulting shadows. Whereas I used commercial acrylic paints, the Indians who made the vessels used materials that they gathered in nature: from clay banks for the vessels themselves, from red iron oxide deposits, and by collecting and boiling down the leaves and stems of plants (such as the Rocky Mountain bee plant) for painting the designs. For me, the final step in the painting process was simply to let the paint dry. For the Indians, the final step was to harden the vessels in an open-air fire.

During this last step, some vessels were so badly cracked as to be useless. Others that cracked from the rim down into the body of the vessel could be made useful anyway: a network of wet rawhide was tied around the vessel; when it dried, it shrank enough to pull the edges of the crack tightly together. Two jars in this painting show the pattern of rawhide attachment that was commonly used. Sometimes, when the rim of the vessel was strongly flared, a single strip of rawhide at the base of the neck was sufficient for accomplishing the desired effect. Another common procedure was to use a sharply pointed rock to drill a hole on each side of the crack and to tie the two sides together. For me, the challenge was to make the rawhide strips look three-dimensional.

The painting in figure 66 is rather different from the composition and choice of objects that I usually use. I almost always have the objects confined by the edges of the painting, but here several of them extend beyond that confinement. The objects in this still life are varied: a Grecian pitcher, a Pueblo dance kilt, a pair of gloves, a shelf made of wood planks, and an ancient Mexican sculpture. There are, in addition, several pieces of Pueblo pottery, including a Hopi bowl (left), a Four-Mile Polychrome bowl (center), a Wingate Black-on-red bowl (far right), and an ancient black-on-white bowl in the left foreground.

The picture in figure 67 shows a pottery storyteller figure, with numerous children enjoying the presentation. The piece was created at Cochiti Pueblo, likely by Helen Cordero, during the latter part of the 1900s. (Storyteller figures were first crafted in 1964 by Cordero, a Cochiti Pueblo potter, in honor of her grandfather, a tribal storyteller. They have since become very popular, and potters at many pueblos produce similar figures.) Patricia and I once owned a pottery storyteller, but it got broken, so I decided to make this painting, which has been prominent on one of the walls in our living room for many years. This is not an image of the figure we lost; I don't recall where I saw the figure I recorded in my painting. Here I used a dark gray background to emphasize the coloring of the object of interest.

Maria Martinez, perhaps the most famous of the recent Pueblo Indian potters, became a good friend of mine, as discussed in chapter 8. In my numerous visits to her home at San Ildefonso Pueblo, she very much enjoyed giving me comments about the early days of her life and letting me take pictures of her, usually with pottery from her village. In the painting in figure 68, I show her with two examples

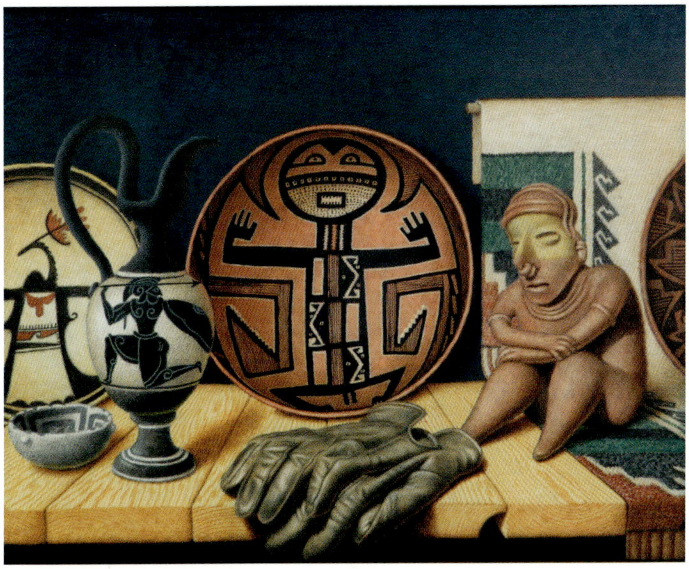

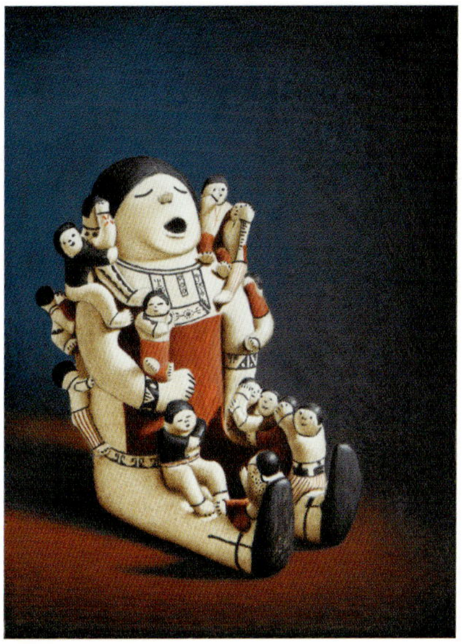

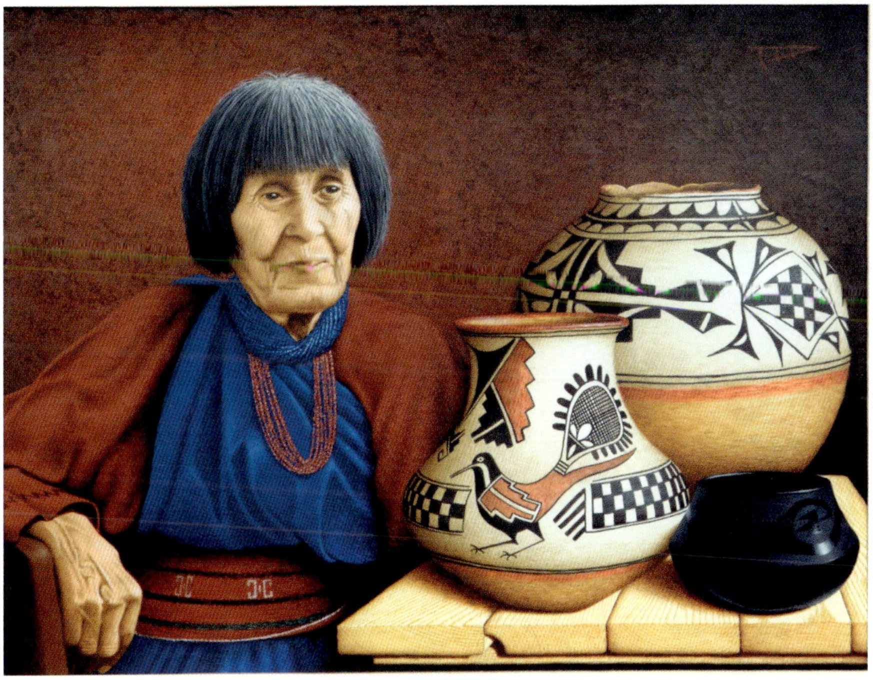

Figure 66 (*top left*). *Still life*, November 1997, 16 x 20 in. (Photo by Mike O'Keefe. LACC, FH-1475.)

Figure 67 (*top right*). *Cochiti Storyteller*, April 1979, 12 x 9 in. (Photo by Addison Doty. Frank Harlow collection, FH-1121.)

Figure 68 (*bottom*). *Maria Martinez*, June 1977, 18 x 24 in. (Photo by Mike O'Keefe. Keith Harlow collection, FH-1065.)

she made, along with a large storage jar that was likely made by an ancestor of hers. Especially noteworthy is the jar with what I call the tennis-racket-tail bird, which was painted by her husband, Julian.

An interesting feature of this jar is the surface on which the designs were created. Most Pueblo Indian pottery is covered with a thin layer called slip. For many centuries, the slip at San Ildefonso was polished with a smooth stone rubbed across the surface. Such was the case with this jar, although in the early 1900s, Maria and the other potters were experimenting with a slip imported from Cochiti or Santo Domingo Pueblo that could be polished with a cloth or soft leather with much less effort.

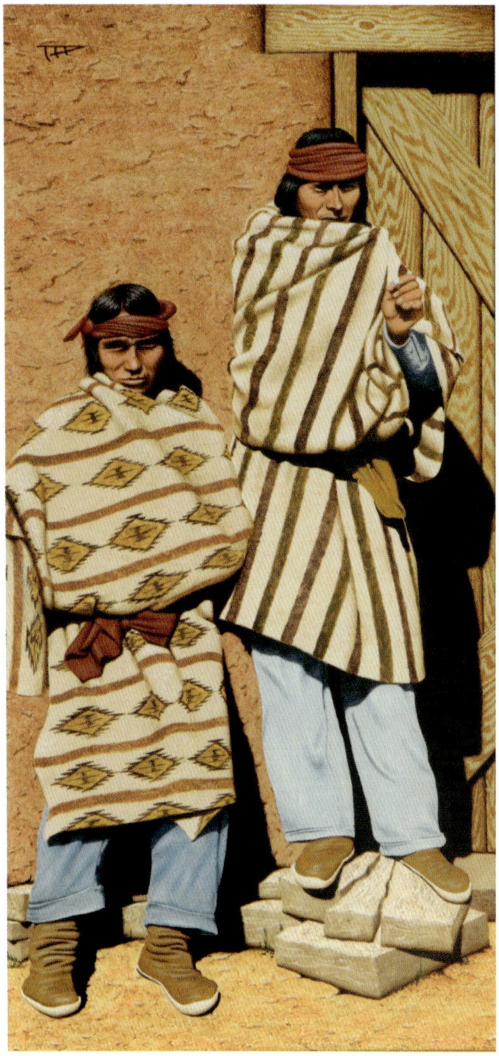

Figure 69. *Two Pueblo Men*, July 1976, 18 x 36 in. (Photo by Mike O'Keefe. LACC, FH-1033.)

How do I show in the painting the type of slip used on this jar? I never figured out how to accomplish this for light-colored slips. Also in the painting is a smaller black jar. I show its polished surface by means of a reflection of light from the right side of the vessel.

I also want to mention the perspective of the depiction of table and pots. I had learned by experimenting that an intentional inconsistency of the horizon can lead to a much better feeling of stability for the pots on a table. Notice that I put the vanishing point for the boards on the table *below* that of the opening at the top of the larger jars. Notice also that the wall is red in this painting, whereas I usually use a dark blue or gray color for that background. Our son, Keith Harlow, now owns both this painting and the tennis-racket-tail jar.

The Indian men in the painting shown in figure 69 are guarding a doorway and also enjoying the warmth of the winter sunshine. Most of the surfaces in this painting are smooth, while the adobe wall and the ground have been textured. It was an interesting exercise to show the different surfaces of the blanket, the blue jeans, the moccasins on their feet, and the red bands around their heads.

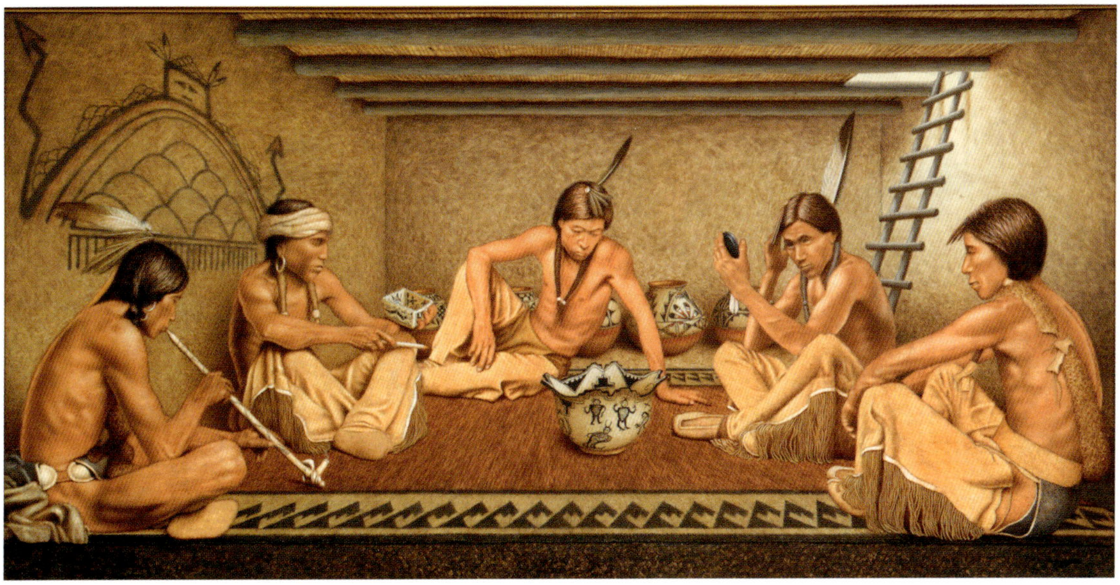

Figure 70. *Pueblo Indian Men*, April 1994, 24 x 48 in. (Photo by Mike O'Keefe. LACC, FH-1419.)

The title of the painting in figure 70 is *After Exercises to Build Up Strengths*. I like this descriptive phrasing because it contains the only English-language word I know with one vowel and seven consonants, or eight consonants if you include the plural.

The composition contains numerous elements that were chosen and arranged in a pattern invented by my own imagination. I've never seen a room like this, and I doubt that one exists.

Michael Steinkamp (fig. 71) was a pitcher for the Salt Lake Trappers and was developing rapidly in his goal of becoming a pitcher on a major-league team. This idea, however, was ended by a severe injury to his back, so Michael applied a different set of talents to the goal of a scientific career. He and I met when he received a position at Los Alamos National Laboratory, with the task of completing his research for obtaining a PhD while working with me on the development of a mathematical model for describing the behavior of turbulence in complicated fluid flow and proving the validity of this work by solving some significant problems on the Lab's supercomputers. He now holds an important position in the Lab's scientific administration.

The painting in figure 72 is my adaptation of a self-portrait of the English artist Stanley Spencer, which he painted in 1914 and which is now in the Tate

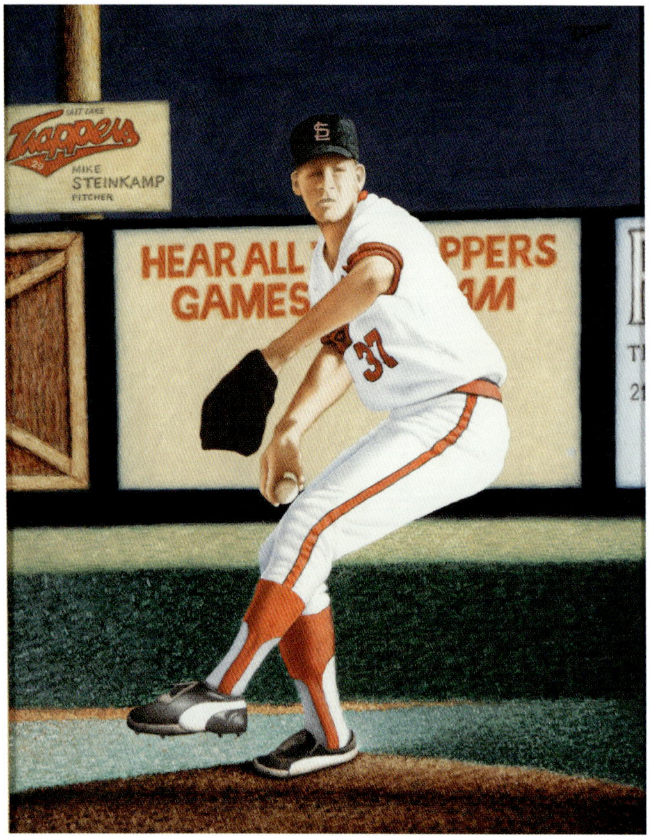

Figure 71. *Baseball Pitcher*, June 1993, 16 x 20 in. (Photo by Addison Doty. Michael Steinkamp collection, FH-1410.)

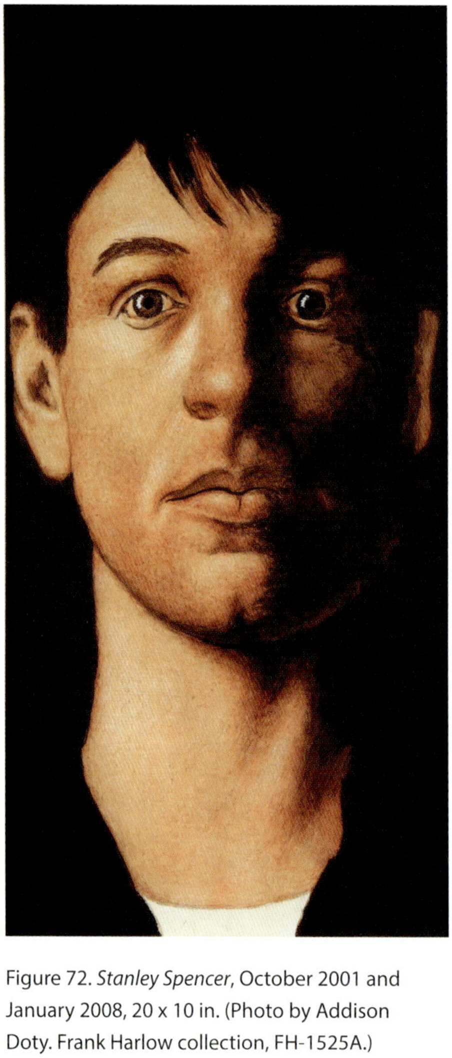

Figure 72. *Stanley Spencer*, October 2001 and January 2008, 20 x 10 in. (Photo by Addison Doty. Frank Harlow collection, FH-1525A.)

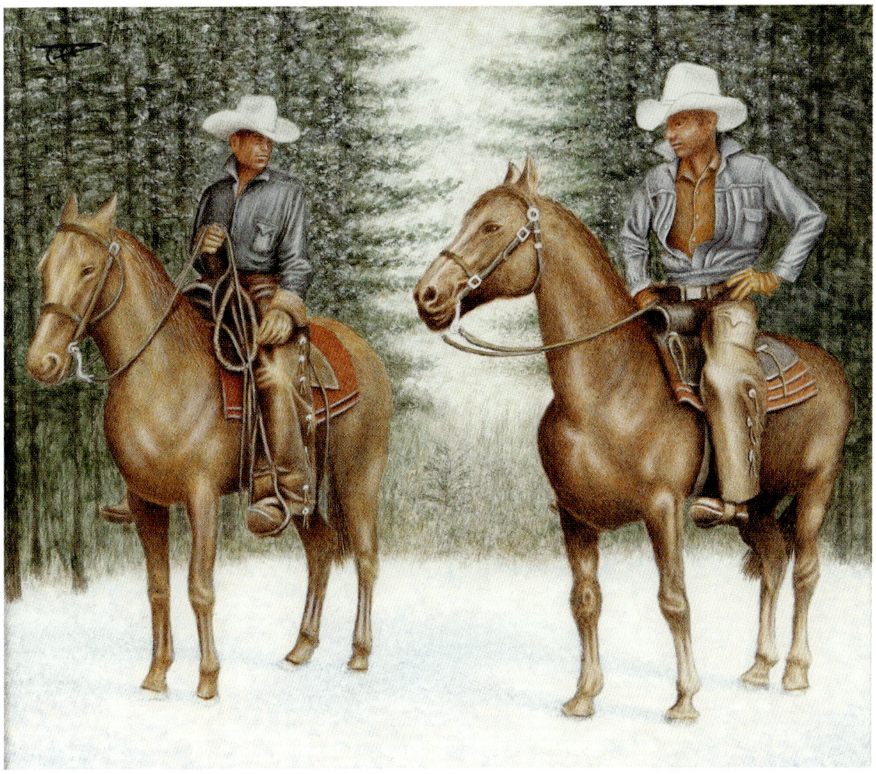

Figure 73. *John Grady Cole and Lacey Rawlins*, January 2001, 20 x 24 in. (Photo by Addison Doty. Frank Harlow collection, FH-1515.)

Gallery in London. I like my version better than his original and keep it in my own collection for technical reference. Actually, I made two paintings that are almost identical; the other is in the Los Alamos County collection.

I like painting pictures of horses. I painted the picture in figure 73 to show my interpretation of John Grady Cole and Lacey Rawlins, who went on horseback to Mexico, as is written by Cormac McCarthy in *All the Pretty Horses*. This is one of my all-time favorite paintings, and I always keep it prominently in my collection. (See fig. 61, chapter 11.) Note that the background is intentionally impressionistic to suggest distance. I know that I could not duplicate this painting at this late stage of my life.

The painting *Pony Express* in figure 74 is another of my favorites, so I also keep it in my home. Here the background depicts the flat-topped mesas of the Pajarito Plateau, on which the town of Los Alamos is located. Dimly showing in the background are the Jemez Mountains, which were formed about a million years

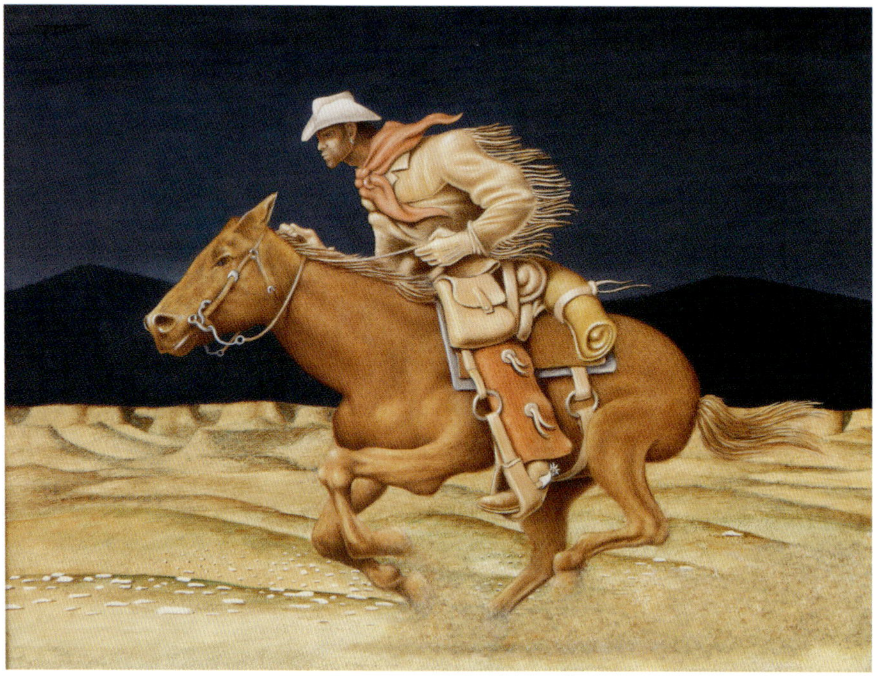

Figure 74. *Pony Express*, September 1990, 18 x 24 in. (Photo by Addison Doty. Frank Harlow collection, FH-1385.)

ago as a result of a huge volcanic eruption spewing enormous amounts of lava and ash, in some places about six hundred feet thick. Not visible in the painting is the famous Rio Grande flowing from Colorado (around one hundred miles to the right) and to the Gulf of Mexico (about four hundred miles to the left). I hope you like this painting as much as I do.

The three young men in figure 75 seem oblivious of each other. This painting was designed to express feelings of detachment that can occur with the complexity of society. Major challenges for me included depicting the fire and the isolation of each person's feelings. The reflection of the moon on the lake helps portray loneliness without desperation. To me, the goals I set for the painting were nicely achieved.

In 1955 Patricia and I took our daughter Catherine, then six months old, to see the Grand Canyon in northern Arizona. We took some nice photographs, and I walked down to the plateau above the river. Coming back up was exhausting, and I needed several hours of sleep to recover. About twenty years later, I used one photograph from that trip as a basis for the painting in figure 76. I think the clouds look nice in this depiction. Our son, Keith, liked the painting so much that we gave it to him.

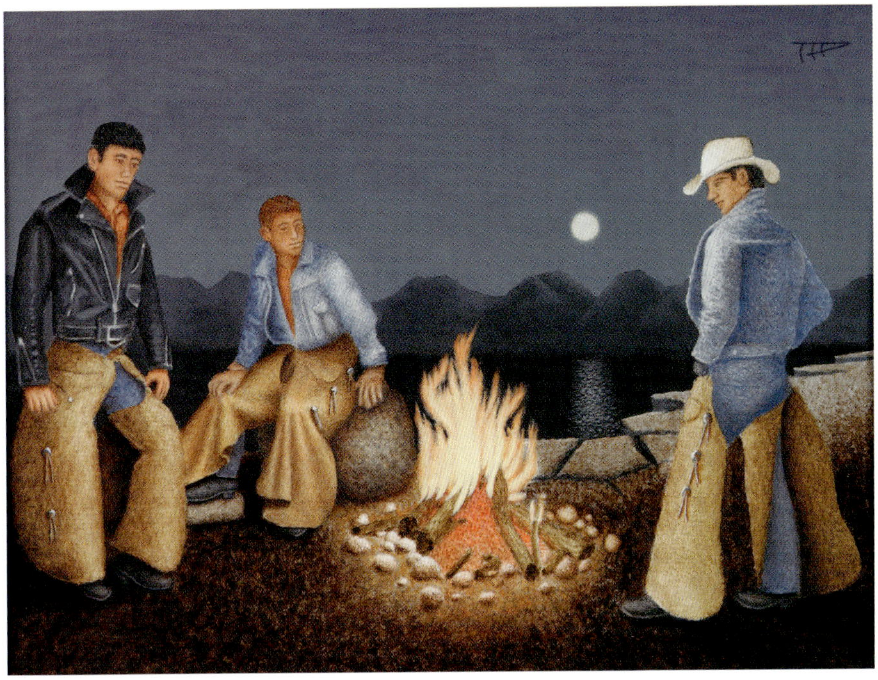

Figure 75. *A Campfire on a Moonlit Night*, June 2011, 18 x 24 in. (Photo by Addison Doty. Frank Harlow collection, FH-1590.)

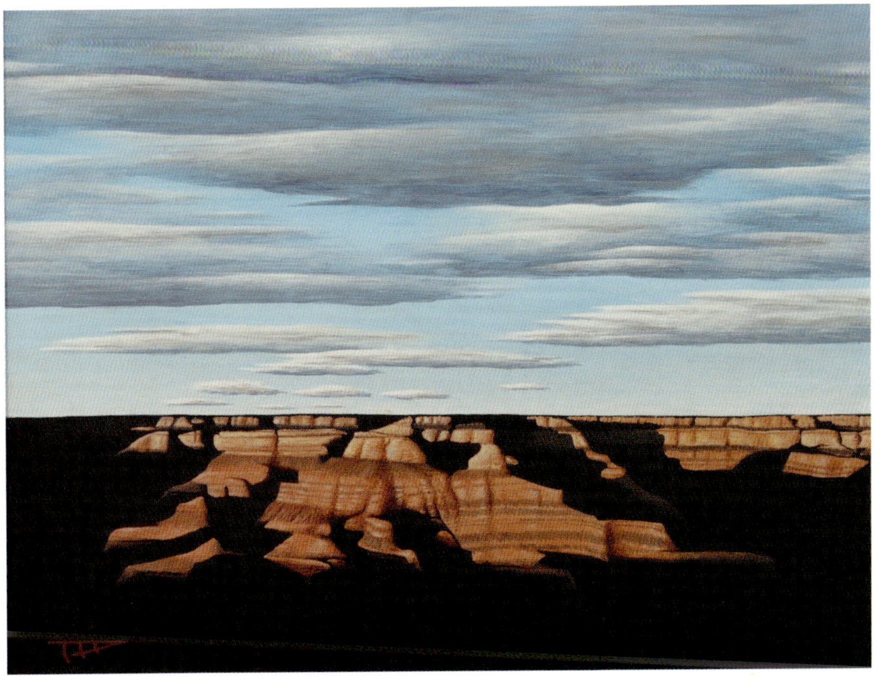

Figure 76. *Grand Canyon*, October 1976, 18 x 24 in. (Photo by Addison Doty. Keith Harlow collection, FH-1041.)

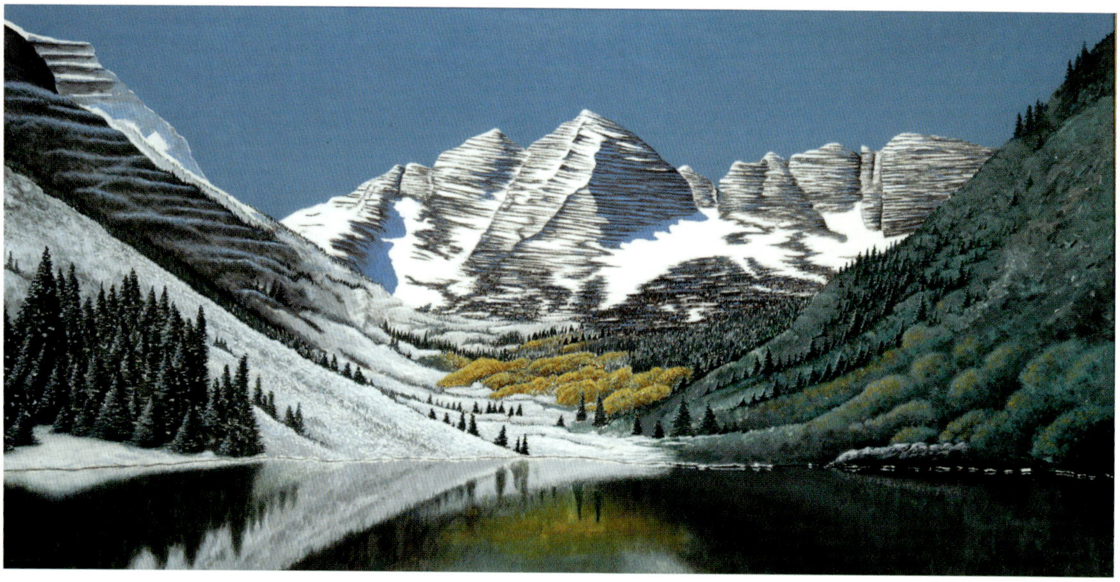

Figure 77. *Maroon Bells*, April 1989, 24 x 48 in. (Photo by Mike O'Keefe. LACC, FH-1365.)

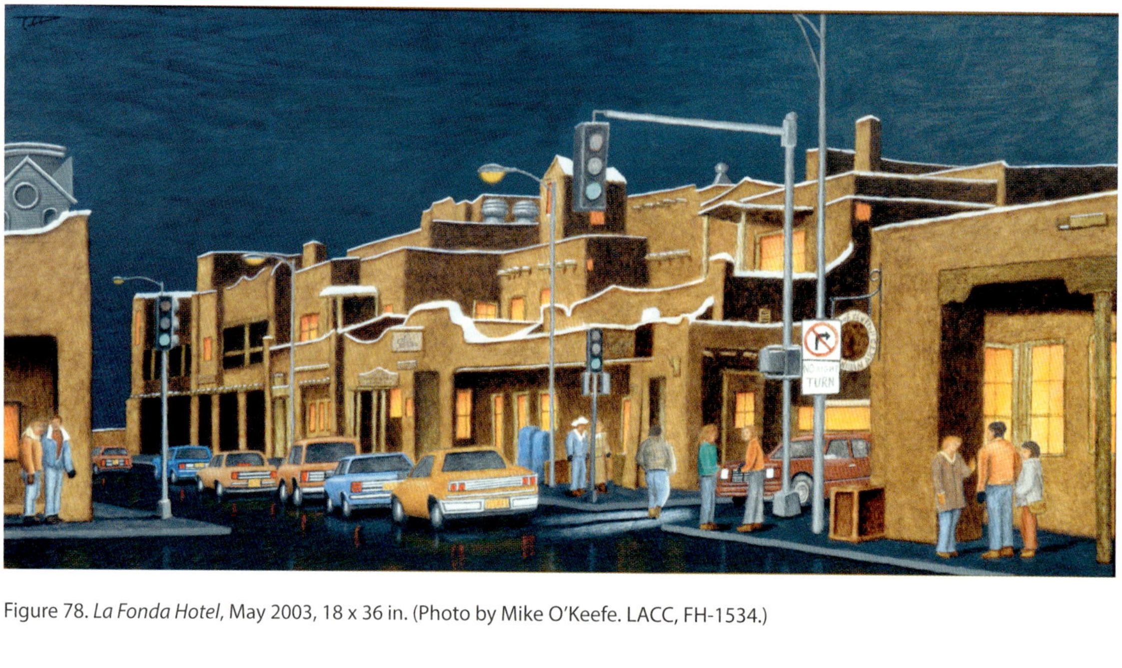

Figure 78. *La Fonda Hotel*, May 2003, 18 x 36 in. (Photo by Mike O'Keefe. LACC, FH-1534.)

I've never been to the Maroon Bells peaks in Colorado, but I wanted to try painting them, so I used some photographs of this famous view. I took a few liberties with the slopes on the left and right sides of the painting (fig. 77), but I nevertheless think that the results turned out quite nice. Many people have agreed that the painting is beautiful, and I have given it to the permanent collection of Los Alamos County.

Here (fig. 78) is a painting of La Fonda Hotel in Santa Fe. Chapter 7 contains another with the same view (see fig. 24) but with entirely different lighting and a group of motorcycle riders on the street. The idea is to show how the mood of a painting can be altered with relatively small changes. I like them both very much.

This street scene in Santa Fe (fig. 79) was completely invented in my imagination. The two shops are both catering to art lovers. The one on the left sells abstract paintings; the one on the right caters to people looking for American Indian art. A close examination of the objects for sale shows how detailed I could paint some number of years ago. Such fine-scale brushstrokes are completely impossible for me to accomplish now. The motorcycle parked in the street is my 1940 Harley-Davidson, which I have depicted in half a dozen paintings. I like the reflections of light on the wet street and have added pedestrians to give life to the

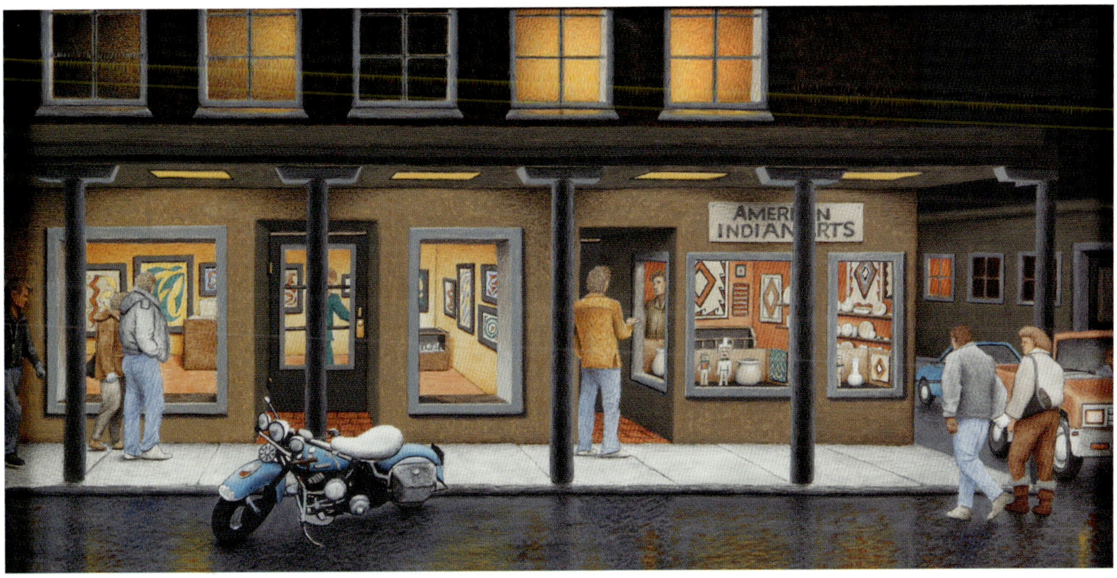

Figure 79. *Santa Fe Scene*, February 1996, 12 x 22 in. (Photo by Addison Doty. Frank Harlow collection, FH-1453.)

composition. Who might be the residents living behind the upstairs window is a question for everyone who looks at the painting to guess. I like what the picture says to me and keep it on the wall of my studio.

The abstract depiction in figure 80 is titled *Constellation of Gloves.* I'm reminded of the song "Beautiful Noise" as sung by Neil Diamond, with the lyrics "It makes me feel good, like a hand in a glove." There are various reasons for painting this scene. One is the fact that ever since I was a teenager, I've enjoyed wearing gloves on my cold fingers. From the standpoint of painting, the shading of light and shadows was an interesting challenge for me. Notice that the objects around the edge of the painting are not bounded by the frame, in a similar fashion to figure 66.

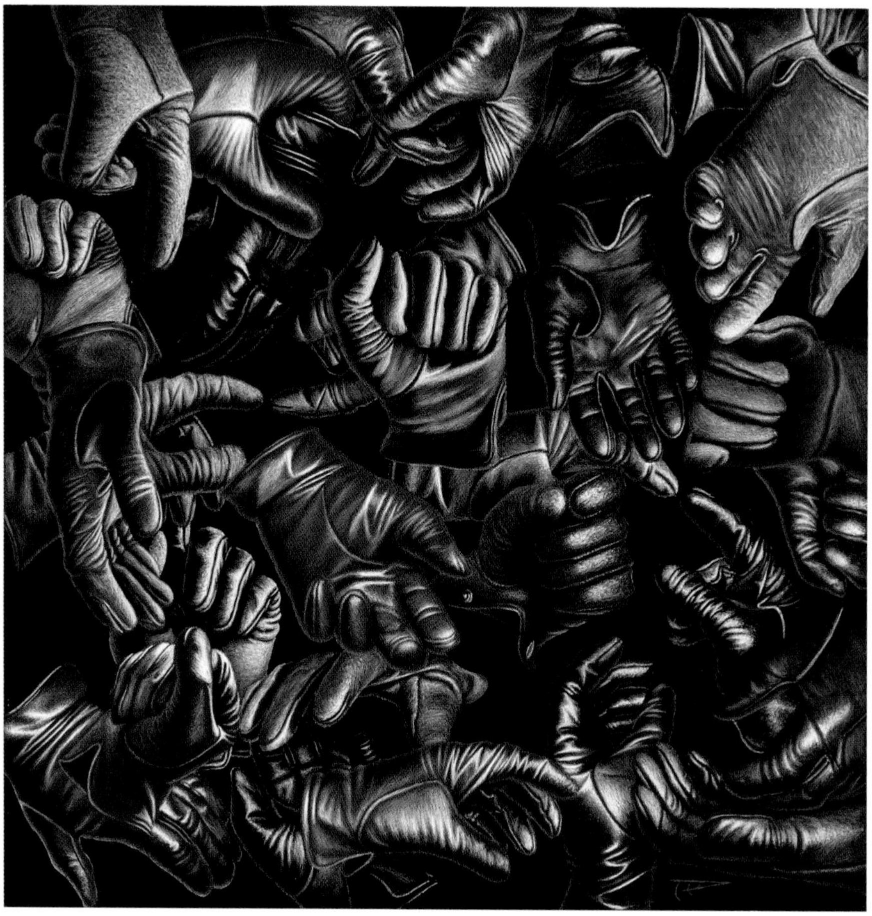

Figure 80. *Constellation of Gloves*, October 1994, 16 x 16 in. (Photo by Craig Smith. Dwight and Lorri Lanmon collection, FH-1430.)

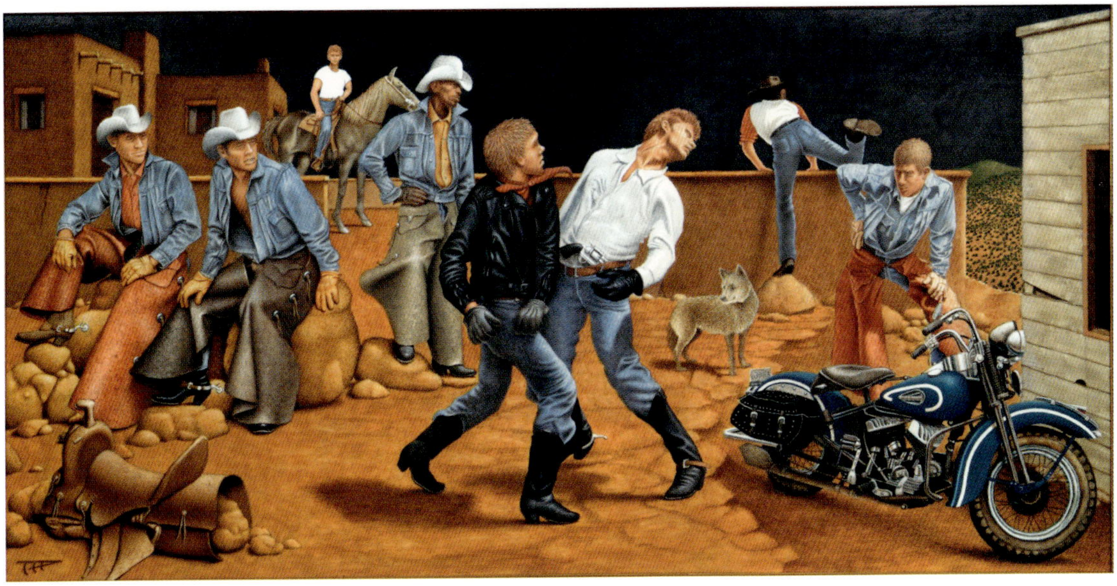

Figure 81. *A Fight*, December 1994, 24 x 48 in. (Photo by Mike O'Keefe. LACC, FH-1409.)

Most of my paintings are more or less static, but in figure 81 there is a fast-moving fight between a sole biker and a cowboy, with a number of other cowboys standing or sitting around the battle, which the biker seems to be winning. The only other motion is that of the person climbing the wall. Note that the two guys sitting on the rocks to the left are identical twin brothers. The motorcycle a little lower on the right is, of course, my third bike, which is shown in chapter 7 (figs. 27, 29, and 30). The composition of the painting was at first rather awkward, from the falling cowboy to the right edge of the picture, so I covered that area with gesso and painted a different arrangement that I think looks just right. I couldn't resist the idea of a horse and rider in the far background, although their presence is not very strongly constructed.

The painting in figure 82 brings together many of the things that describe my personality. Outside the window you can see my third motorcycle, again as shown in chapter 7. Its presence is complemented by the leather jacket on the left, plus the helmet and gloves on the shelf by the window. Cowboy boots like the ones I wore for years are at the left end of that shelf. On the right end is a bronze sculpture, somewhat reduced in size from the true height, so as to fit into the composition. It shows the talent of the sculptor, Buck McCain. On the wall hangs a saddle ring carbine reminiscent of the Civil War, a pair of old spurs given

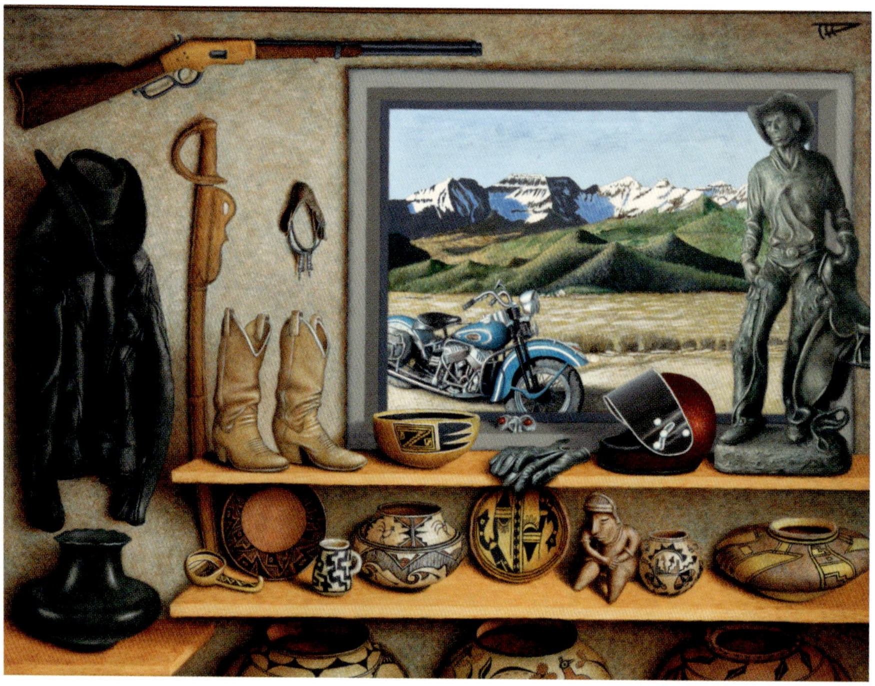

Figure 82. *Still life*, November 2000, 30 x 40 in. (Photo by Mike O'Keefe. LACC, FH-1512.)

to me by Kenneth Chapman, and an interesting sword of undetermined origin, its handle covered with leather that shows many years of aging and tough usage. On the shelves below are, of course, many examples of Pueblo Indian pottery, plus a pottery sculpture of a sitting warrior made many years ago in west-central Mexico. The San Juan Mountains are visible in the distance, covered with snow.

During the early years of the 1980s, Patricia was sewing some needlepoint pictures that were turning out to be very attractive. So I thought, "Hey, this looks like fun. It's not painting but nevertheless is a close relative of the process." So I decided to try my hand at that method of creating art and actually ended up completing two needlepoints before I realized how much time was required for each one. Figure 83 is one that I completed in February 1984; it took about sixty or seventy hours. The canvas used in this project has fourteen holes per inch, so the total number of stitches is 21,168.

In each case, I had designed, sewn, and blocked the image and mounted it into a frame. It illustrates quite well the need for shading with discrete areas of color, which is quite different from painting.

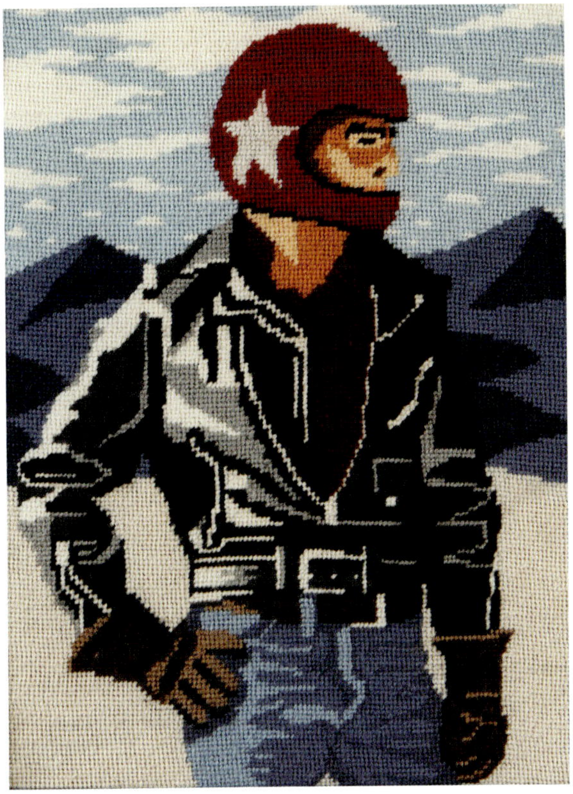

Figure 83. *Needlepoint picture*, February 1984, 9 x 12 in. (Photo by Addison Doty. Frank Harlow collection, FH-1602.)

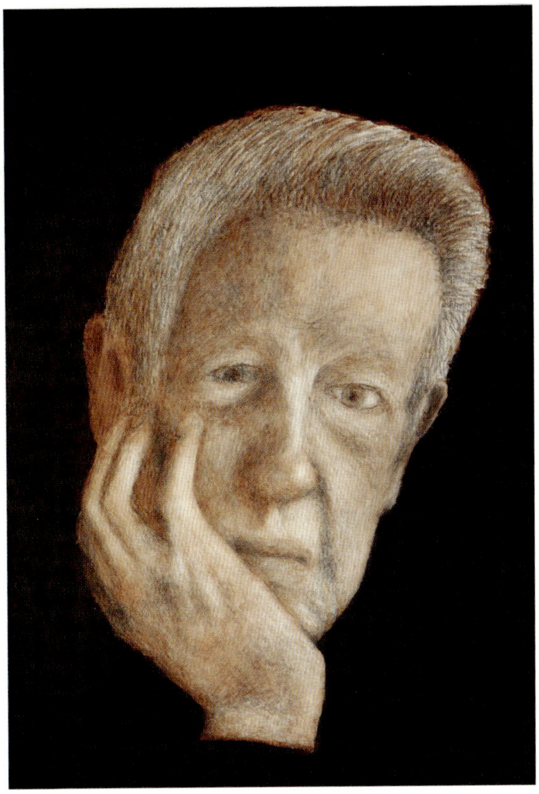

Figure 84. *Self-portrait*, April 2015, 14 x 10 in. (Photo by Addison Doty. Frank Harlow collection, FH-1262.)

The blocking is especially challenging. I had used only one direction for each stitch, and the result was very awkward, with the overall configuration departing very strongly from rectangular. Patricia solved that problem by suggesting that the canvas be wetted and then stretched over a nine-by-twelve-inch piece of Masonite and tied in place until it dried. Even today, the strings hooked into the canvas are still on the back, presenting the appearance of a cubist configuration of a distorted chainlink fence. Yes, each of the two was fun, but I've never tried another and likely will not do so in the future.

As in figure 75, my expression in figure 84 is meant to depict a sense of deep concentration on the mysteries of life and getting older. To achieve this, I felt that both the color and the messy shading were important departures from my actual image, and also from any techniques I had ever tried before. It's also possible that this is close to being the last painting I shall ever undertake.

BIBLIOGRAPHY OF HARLOW PUBLICATIONS ON PUEBLO POTTERY AND PALEONTOLOGY

FRANK, LARRY, AND FRANCIS H. HARLOW

Historic Pottery of the Pueblo Indians, 1600–1880. Boston: New York Graphic Society, 1974.

HARLOW, FRANCIS H.

"An Enormous Painted Jar from Modern Santo Domingo Pueblo." *El Palacio* 74, no. 3 (1967): 44.

"Glazed Pottery of the Southwest Indians." *American Indian Art Magazine* 2, no. 1 (1976): 64–70.

Historic Pueblo Indian Pottery. Los Alamos: Monitor Press, 1967. Reprinted 1968 by Monitor Press; reprinted 1970 by the Museum of New Mexico Press.

"An Introduction to Hopi Pottery." In *An Introduction to Hopi Pottery*. Flagstaff: Museum of Northern Arizona Press, 1978.

Matte-Paint Pottery of the Tewa, Keres, and Zuni Pueblos. Papers in Anthropology. Santa Fe: Museum of New Mexico Press, 1973.

Modern Pueblo Pottery, 1880–1960. Flagstaff: Northland Press, 1977.

"The Pottery of San Ildefonso Pueblo." Supplementary text in Kenneth M. Chapman, *The Pottery of Santo Domingo Pueblo*. Santa Fe: School of American Research Press, 1969.

Pueblo Art: Southwestern Indian Pottery. Dallas: Somesuch Press, 1983.

"Pueblo Indian Pottery Traditions." *Viltis* 3, no. 3 (1978): 6–7.

"Pueblo Pottery on United States Postage Stamps." *New Mexico Philatelist* 31, no. 2 (1978): 5.

"Rio Grande Glaze Ware." Invited lecture and published proceedings, Seminar on Southwestern Native American Ceramics, Santa Fe, June 24–26, 1981.

"Tewa Indian Ceremonial Pottery." *El Palacio* 72, no. 4 (1965): 13–23.

"Transitional Pueblo Pottery, 1500–1700." Invited lecture and distributed lecture notes, Concourse of Southwest Ceramics, Recursos de Santa Fe, 1988.

Two Hundred Years of Pueblo Pottery: The Gallegos Collection. Santa Fe: Morningstar Gallery, 1990.

HARLOW, FRANCIS H., DUANE ANDERSON, AND DWIGHT P. LANMON

The Pottery of Santa Ana Pueblo. Santa Fe: Museum of New Mexico Press, 2005.

"The Pottery of Santa Ana Pueblo." *El Palacio* 110, no. 4 (2005): 32–36.

"Santa Ana Pueblo Pottery." *American Indian Art Magazine* 31, no. 1 (2005): 42–53.

HARLOW, FRANCIS H., AND DWIGHT P. LANMON

"The Colored Pottery of San Lazaro Pueblo." In Forrest Fenn, *The Secrets of San Lazaro Pueblo*. Santa Fe: One-Horse Land and Cattle Co., 2004.

The Pottery of Zia Pueblo. Santa Fe: School of American Research Press, 2003.

"Pueblo Indian Storage Jars of the 1700s." *American Indian Art Magazine* 35, no. 4 (2010): 52–59.

HARLOW, FRANCIS H., AND J. SILVERMAN

Pueblo Indian Pottery. Santa Fe: Silverman Museum, 2001.

LANMON, DWIGHT P., AND FRANCIS H. HARLOW

"The Potters of Zuni Pueblo of the 1920s and 1930s." *American Indian Art Magazine* 33, no. 3 (2008): 58–67.

The Pottery of Acoma Pueblo. Santa Fe: Museum of New Mexico Press, 2013.

"The Pottery of Acoma Pueblo, Part One: Glazewares, Ako Polychrome and Acomita Polychrome (1300–1860)." *American Indian Art Magazine* 37, no. 4 (2012): 50–57.

"The Pottery of Acoma Pueblo, Part Two: Acoma Polychrome (1840–Present)." *American Indian Art Magazine* 38, no. 1 (2012): 66–74.

The Pottery of Zuni Pueblo. Santa Fe: Museum of New Mexico Press, 2008.

"Reyes Galvan: A Master Zia Potter." *American Indian Art Magazine* 28, no. 3 (2003): 48–59.

"Zuni Pueblo Pottery: An Overview." *American Indian Art Magazine* 33, no. 2 (2008): 40–51.

SUTHERLAND, PATRICK K., AND FRANCIS H. HARLOW

"Late Pennsylvanian Brachiopods from North-Central New Mexico." *Journal of Paleontology* 41, no. 5 (September 1967): 1065–1089.

Pennsylvanian Brachiopods and Biostratigraphy in Southern Sangre de Cristo Mountains, New Mexico. Memoir 27. Socorro: New Mexico Bureau of Mines and Mineral Resources, 1973.

YOUNG, J. V., AND FRANCIS H. HARLOW

Contemporary Pueblo Indian Pottery. Popular Pamphlet Series. Santa Fe: Museum of New Mexico Press, 1965.